W9-CLI-833

To Dare More Boldly

❖❖❖❖❖

To Dare More Boldly

❖❖❖❖❖

THE AUDACIOUS STORY
OF POLITICAL RISK

John C. Hulsman

PRINCETON UNIVERSITY PRESS

Princeton and Oxford

Published by Princeton University Press,
41 William Street, Princeton, New Jersey 08540

In the United Kingdom: Princeton University Press,
6 Oxford Street, Woodstock, Oxfordshire OX20 1TR

press.princeton.edu

Jacket art: Detail of Portrait of Sir Francis Drake (1540–96), oil on panel
by unknown artist, c. 1581. IanDagnall Computing / Alamy Stock Photo

Jacket design by Kathleen Lynch / Black Kat Design

ISBN 978-0-691-17219-4
Library of Congress Control Number: 2017962507

British Library Cataloging-in-Publication Data is available

This book has been composed in Minion Pro

Printed on acid-free paper. ∞

Printed in the United States of America

1 3 5 7 9 10 8 6 4 2

This book is for Benjamin, Matilda, and Samuel; you are all I have to offer the world, but you are far more than enough.

Disturb us, Lord, when we are too well pleased with ourselves
When our dreams have come true because we have dreamed
  too little
When we arrive safely because we sailed too close to the shore.
Disturb us, Lord, to dare more boldly, to venture on wider seas
Where storms will show your mastery
Where losing sight of land, we shall find the stars.

—Excerpts from Sir Francis Drake's prayer, 1577 (apocryphal)

❖ CONTENTS ❖

❖ **CHAPTER ONE**

**480 BC: Introduction—The First Political
Risk Analysts: The Pythia of Delphi**   1

The Pythia as the World's First Political
   Risk Consultant   1

The Pythia Masters the Persians   2

The Merits of History   6

A Potted History of the Modern Political
   Risk Business   11

Hans Morgenthau, Realism, and Modern
   Geopolitical Risk   27

Brian Wilson and Greek Attributes   31

Back to the Past of the Pythia's Lair to Glean
   the Future of Geopolitical Risk Analysis   36

❖ **CHAPTER TWO**

**31 AD: We Are the Risk; The Decline and
Fall of the Roman Empire**   42

Edward Gibbon and How Political Risk
   Analysts Think   42

The Rise of Sejanus and the Fall of the
   Roman Empire   46

An Avoidable Tragedy in France and the
   Root Cause of Europe's Decline   49

Europe's Ticking Demographic Time Bomb   52

Karl-Theodor zu Guttenberg and Germany's
   Distrust of Success   56

The Sudden End of Europe's Sunny Way of Life 59

The Political Naïveté of Lying about Europe's
Gloomy Future 61

Rome Dies from Within 65

❖ CHAPTER THREE
**1192 AD: Gaming Out Lunatics; The Assassins and the
Old Man of the Mountain** 68

The Old Man of the Mountain Demonstrates
What Power Actually Is 68

Rashid ad-Din Sinan and the Benefits of Being
Seen as Crazy 70

The Elusive Madness of Charles Manson 73

The Method of ISIS's Madness 78

Sinan Bests Saladin 84

Sinan Bests the Crusaders 86

❖ CHAPTER FOUR
**1503 AD: Gaming Out Chess Players; Machiavelli,
Cesare Borgia, and Pope Julius II** 92

Machiavelli Attempts a Comeback 92

Machiavelli Backs the Wrong Horse 95

Cesare Borgia's Overrated Bond Villain Luster 99

Washington and Hamilton as Chess Players 103

Washington's Farewell Address as Geopolitical Strategy 108

Julius Runs Rings around Borgia 112

The Prince with Julius as Hero 115

The Analytical Riches That Come from
Spotting Chess Players 119

❖ CHAPTER FIVE

1776: Everything to Play For; John Adams and Game-Changers   121

Adams Sees the Future, Jefferson Buys Gloves   121

The Political Miracle of the Fourth of July   124

Churchill Rejoices over Pearl Harbor   132

Hitler's Fatal Error   138

The Declaration of Independence as Improbable Game-
Changer   141

The Limits to Even Adams's Sagacity   145

❖ CHAPTER SIX

1797: Getting to Goldilocks; Napoleon and the Venetian Republic   147

The Dangers of Analytical Overreaction   147

Venice's Slow Castration   149

Manin Goes Out with a Whimper   151

Napoleon's France as a Country on
Military Steroids   155

Bonaparte's Predictable Fall as a Leader of a
Revolutionary Power   161

The Benefits of Balance   165

❖ CHAPTER SEVEN

1863: The Losing Gambler Syndrome; Robert E. Lee at Gettysburg   167

Why Casino Magnates Get Rich: Gettysburg
and Vietnam   167

Joshua Lawrence Chamberlain Saves the Union   168

The United States Tragically Doubles Down in Vietnam   174

Lee Fatally Goes for Broke with Pickett's Charge   181

The Losing Gambler Syndrome as Beguiling
    Analytical Trap   187

❖ CHAPTER EIGHT
**1895: Knowing Your Country's Place in the World;
Lord Salisbury Saves the British Empire**   188

The Analytical Imperative of Seeing the
    World as It Is   188

Salisbury's Intellectual Courage in Confronting
    His Changing World   189

The Merits of Off-shore Balancing   193

The Meiji Restoration Saves Japan   197

The *Genrō* Face the World   201

Salisbury Finesses America over the
    Venezuelan Crisis   203

Salisbury Saves His Country, Long after His Death   207

❖ CHAPTER NINE
**1898–1912: The Promised Land Fallacy;
Von Tirpitz Disastrously Builds a Navy**   209

The Dangerous Mirage of the Promised Land Fallacy   209

Von Tirpitz Recklessly Challenges British
    Naval Dominance   210

Khrushchev and the Limits of Brinkmanship   217

Khrushchev's Ill-Fated "Wars of National
    Liberation" Strategy   223

The Haldane Mission as the End of Tirpitz's
    Promised Land   229

❖ CHAPTER TEN

**1970: Knowing the Nature of the World
You Live In; Or the Trials and Tribulations
of George Harrison**   233

The Imperative of Understanding Time in the
    Analytical Equation   233

The Beatles' System Falls Stunningly Apart   234

The Rise of George Harrison   236

The Rolling Stones Regroup   238

The Fall of Brian Jones   239

The Beatles as a Frightening Metaphor for
    Today's World   246

How the West Can Avoid the Beatles' Fate   250

The Analytical Imperative to Closely Track Changes
    in Systems   251

❖ CHAPTER ELEVEN

**1978: The Butterfly Effect in Political Risk;
Or Deng Xiaoping and the Perils of a Drunken
Sea Captain**   254

Mastering Real-World Bolts from the Blue   254

Deng Xiaoping Crafts China's Successful Mercantilist
    Foreign Policy   256

Deng Survives Mao and Transforms China   259

Macmillan Salvages Britain's Place in the World   268

The Present Tinderbox in the Waters
    Surrounding China   274

Today's Asia as 1914   279

History Is Never Finished   283

❖ CHAPTER TWELVE

Conclusion: Back to the Pythia's Lair; Mastering Geopolitical Risk 284

Can the Future Be Foretold? 284

Kenneth Waltz and the Systemic Realism Underlying
Geopolitical Risk Analysis 284

"Know Thyself" as the Base of the Geopolitical Risk
Analysis Typology 287

"Nothing in Excess" as a Branch of the Geopolitical Risk
Analysis Typology 292

"Make a Pledge and Mischief Is Nigh" as a Branch
of the Geopolitical Risk Analysis Typology 297

The End of the Pythia and the Beginning of Political
Risk Analysis 303

Acknowledgments 305

Bibliography 307

Index 313

To Dare More Boldly

❖❖❖❖❖

480 BC: Introduction

THE FIRST POLITICAL RISK ANALYSTS: THE PYTHIA OF DELPHI

The Pythia as the World's First Political Risk Consultant

In 480 BC, the citizens of Athens found themselves in more trouble than the modern mind can imagine. Xerxes, son of Darius the Great of Persia, King of Kings, King of the World, had some unfinished business left to him by his all-powerful father. A decade earlier, at the Battle of Marathon in August 490 BC, the impossible had happened.[1] The little-regarded Athenian army had seen off Darius and his mighty horde, saving the fragile city-state from certain destruction. Now Xerxes had invaded the Greek mainland again, to finish what his father had started.

Judging by his past record, the Athenians knew better than to expect mercy from the great king. Upon ascending the throne, Xerxes had savagely crushed two rebellions by portions of his empire then thought to be infinitely superior to the little city-state that was Athens. In 484 BC, Xerxes had quashed a revolt in Egypt, devastating the Nile delta. Soon after, he decisively put down efforts to throw off his yoke in Babylon, going so far as to pillage the sacred Babylonian temples. Xerxes was a man who saw every form of dissent as

---

[1] Recently the likely date of the battle has been revised to August 490 BC from September of that year. See Mark Peplow, "Battle of Marathon Date Revised," *Nature*, July 19, 2004.

sacrilege; the Athenians knew they could expect no quarter from the Persian king should they fail.

Just to make sure that this time Athens did not escape the wrath of the Persian Empire, Xerxes assembled the largest invading force the world had ever seen. While the Greek historian Herodotus—typically exaggerating—put the Persian numbers at 5 million, modern-day historians still place them at an overwhelming 360,000, with a gigantic armada of 700 to 800 ships in support of this vast host.

Confronted with almost certain annihilation, what did the Athenian leadership do? What was their response to a problem that in terms of both its size and its likely devastating impact seemed insurmountable?

Simple. They requested the services of the world's first political risk consultant.

The Pythia Masters the Persians

By 480 BC, the Pythia of Delphi already amounted to an ancient institution. Commonly known now as the Oracle of Delphi (when in fact the "oracles" were the pronouncements the Pythia dispensed), the Pythia were the senior priestesses at the Temple of Apollo, the Greek God of Prophecy.

The temple, sitting precariously (and beautifully—the site is still a wonder to behold) on the slope of Mount Parnassus above the Castalian Spring, had long been the center of the Greek world, going back into the mists of time. The site may well have had religious significance as early as 1400 BC, during the forgotten days of the Mycenaeans, with devotions to Apollo being established in the eighth century BC. Delphi remained a center of worship until 390 AD, having been in use for at least 1,100 years.

During this long period, the Pythia was seen as the most authoritative and important soothsayer in Greece. Pilgrims descended from all over the ancient world to visit the temple and have their questions about the future answered. Sitting in a small, enclosed chamber at the base of the edifice, the Pythia delivered her oracles in a frenzied state, most probably imbibing the vapors rising from the clefts of Mount Parnassus.

We know a good deal about how the oracles came to pass. For a time during the period of Roman domination, the Greek historian Plutarch served as high priest at Delphi, assisting the Pythia in her mission. Perched above the major cleft in the rock, the Pythia would be sitting in a perforated cauldron astride a tripod. It was reported by pilgrims that as the Pythia imbibed the vapors rising from the stone her hair would stand on end, her complexion altered, and she would often begin panting, with her voice assuming an otherworldly tone, not quite human.[2] In classical days, it was asserted that the Pythia spoke in rhyme, in pentameter or hexameter.

To put it in modern terms, there is little doubt that the Pythia did see visions and underwent a dramatic transformation while in the temple; she was clearly as high as a kite. Plutarch himself believed that her oracular powers were directly associated with the vapors that emanated from the Kerna spring waters that flowed underneath the temple, vapors that may well have been full of hallucinogenic gas.

We now know that two tectonic plates intersect beneath Mount Parnassus; such a fault line creates many crevices in the earth, through which gases can rise. Recent tests have found ethylene in the spring water near the site of the Temple of Apollo. It is the most likely cause of the Delphic prophesies.

Ethylene is characterized by its sweet smell and produces a narcotic effect described as floating or disembodied euphoria.

[2] William Goodwin, *Lives of the Necromancers* (London: F. J. Mason, 1876), p. 11.

As described in detail by Plutarch, the experiences of the Pythia in action match the effects of ethylene. Under the influence, a person's tone of voice alters and speech patterns change, yet they retain the ability to answer questions logically. With exposure to higher doses of the drug, the person thrashes about wildly, groaning in strange voices, frequently falling to the ground, all behaviors tracking with eyewitness accounts of the Pythia's behavior.

The Greeks believed that Apollo possessed the Pythia's spirit when she was delivering her oracles—a point at which she was intoxicated by the vapors. They saw her prophecies as religious in nature, but let's look at them afresh. For I think the Temple at Delphi amounts to nothing less than the world's first political risk consulting firm.

At least since the days when the Athenians consulted the Pythia during the height of the Persian Wars, political and business leaders have looked to outsiders blessed with seemingly magical knowledge to divine both the present and the future. While the tools of divination have changed through the ages, the pressing need for establishing rules of the road to manage risk in geopolitics have not. The question remains: through superior knowledge (either intellectual or spiritual in nature), can we reliably do this?

During the period of the Pythia's ascendance, pilgrims brought animals to Delphi for sacrifice to Apollo, as well as a monetary fee for the privilege of using the Pythia's services. Of the petitioners who waited for the one day of the month the Pythia deigned to reply to their questions, those who brought larger donations to the god secured an advanced place in line. Political risk has always been a business that directly links analysis to monetary rewards.

And since the days of the classical Greeks, such special knowledge and policy advice have always been essential for governments and businesses, as well as individuals. At the time of the Battle of Salamis in Greece, no expedition was undertaken, no new colony established, and no major event involving distinguished individuals went by without the Pythia being consulted.

The Pythia (three of them were "on call" at any one time) gave advice to shape future actions, practical counsel that was to be implemented by the questioner. This is exactly what political risk analysts still do today, though we'd use modern jargon and call it "policy" in the public sphere and "corporate strategy" in the business world. But what the Pythia was doing is recognizably the same thing my political risk firm does today, save for the substance abuse.

Given the pharmacological basis for the Pythia's special insights, it is amazing how good a political risk record the priestesses actually had. Between 535 and 615 of the oracles have survived to the present day, and well over half of them are said to be historically correct. I can name a goodly number of modern firms that would kill for that record, high or not.

Crucially, on the biggest political risk question Delphi was ever presented with—the invasion of Xerxes—the Pythia came through with flying colors. When the Athenians first asked the Pythia what to do, she gave them the foreboding reply: "Drown your spirits in woe." In other words, there was nothing to do, as Xerxes was unstoppable.

When persuaded to see them a second time, the Pythia outlined a policy that would provide the Athenians with a way to practically escape from their impending doom. She recounted that when Athena—the Greek Goddess of Wisdom and the patron of her namesake city—implored her father Zeus, the King of the Gods, to save her city, Zeus replied that he would grant that "a wall of wood shall be uncaptured, a boon to you and your children."

Back in Athens, Themistocles, the paramount Greek leader in their fractious democracy, successfully argued that a wall of wood specifically referred to the Athenian navy, and he persuaded the city's leaders to adopt a maritime-first strategy. This policy—concocted by the Pythia and put into concrete action by the decision-maker Themistocles—led directly to the decisive naval Battle of Salamis, the turning of the tide that brought about the end of the Persian risk to Athens's survival. To put it mildly, the Pythia had proven to be well worth her political risk fee.

The Merits of History

Geopolitical risk analysis is an increasingly sexy topic today, striding like a colossus athwart the arenas of global business, international relations, and the general public, all beguiled by its siren song of making sense of both the present and the future in our uncertain new age.[3] But for all the hoopla, there has been precious little written about how practical rules of the game can be applied to managing risk in geopolitics, and even less on the core components, or elements, that comprise this latest attempt at soothsaying.

This book, following in the footsteps of the unimaginably bold prayer that opens it, attempts to do this, using the potent brew of political realism, geopolitics, and historical analysis (particularly relating to lessons learned from history and the relevance of historical analogies), as these analytical tools remain vitally important for understanding our perplexing contemporary world. Such a historical analysis can help lay

[3] A good general definition of geopolitical risk is: "Events, countries and groups that can upset a state's equilibrium, through upsetting its political or social policy, as well as its goals based on its national interest." See Colin Moore, "Geopolitical Risk—The Fear and Reality for Free Markets," *Global Perspectives* (Columbia Management Global Advisers), March 2015.

bare the rules of the road as to how leaders ought to deal with geopolitical risk. For there has not been a good fusion of historical analysis to the study of international relations since Dr. Kissinger was in his heyday.[4]

Kissinger, particularly in *A World Restored* and *Diplomacy*, was a master at developing an operational set of realist-inspired maxims, based on his historical analysis, for decision-makers to use in generally interpreting the geopolitical world around them. However, much of his thinking was unsurprisingly rooted in the bipolar era of the Cold War of his time, and then in the brief unipolar moment following on from the demise of the Soviet Union. With the dawn of our new multipolar age—following the dual calamities of the Iraq War and the Lehman Brothers Great Recession—new thinking along these highly productive lines is very necessary. For this creative rules-of-the-road approach, based on rock-solid historical analysis, remains a neglected aspect of contemporary thought about international relations.

Before forging on, here is what I and *To Dare More Boldly* will not do. This book is not an exploration of realist theory (I have written a book on this topic already), another salvo in the endlessly tired fight between history and political science (despite my strong views on this); neither is it a literature review of what has gone on recently in the field of political science.[5]

Instead, the undervalued and enduring relevance of history for formulating a successful interpretation of contemporary international politics will be a central theme, both for corporate entities grappling with geopolitical risk and for

[4]See Henry A. Kissinger, *A World Restored: Metternich, Castlereagh, and the Problems of Peace, 1812–1822* (Boston: Houghton Mifflin, 1996); and Kissinger, *Diplomacy* (New York: Pocket Books, 1994).

[5]See Anatol Lieven and John Hulsman, *Ethical Realism: A Vision for America's Role in the World* (New York: Pantheon Books, 2006).

political actors combating simplistic foreign policies and the decision-makers who all too often now are propagating them. Specifically, this book will put forward a rules-of-the-game approach (based on historical analysis) to mastering geopolitical risk or any other risks that impact the national interest or the politics (domestic and international alike) that impact foreign policy and strategic considerations of policy-making.

This rules-of-the-game historical approach has been a neglected aspect of political risk analysis generally and geopolitical analysis more specifically (of which it is a vital sub-set). The strength of the method lies in avoiding the otherworldly models of political science and instead remaining grounded in the empirical realities of a real world we have already experienced as fact.

While there is much truth in the assertion that there are multiple variables that have gone into every single major historical occurrence and output across time, it is well we should not get bogged down in the infuriating, self-perpetuating nihilism of post-modernism, for lessons can still be truly learned from the world as we have lived it and definitive statements made about them.

Some lessons from history truly are self-evident. Waterloo genuinely was a disaster for Napoleon. The Great Depression did not help European democracies of the 1930s cope with extremism. Franklin Roosevelt was a more successful politician than Jimmy Carter. I have little time and less patience for the cottage industry of post-modernists in the academy who say that nothing true or universal can be learned from history or from intellectual thought in general.

The real-world, commonsense way out of this seeming intellectual thicket is to accept that history does have universal and applicable lessons to teach us, but that any analyst's use of history to assert such maxims for outlining a rules-of-the-game approach to the study of risk in geopolitics should be held to the highest analytical standards. While there may be many other perfectly applicable interpretations of the events that analysts chronicle, their specific interpretation of any event must at a bare minimum be highly plausible.

While there certainly will be other alternate historical analytical points to be made about all the eras and historical instances we recount in *To Dare More Boldly*, that is not the point. The point is: do the historical lessons learned and analogies I draw on work to illuminate, buttress, and underline the rules of the game I propound for dealing with risk in geopolitics?

The historical analogies and interpretations employed in *To Dare More Boldly* must work in highlighting and underlining broader, more universal maxims that can apply to understanding and managing geopolitical risk in a more general way. If they do, and if the maxims hold across time and space, then all is well and I can leave alternate assessments of all these historical eras and events to others to work on. If they do not, then I have failed.

But there is much to be gained by using this historical approach to more deeply understand contemporary international politics. In employing the historical lens—looking at real-world, empirical, historical examples of good and bad performance in the face of geopolitical risk across time— these analogies strikingly highlight a specific, more universal set of rules of the game for understanding geopolitical risk in our contemporary era. The hope is that these rules of the road—underlined and amplified by the use of copious historical analogies—can help today's decision-makers be better able to deal with geopolitical risk, while underpinning a "do's and don'ts" list—ten commandments of geopolitical risk that transcend time and space and help make sense of the multipolar world we now happen to live in.

Finally, such a historical approach to understanding risk in geopolitics simply allows us to learn from hindsight, much as individual humans attempt to do every day. Each chapter of *To Dare More Boldly* will use a variety of historical examples as it underlines a specific element—a "commandment"—of this larger rules-of-the-game approach to mastering risk in geopolitics. The chapters are grouped around specific elements of both what geopolitical risk analysis is and what it must not be. By the time we reach the end of our tale, having looked in detail at the specific factors that go into mastering risk in geopolitics, it will be possible to determine the nature of the beast we have been thinking about.

The benchmarks for assessing geopolitical risk involve geography, history, and time. The study of geopolitics—the assessment of how geography affects a country's foreign policy over its history—is an essential part of the larger intellectual toolbox of political risk analysis because, as was true of the Pythia, modern geopolitical risk analysts dare to think that there are broadly fixed rules to foreign policy analysis, discernible patterns of history that make human endeavor broadly predictable over time. George Friedman, a major modern geopolitical risk thinker, defines geopolitics as "the craft of understanding the forces at play well enough to generally predict where we are going."[6]

But even given this startling conclusion, a large dose of humility is in order, as it has been since the Pythia helped defeat the Persians. In essence, geopolitical risk analysis is like nothing so much as baseball: there is an undoubted element of chance to the game, and even the best player strikes out with soul-destroying regularity.

---

[6] George Friedman, "How Important Is the US President—or Any Leader?" *Geopolitical Futures*, November 10, 2016.

Saying this, it is not dumb luck that the legendary Ted Williams was the last man to hit .400, or that Yankee great Joe DiMaggio accomplished the unmatched feat of hitting safely in fifty-six straight games. The immortals in both geopolitical risk and baseball invariably do the best over time; there is a lot more skill than randomness driving both fields of endeavor. If the soothsaying perfection of the mythical Merlin is out of the question, mastering geopolitical risk—and putting it to use for the businesses and governments in today's world—assuredly is not.

But the way to get to the mountaintop is more an art than a science; the swashbuckling boldness of the best practitioners in managing such risk is tempered with their acute awareness of what they don't know. The basic problems of geopolitical risk in today's new and bewildering age are the same as in eras gone by, involving very human, timeless, and universal analytical failings.

This will be a worthwhile intellectual journey. For all the copious amounts of snake oil being peddled both today and in the past, for all the false starts and embarrassing limits that have cursed those who claim such an ability, my surprising and (dare I say it) Drakean conclusion is that into the medium-term, and over specific issue areas, the answer is, "Yes, the geopolitical future can be foretold," if imperfectly.

A Potted History of the Modern Political Risk Business

In the public consciousness, political risk firms—those that rely on assessing geopolitical risk as part of their overall analytical toolbox—have seemingly sprung up fully grown: powerful, if secretive, organizations providing vital soothsaying knowledge about the future of the world to their clients and even to countries. A large part of the recent fascination with political risk analysis stems from this abrupt emergence, coupled with the industry's unseen power. As almost nothing has been written about the genesis of political risk firms, a brief history is in order.[7]

The Economist Intelligence Unit (EIU), one of the oldest examples of a world-class political risk firm, specializes in forecasting as well as economic research and analysis. For seventy years, the EIU has assisted businesses, financial firms, and government clients in understanding change in the global order and how these shifts create both opportunities to be taken advantage of as well as risks to be managed.

Established after World War II in 1946, this British sister company of the famous magazine follows in its cultural footsteps, preferring to safeguard the anonymity of its best analysts rather than publicly promoting home-grown public superstars. Compared with some later major political risk firms, the EIU is corporate, anonymous, and secretive. Much of its work for clients is bespoke and confidential.

Presently, the EIU has twenty-four offices around the world, employing 130 full-time analysts. It makes its money through advisory and forecasting services, tailored research and analysis, monthly country political risk reports, longer-term five-year country macroeconomic assessments, and micro-level industry reports. The EIU has a subscription service for many of its more generic analytical products and possesses a long-standing client base eager to buy its wares. As it is one of the oldest political risk firms, the

[7] As this history of political risk firms is not the primary focus of the book, this sampling is by its nature bound to be impressionistic and incomplete. It omits other important risk firms such as Control Risks Group, Oxford Analytica, Roubini Global Economics, the PRS Group, and Teneo. Saying this, our brief survey does delineate the major sorts of risk firms and the industry's genesis and evolution.

EIU's basic format for what it actually does has become the standard template for the political risk industry in general.

Over the years, the EIU, with three offices in China, including one in Hong Kong, has developed a specific competitive advantage in the analysis of Asia. A specific product emanating from this intellectual strength is the much-lauded "Access China White Paper on the Top 20 Emerging Cities in China," a comprehensive guide to the internal workings of the rise of the Dragon itself.

The EIU sets great store by its commitment to its own intellectual independence and integrity, a mantra that has become a selling point for the industry as a whole. By remaining wholly ignorant of a client's specific internal bureaucratic politics, political risk firms have no vested interest in the promotion of any specific policy recommendations they make, basing their views wholly on their own geopolitical analysis. This lack of skin in the game makes them an invaluable asset to business leaders looking for dispassionate analysis of how the world really works.

If the EIU can be thought of as a group of powerful, faceless, and anonymous (if quite effective) analysts toiling away in much-desired obscurity, the emergence of Kissinger Associates in 1982 follows a very different model: the rise of the rock star analyst. Formed by the most famous statesman of the Cold War era, Kissinger Associates is a New York–based international consulting firm founded and run by the former secretary of state with his partner, former National Security Adviser Brent Scowcroft, a man almost equally famous in foreign policy circles. Through the years, former Secretary of State (and long-time Kissinger hand) Lawrence Eagleburger and former Treasury Secretary Timothy Geithner have also played senior roles in the organization.

Backed by their formidable rolodexes as well as their vast practical government experience, the firm founded by

Kissinger and Scowcroft assists clients in identifying the global weather—the strategic parameters that affect investment opportunities. While the EIU has always had more of a macroeconomic bent, Kissinger Associates specializes in advising clients on governmental and political relations throughout the world.

Kissinger Associates, following in the image of Kissinger himself, shares with the EIU a penchant for working off the record; its specific activities are a closely guarded secret. Kissinger Associates does not disclose a list of its corporate clients, whom it bans from acknowledging either the relationship or the services provided by the firm.

An illuminating example of this passion for secrecy was an incident in the wake of 9/11. President George W. Bush had appointed Kissinger the chairman of the National Commission on Terrorism. Hearing of the appointment, congressional Democrats insisted that Kissinger disclose the names of his clients, to avert possible conflict of interest issues. Rather than do this, to preserve the secrecy of his firm, Kissinger stepped down as chair.

The Kissinger Associates approach to political risk has both advantages and drawbacks compared with the EIU's. The "great man" management style provides almost endless free publicity for the firm, as well as intellectual security for clients, who can be confident that the analysis is a known and highly regarded quantity, being backed up by peerless contacts throughout the world. However, the ultimate establishment political firm may have real difficulties in seeing real changes (and failings) in an elite in which it is an integral part. Kissinger Associates lives in perpetual danger of being too close to the global elite it is supposed to be objectively analyzing.

The other danger involves the succession when these pillars of the foreign policy establishment pass from the scene. As the firm is founded on notoriety and name recognition, it is an open question as to whether it can healthily survive the generational change that is bound to occur. As there are literally almost no other statesmen in the younger set out there with the name recognition of either Kissinger or Scowcroft, the longevity of this rock star firm is an open question.

For all the undoubted success of the EIU and Kissinger Associates, it was with the rise of Ian Bremmer and the Eurasia Group that political risk analysis burst upon the public consciousness. Best thought of as the first major post–Cold War political risk firm, Eurasia to some extent fuses the management styles of Kissinger Associates (with Bremmer as the media-savvy rock star) and the EIU (reflected in Eurasia's more corporate approach).

Originally focusing on the emerging countries of the former Soviet Union, the Eurasia Group is now the world's largest political risk consultancy. Founded in New York by Bremmer in 1998, Eurasia now has more than 150 full-time employees, with offices around the world in New York, Washington, London, Tokyo, São Paulo, and San Francisco.

The Eurasia Group is recognized as being the first major political risk firm to systematically apply the discipline of political science to its analysis, bringing this approach to Wall Street and the investment community. Whereas the EIU has an economic bent, Kissinger Associates relies on its rolodex for assessments, and smaller modern firms engage in history-centric analysis, Eurasia has led the intellectual charge for treating political risk analysis as more of a science than an art.

For example, the Eurasia Group Global Political Risk Index (GPRI) is designed to measure stability in emerging markets, a very practical concern for large multinational companies. In general, as is true for the other firms, Eurasia makes its money by providing clients with analytical publications, tailored consulting and advising, and direct access to its army of analysts. It tracks global political trends, analyzing their impacts on business, markets, and the overall investment climate. Bremmer is blessed with a genius for marketing his wares: in January of every year, Eurasia releases a highly anticipated list of the top ten global risks for the coming year. In general, Eurasia's clients include major investment banks, institutional investors, multinational corporations, and governments around the world.

Bremmer, born in November 1969 in the inhospitable climate of the Boston housing projects, has been a prodigy for much of his life: he was awarded a PhD from Stanford at the eye-catchingly young age of twenty-four. The youngest-ever national fellow of the Hoover Institution, Bremmer went on to found the Eurasia Group when he was only twenty-eight. Eurasia's specific expertise is in providing analysis and in-depth knowledge about how national security and political developments shape the investment environment across the world.

Boyish, driven, and quietly if compellingly enthusiastic about what he does, Bremmer had an important management insight early on: writing in open-source publications provides the best form of advertisement for a political risk firm. This practice elevated him to rock star status and also helped brand Eurasia as the next big thing. As such, Bremmer is presently foreign affairs columnist and editor-at-large for *Time* magazine, which serves as a major platform for both him and his company. And as global research professor at New York University, Bremmer provides the template for the political risk industry's present incarnation, with academics becoming leading entrepreneurs.

Bremmer is also the author of a number of well-known foreign policy concepts. His notion of the "J Curve"—that, counter-intuitively, it is when dictatorships open up that things fall apart—became the trendy political idea of the

moment in 2006.[8] On one side of the graph (in good political science fashion) sits political stability, on the other side
a society's openness.

Bremmer not only acutely pointed out that dictatorships rarely make the transition from a closed to an open
society effortlessly, but also delineated the hinge points of
maximum political risk along the way. While critics saw this
as merely a statement of the obvious, there is no denying
the power of the J Curve concept as a masterful marketing
tool. Bremmer, more than any other major political risk
analyst of his time, has realized how all his many intellectual platforms—articles, books, television appearances,
speeches—feed back into very successfully marketing his
company. Bremmer blazed the trail that most subsequent
political risk firms have since followed.

Bremmer's other major insight is that, with the decline
of America (and the international institutions it created) as
the world's ordering power, we are now living in a "G-Zero"
world of increased risk, as there is no overarching power to
provide global stability.[9] Historians (such as myself) have
growled that this is simply untrue, as at any given moment
in time there is some sort of global distribution of power,
that power does not simply evaporate but is redistributed.
Still, Bremer's thesis struck a nerve, coinciding with a general
sense that political risk has grown in the world as the notion
of America as global cop has faded. As he put it, "What we
need to realize is that, if the world moves faster, then the
speed with which things can go wrong picks up."[10]

---

[8]Ian Bremmer, *The J Curve: A New Way to Understand Why Nations Rise and
Fall* (New York: Simon & Schuster, 2006).

[9]Ian Bremmer, *Every Nation for Itself: Winners and Losers in a G-Zero World*
(New York: Portfolio, 2012).

[10]Damian Thompson, "Here's How the World Works," *(London) Daily Telegraph*,
September 30, 2006.

In line with the practices of Kissinger Associates, Bremmer makes it a point to meet the rulers of the developing countries his firm is assessing, whether they are the sort you want dating your daughter or not. This belief in specialized, personal knowledge is matched by a Kissingerian penchant for secrecy: much of Eurasia's work for its more than 300 clients is conducted off the record.

Future analytical problems for Eurasia and Bremmer are exactly the sort you wish to have: they are all the result of its phenomenal success. The intellectual danger ahead lies in Eurasia's growth: with size, intellectual quality control becomes harder and harder to manage. The fact is that if we were to survey any group of one hundred people, some would be excellent, some mediocre, and some downright poor. As a corporate entity, Eurasia will have to worry incessantly about maintaining the cutting-edge analysis that is much easier to produce when there are only four or five swashbuckling, but very capable, senior analysts at the table.

In 1996, Stratfor and George Friedman followed quickly on from Eurasia's trailblazing success. With Friedman as chairman and founder, Stratfor—a private global intelligence forecasting company and consulting firm—has grown to have, as of December 2015, 100 employees who advise business and political leaders about political risk. If the other political risk firms conjure images of anonymous Brits circling the globe in pinstriped suits (EIU), the grand old men of the foreign policy establishment gravely gathering to put the world to rights (Kissinger Associates), and the academic as entrepreneur (Eurasia), Stratfor brings to mind military-intelligence types, complete with shades and the requisite trench coats.

Seen as a sort of shadow CIA, Stratfor hires analysts from the military and intelligence worlds. Its revenue stream is broadly similar to its competitors': Stratfor makes its money from subscriptions to its website and from advising its corporate clients. In typically bombastic Friedman fashion, Stratfor has described itself as the world's leading intellectual platform, bringing an invaluable geopolitical context to the assessment of global events, empowering businesses and governments to more expertly navigate their way through the increasingly complex world of international relations. Stratfor develops comprehensive, systemic, and independent political risk analysis for its clients focusing on offering them actionable insights; this practical approach is highly favored in the business world and moves Stratfor away from more strictly esoteric academic analysis.

Founded on the bold notion (shared by the Pythia) that world events can be predictably assessed, Stratfor takes an approach in stark opposition to the political science focus of Eurasia: the consultancy's analysis of open-source information through the lens of geopolitics relies far more on a deep study of history, politics, and geography. In line with its secretive reputation, Stratfor's client list is confidential. It is known that it serves both corporate and US military clients.

Despite its cloak-and-dagger background, Stratfor not only focuses on analysis of open-source data collection but also prides itself on its distance—both socially and intellectually— from the Washington establishment, allowing (it feels) for more dispassionate analysis. It is not a mistake that the firm's headquarters is in far-away Austin, Texas. Friedman has personally said that the firm's outsider (non-Washington) status is a major reason for its success, allowing it to avoid having its independent voice corrupted. As Friedman has proudly proclaimed, "We never go to cocktail parties."[11]

In military style, Stratfor publishes a daily intelligence briefing. It made its name during the Kosovo crisis of 1999, also accurately predicting the 1997 regional economic crisis

[11] Sam C. Gwynne, "Spies Like Us," *Time*, January 25, 1999.

in Asia. Less intellectually glorious was Friedman's insistence that serious conflict between America and Japan was just over the horizon.[12]

Like Bremmer, Friedman started as an outsider to the establishment. Born in 1949 in Budapest to Holocaust survivors, he fled the country with his family when he was a child to escape communism, emigrating to the United States. Also like Bremmer, Friedman excelled intellectually; he holds a PhD in government from Cornell. An early designer of computerized war games—strategic simulations that weigh up the risks of various policy approaches to crises as well as their likely outcomes—Friedman regularly briefed senior armed services commanders, the US Army War College, the National Defense University, and RAND Corporation, developing an easy familiarity with the military intelligence types who have come to dominate Stratfor.

Prior to founding Stratfor, Friedman spent almost twenty years teaching political science at Dickinson College. Despite this background, as a political risk analyst he has more often than not stressed the political philosophy approach of his early briefing days, seeing geopolitics, rather than political science, as the way forward for the political risk discipline.

A charismatic public speaker with easy, imperious command of his audience, Friedman uses public speaking, his books, and his prolific public articles as platforms for business. His most famous effort is probably *The Next 100 Years*, a book that reflects both his belief in the power of forecasting as well as his predilection, in contrast to Bremmer, for long-term historical analysis.[13]

[12] George Friedman, with Meredith LeBard, *The Coming War with Japan* (New York: St. Martin's Press, 1991).

[13] George Friedman, *The Next 100 Years: A Forecast for the 21st Century* (New York: Doubleday, 2009).

Friedman retired from Stratfor in May 2015 to set up *Geopolitical Futures*, a far more public online publication that analyzes and forecasts global events. It is an effort to bring political risk analysis to a far wider and less secretive audience, in line with what a number of other smaller firms have been doing over the past decade.

This leaves Stratfor in a bit of a quandary. As the modern political risk business is so new, most of the firms created are still very much a reflection of the vision and the image of their founder. Stratfor is continuing on as before, but it has lost easily its most recognizable analyst in Friedman, who is nothing less than a totemic symbol of the company itself.

Worse still from the consultancy's point of view, Friedman has re-emerged as a sort of competitor, armed with a more open and modern take, through *Geopolitical Futures*, on what political risk analysis ought to look like. While Stratfor remains supreme in its military intelligence niche, the end of its founder's reign calls into question whether the company can expand into other areas in the future.

A number of substantial but far smaller firms have sprung up in the wake of the stunning success of both Bremmer and Friedman. Amongst these is my own political risk company, John C. Hulsman Enterprises, founded in Berlin in 2007. As is true for most of these smaller risk firms, mine is more like a medieval guild than a corporation. The staff is smaller in number, younger, trading their many hours of toil largely for mastery of the craft of political risk analysis itself.

Also like a renaissance artist's studio, these smaller firms tend to pull in outside experts on a one-off basis. For my own firm this is easy, as I call upon my many friends made through years of working in senior analytical positions in think tanks on both sides of the Atlantic. Metaphorically, for example, if the pope (a modern client) wants a specific ceiling painted and I happen to know the best angel painter, we work together in harmony on this one project, then go our separate ways again.

As opposed to Eurasia, Stratfor, and Kissinger Associates, the smaller firms tend to be more open about what they do, more public, and more analytically (and less rolodex-) driven. At my firm, and in direct contrast to Eurasia and more like Stratfor, we come down strongly on the historical and geopolitical side of the ledger, seeing this analytical approach as the best way to view the political risk world.

However, we have followed in Bremmer's footsteps in using our various public platforms to both advertise our business and showcase our analytical work. In contrast to the bigger, more closed shops that preceded me, much of the written work I do is posted for free on the company website.

This more open approach explains why I have been the senior columnist for foreign affairs and political risk for *City AM*, the newspaper of the City of London, written all or part of 14 books as well as 600 articles, and given over 1,500 television and radio interviews. I have appeared on programs as varied as *The Daily Show with Jon Stewart* and the offerings of C-SPAN, ABC, CBS, FOX, MSNBC, CNBC, and the BBC.

While I have the academic background of both Bremmer and Friedman, holding a PhD from St. Andrews University in Scotland, like them, I am now an intellectual entrepreneur. This is all part of the present trend of political risk analysis: leaving the Kissingerian shadows behind, firms are now competing more openly in the marketplace of ideas.

A final breakthrough has been my firm's design of cutting-edge war games like the ones I used to play during my days in official Washington. These games have become our most popular product with corporate clients; international banks, hedge funds, and insurance companies are all eager to look at global crises in depth, working out both their likely outcomes and the key hinge points of political risk along the way that will determine the trajectory of specific geopolitical events. Beyond our war game innovation, my firm follows the Eurasia path of engaging in boardroom consulting, writing as well as communicating bespoke commissioned analysis, and giving corporate keynote addresses.

The basic managerial problem for smaller political risk firms such as mine is twofold. Even more than is true for the larger companies such as Stratfor and Eurasia, the smaller firms tend to be entirely dependent on one relatively well-known principal. In the corporate consciousness, they are one-man bands that rise or fall on the vagaries of the health and ability of just one person.

The other danger comes when this renaissance guild model begins to succeed because the small number of analysts all happen to do very good work. With success, the pressure to grow, diluting this great analytical competitive advantage, becomes intense. However, given the booming market for first-rate political risk analysis, if smaller firms can escape the Scylla of over-dependence on their founder and the Charybdis of throwing away the competitive advantage of controlling content, the corporate world is theirs for the taking.

Whatever the analytical approach or size of a particular modern political risk firm, the reasons CEOs have for hiring them are fairly uniform. As outside advisers to large corporations, political risk firms operate like corporate strategists or investment advisers, long a part of the business landscape. Rather than assembling a kitchen cabinet of PhDs, lawyers, career diplomats, retired military strategists, or political advisers they personally know well to advise them regarding specific initiatives, corporate executives have found that it is far better to rely on impersonal political risk firms to deliver systemic, dispassionate analysis.

Internal bureaucratic office politics inevitably slants a lot of political risk analysis to suit whatever the corporation or government is doing, making objective, independent political risk advice a godsend for CEOs. Such advice gives decision-makers access to the insights of world experts from outside who, knowing nothing about a corporation's politics, give them straight analysis instead. Over the past decades, as political risk firms have boomed and entered the public consciousness, it has become abundantly clear that such outside political risk assessments are invaluable, and this basic selling point explains the mania of political risk firms for trumpeting their independence.

The second major selling point for all modern political risk firms is that they provide a desperately needed service to a corporate world with a surprising dearth of analytical power. Few organizations have the capacity to conduct the kind of research that a serious political risk firm does every day. After the tech bubble burst, and then again after the Lehman Brothers crisis, many larger corporations downsized their research staffs or got rid of them altogether; now they must outsource such vital work to political risk consultants. The fact that doing so often remains much cheaper than maintaining their old in-house research staffs has only added to the bottom-line incentives driving the boom in the political risk business.

Given these drivers, many large corporations feel that they have no alternative but to bring in outside political risk firms for advice, particularly given the recent jarring change in the overall structure in the global order, a world of many powers having replaced the more comfortable, understood era of American dominance. As many of the pieces of the old global power puzzle—be it the United States, China, India, Russia, or Europe—now have different weights and functions in the multipolar era, the added value of political risk firms is far more obvious. Everyone is aware not only that has the world changed, but also that almost no one knows what it means. There has rarely been a better time for a Pythia to emerge to restore intellectual order to seeming global chaos, for investors and governments alike. This is the generic commercial opening all good political risk firms have at the moment.

In a larger sense, political risk firms provide their clients with a form of intellectual insurance—secure analytical compass points on the stormy seas of a new era. In general, modern society itself would be impossible without insurance. This basic insight lies beneath all financial risk management, of which political risk analysis amounts to an important and growing sub-set. Political risk firms provide intellectual insurance for countries, corporations, and other institutions to do what they do, explaining the global geopolitical weather they all must live in. Beyond this essential, if negative, function, political risk insights also allow corporations to grasp positive opportunities they might not see without such Delphic insights.

Yet truth be told, for all this shiny new professionalization, the recent record of top political risk thinkers regarding the highly uncertain, even shocking, political times we are living through is nothing short of abysmal. (Over two of the most important and hardest recent geopolitical events to predict—Brexit and the surprise election of Donald Trump—an overwhelming number of predictions have been botched.)

For example, Ian Bremmer was flatly wrong about both.[14] George Friedman, long a skeptic of the EU, nevertheless hedged on the Brexit outcome, and also misunderstood the Trump phenomenon.[15] Looking directly in the mirror,

[14]See "Bremmer Sees 30% Chance of a Trump Presidency," *Bloomberg*, September 20, 2016; and Peter Foster, "Bremmer on Brexit: Why Britain, Reluctantly, Is Likely to Vote to Stay in the EU," *(London) Daily Telegraph*, January 28, 2016.

[15]George Friedman, "The Crisis of the Well-Crafted Candidate," *Stratfor*, September 22, 2015.

even though my firm had a very good 2016—we called the Colombian, Dutch, and Italian referenda correctly—we were off the mark about Trump; in speeches I echoed Bremmer in saying that Trump had only around a one-in-three chance of winning. We did cover ourselves in some glory by rather uniquely calling Brexit in our January 2016 predictions column.[16]

Taken as a whole, the political risk industry has not recently lived up to its hype. This is a major reason I have written *To Dare More Boldly*: to highlight the elemental principles of geopolitical risk—the ten analytical commandments—that must never be forgotten if we are to do better.

Why has political risk analysis gone so wrong? I have long held heretical views about the industry, which cluster around what I call the "plumber's test." However bejeweled or slick at marketing a political risk firm may be, what matters in the end is delivering correct analysis to its clients.

Just as I don't invite back my local plumber if he fails to fix the pipes, nor should businesses put up with political risk firms that missed the war in Iraq's predictable outcome, failed to see the coming of the Lehman Brothers crisis, or (more recently) failed to predict that Britons would leave the EU. What holds true for my plumber ought to hold for what I do for a living as well.

The general Brexit political risk analysis failure revolved around the "Pauline Kael fallacy." The legendary cinema critic of the leftish *New York Times* supposedly wondered, following Richard Nixon's landslide forty-nine-state victory in 1972, how it was possible that the incumbent won when everyone she knew voted for the hapless Democrat George McGovern.

---

[16]John Hulsman, "The End of the West: 2016 Is the Year a New Order Begins to Rise," *City AM*, January 4, 2016.

There we have it in a nutshell. Top political risk analysts are generally now part of the elite they are supposed to assess, an elite who uniformly called your sanity into question if you so much as broached the possibility of Brexit happening. These analysts too often go to the same cocktail parties, read the same books, intermarry, and share the same "right thinking" views with global elites, all without wondering over much about the wider world outside the cocoon of conferences at nice hotels. All too often intellectually trapped within an elite they are supposed to objectively analyze, much political risk analysis has lost the precious objectivity needed to think about our rapidly changing world.

This danger is balanced by the lure of the glittering rewards of being amongst the few to truly understand the new multipolar era that is dawning. For there are endless commercial and political opportunities to be reaped in mastering our present complicated world, as political risk analysis can uniquely guide businesses to see the myriad glittering opportunities on the global chessboard. With the world in transition, there has never been a better or more lucrative time for political risk analysts to get their act together.

Hans Morgenthau, Realism, and Modern Geopolitical Risk

Strikingly, the lion's share of political risk firms and their star analysts share a further commonality: almost all of them adhere to the realist foreign policy school of thought, an enduring if minority point of view in the modern world. Given the need in geopolitical risk analysis to focus dispassionately on the realities of power—on how the world actually works rather than on how one might wish it did—a realist point of view is necessary for effective geopolitical risk analysis in particular, and for managing the ship of state more generally. This is especially true in our non-ideological multipolar world, where power alone—rather than ideological considerations—more often determines outcomes. Either directly or indirectly, all modern realists sit at the feet of Hans J. Morgenthau, the preeminent political philosopher of modern realism.

As my colleague Wess Mitchell and I have made clear, "At its root, realism can be reduced to a simple proposition: that, in order to anticipate and adapt to change in international politics, you must first understand the nature, uses, and limitations of power, tailoring strategies to the actual capabilities a country possesses."[17] In other words, to expertly analyze the world, realism commands that a geopolitical risk analyst must see the world as it actually is.

This book is an adventurous exploration of the modern trinity of geopolitical risk analysis, a vital sub-set of overall political risk analysis: principles, progenitors, and philosophy. The book focuses more on the first two parts of this trinity, as they are far less discussed, but no discussion of modern geopolitical risk could be complete without revisiting Morgenthau and his realist descendants, especially Kenneth Waltz,[18] who provide its absolutely necessary philosophical underpinnings.

Morgenthau was born in Coburg, Germany, in 1904, attending the universities of Berlin, Frankfurt, and Munich. Along with George Kennan and Reinhold Niebuhr, he is one of the three intellectual realist lions of the post-1945 world. In his youth, after bravely opposing the rise of Nazi ideology from its inception, Morgenthau emigrated in 1937 to America, where he spent most of his career at the University of Chicago, from 1943 to 1973.

---

[17] John Hulsman and A. Wess Mitchell, *The Godfather Doctrine: A Foreign Policy Parable* (Princeton, NJ: Princeton University Press, 2009), p. 7.

[18] Waltz is highlighted at length in the conclusion.

In line with future geopolitical risk stars, Morgenthau managed the difficult feat of maintaining his intellectual credibility while working with powerful decision-makers. As a strong supporter of Franklin Roosevelt and Harry Truman, Morgenthau served as a consultant to Kennan at the State Department in the early days of the Cold War and later served in a similar capacity in the Kennedy and Johnson administrations. However, there was never any chance that he would be corrupted by proximity to power. From early on, Morgenthau decisively fell out with the Johnson White House over Vietnam, going so far as to publicly support opposition to the war, then just brewing on America's college campuses.

Though a prolific writer and thinker, Morgenthau's masterpiece, *Politics Among Nations*, came early to him, in 1948.[19] In it, he did nothing less than lay out the philosophical tenets of modern realism, serving as the well-spring for most geopolitical risk analysis today. First, Morgenthau declared that nation-states are the main actors in international relations; they are the main unit of analysis for modern geopolitical risk. Second, nation-states are primarily motivated by their national interests, that of survival above all, as well as maximizing their power in an anarchic world, without an overall global referee.

For geopolitical risk analysts, this means, through the correct analysis of a country's national interest, its behavior can be largely assessed, as well as predicted. For Morgenthau, history's winners were the statesmen who managed to recognize the power realities of their day, and to construct foreign policies attuned to these realities. But the national interest is not an entirely fixed concept. Beyond the specific foreign policy power realities of time and place that a country

---

[19] Hans J. Morgenthau, *Politics among Nations: The Struggle for Power and Peace* (New York: Alfred J. Knopf, 1948).

confronts, the national interest is also determined by the unique political and cultural context of any given state. In other words, history matters in any overall geopolitical risk analysis assessment.

Morgenthau saw the correct assessment of the national interest as the only way forward for the insightful analysis of international relations. To pine for a world that simply does not exist—as the more utopian Wilsonian and neo-conservative foreign policy schools of thought so often do—is to entirely miss the point. As Morgenthau cogently put it, "The choice is not between moral principles and the national interest, devoid of moral dignity, but between one set of principles divorced from political reality and another set of principles derived from political reality."[20]

Third, given this lack of an overall global ordering power, countries will endlessly jockey with each other for power, making peace and stability fragile and dependent on a balance of power between great nations at any given time. This imperative drives geopolitical risk analysts to constantly focus on changes to any international political system, as it is change and not stability that characterizes history itself.

Fourth, and directly in line with the general thrust of this book, Morgenthau—going back to the works of Hobbes and Machiavelli—epitomized the classical realist view that international relations can be explained as a result of the study of human nature. For Morgenthau, foreign policy analysis can attain meaningful insights only if the analyst places himself correctly in the place of specific statesmen in order to predict geopolitical outcomes.

Morgenthau commands that a world-class analyst "must put himself into the other man's shoes, look at the world

[20] Hans J. Morgenthau, *In Defense of the National Interest* (Lanham, MD: University Press of America, 1982), p. 34.

and judge it as he does, anticipate in thought the way he will feel and act under certain circumstances."[21] For geopolitical risk analysts—especially the branch of the tribe that favors a history-first approach—Morgenthau's pioneering work made it clear that geopolitics can be not only assessed but also predicted, and that history and psychology would be the primary guides for doing so. This book will follow gratefully in Morgenthau's ground-breaking footsteps, attempting to delineate the elements that undergird modern geopolitical risk analysis, using his novel realist philosophical insights as our guide.

Brian Wilson and Greek Attributes

As we have seen, while appearing to be the height of modern fashion, in reality geopolitical risk analysis is as old as the Greeks. Every chapter of this book highlights what the ancients would call an element of geopolitical risk analysis, a "do" or a "don't" maxim which taken together provides us with the rules of the game for mastering risk in geopolitics. As a result of our approach, this book will make clear the enduring nature of geopolitical risk analysis, using pivotal historical moments—and the lessons they teach—to illuminate our search for these key elements. Taken together, these elements or maxims—the ten commandments of geopolitical risk—do nothing less than provide a practitioner's handbook for mastering risk in geopolitics, a way of facts-based structured thinking that codifies what up until now has been shrouded in the Pythia's mystery.

The elements in each chapter are precisely the answer as to why geopolitical risk analysts find themselves in such demand

---

[21] Hans J. Morgenthau, "The Limits of Historical Justice," in *Truth and Power: Collected Essays 1960–1970* (New York: Praeger, 1970).

in today's world. Unlike Citibank's in-house researchers or the kitchen cabinet of the Irish *Taoiseach* (prime minister), geopolitical risk analysts ought to come to work armed with history as an intellectual discipline—epitomized by these Greek elements, maxims built around real-world past cases of risk—allowing them to avoid proven historical traps that gifted outsiders may well be unaware of. This crucial advantage leapfrogs its best practitioners' work above that of the gifted amateur.

To Dare More Boldly is not an international relations book per se, but a history of geopolitical risk throughout the ages and the rules of the game that can be derived from that history, understood through historical anecdotes and analogies. The book explains how managing risk in geopolitics has defined the life of nations since the ancient world.

The use of historical analogies as a way of understanding the rules of the road in geopolitical risk analysis is particularly novel and important. The purpose of using such a method is to convey in succinct form, and for academic and more general audiences alike, the broader importance of the primary geopolitical risk rules of the road we propound, while at the same time grounding them in the only intellectual laboratory that matters, the real-world experiences of mankind.[22]

The book is also underpinned by the value of political realism and above all the value of historical analysis (particularly as it relates to lessons and analogies) remaining vital to understanding the contemporary world of international relations and geopolitics. Particularly, such an analysis can help lay bare the rules of the road for how leaders ought to deal with geopolitical risk; transcending time and place, this "do's and don'ts" list is a typology for mastering geopolitical

[22] See Hulsman and Mitchell, *The Godfather Doctrine*, p. 63.

risk itself. I look forward to readers reveling in the adventure of *To Dare More Boldly* with me.

The chapters themselves are baroque in structure, a fond *homage* to the genius of the pioneering musician and peerless producer Brian Wilson of the Beach Boys, particularly his work on his masterpiece, *Pet Sounds*. I have long thought that Wilson's approach to music has more universal applications, working even better in the world of writing. On *Pet Sounds*, Wilson changed how we think about music itself, writing songs that had definable segments that could be moved about in endless, intricate, creative combinations, as their internal consistency was so pronounced.

I have structured *To Dare More Boldly* much like *Pet Sounds*. There is a main historical story in each chapter flowing throughout the book in chronological order, giving *To Dare More Boldly* its narrative thrust forward and allowing it to be daring but structured and understandable. We cover a lot of ground, from 480 BC to 1978 AD, proving that while geopolitical risk analysis may be trendy, it is also far from new. Beneath this clear, elegant historical structure, in Brian Wilson fashion, each chapter also has at least one non-chronological inter-chapter, further historical vignettes buttressing the thematic element, the commandment the main portion of each chapter highlights.

This is not a mistake; Wilson's baroque method focuses attention on themes. In our case, the important fact is that throughout history there have been many examples of the major elements each chapter outlines. We are not cherry-picking history to suit our purposes, using only one historical example over the 2,500 years *To Dare More Boldly* covers to falsely derive the definitive list of geopolitical risk elements, the maxims that form the basis of this book. In essence, our book moves from prayer (the Pythia), to principle (the realist views of Morgenthau), to the historical progenitors of the elements that allow for a mastering of risk in geopolitics.

Instead, the inter-chapter approach underlines that there are several, often many, historical examples of each element beyond the primary one highlighted in every chapter to come. For every Lord Salisbury there is a Meiji Restoration example of the imperative of analysts correctly seeing where their country fits in their world. For every John Adams there is a Winston Churchill underlining the importance for risk analysts of comprehending game-changing events. For every Deng Xiaoping there is a Harold Macmillan highlighting the need for analysts to surmount random, incalculable events. The baroque Brian Wilson approach allows the elements and the book itself to have a more profound, timeless quality.

The baroque method also allows us to focus more on the themes underlying geopolitical risk analysis across time, while at the same time providing enough narrative structure and coherence to keep the show on the road. If properly done, there are great benefits to this unorthodox, less conventional approach by theme, as it makes the timelessness of the elements crystal clear. The conclusion of *To Dare More Boldly* is the moment when we reach the peak of Everest, marshaling the political risk elements derived from our historical stories to codify the ten commandments of geopolitical risk. Following in the footsteps of Morgenthau, the book amounts to nothing less than an opportunity to outline a way of thinking peculiarly suited for the new, unfamiliar multipolar world, fraught with geopolitical risk, that we now all find ourselves in.

Effective statecraft has always been immersed in geopolitical risk—both its promise and its peril—as successful foreign policy analysis always requires both the proper assessment and management of such challenges. Beyond all else, such geopolitical risk management requires a truly global geostrategic perspective in line with our multipolar world, where power is dramatically diffusing away from the long-dominant West to new rising powers across the globe, to unthought of places such as India, China, Turkey, Indonesia, South Africa, and Brazil.

Knowing about the politics of the West is simply no longer good enough. Our choice of historical stories reflects this necessity, going beyond merely an understanding of the Western world to also focus directly on the Middle East, Japan, and China and indirectly (through the Beatles chapter) on the rise of today's non-Western emerging powers.

Drawing on as disparate a group of historical actors as possible, *To Dare More Boldly* will look at Ancient Greece, Rome, the Third Crusade, Machiavelli, the American Founders, Napoleon, Lee at Gettysburg, Lord Salisbury and the British Empire, Wilhelmine Germany, George Harrison, and Deng Xiaoping to both draw out the timeless elements underlying geopolitical risk analysis and illustrate the never-ending efforts throughout history of people to master their world.

We shall set out, using history and the priceless Homeric gift of story-telling as our guides, to assess element by element what is conceptually right and wrong with geopolitical risk today to unlock the analytical key to mastering it in our present age. Indeed, the book's extensive use of vignettes will illustrate the profound advantages of re-acquiring story-telling as a vital, venerable, and underrated tool, to aid human understanding.

By the end of our story, through the use of this unique method, we will have delineated the long and neglected history of geopolitical risk analysis, linking that important tale to the broader efforts of both business and political leaders to master risk in general. After this story has been conclusively laid out, we will attain the summit in terms of understanding geopolitical risk. Now confident in what geopolitical risk analysis has been, is, and can be, we will see that the Delphic dream of soothsaying—in a limited way, over limited issues, and for a limited period of time—can at least be partially fulfilled. Losing sight of land, we will truly find the stars.

Back to the Past of the Pythia's Lair to Glean the Future of Geopolitical Risk Analysis

To Dare More Boldly will make the case that there are ten basic elements comprising the rules of the game, ten commandments that allow analysts to begin to slay the dragon that is geopolitical risk. In chronological order in terms of our story-telling they are:

1. **"We are the risk."** As the history surrounding Sejanus and the decline and fall of the Roman Empire makes clear (alongside the corroborating tale of present-day Europe's decadent decline), geopolitical analysts have a terrible time looking in the mirror and seeing that the society they are part of can itself be the major geopolitical risk problem.

2. **Gaming out "lunatics."** Far too often geopolitical risk analysts let those with very different belief systems off the hook by lazily assuming that they must be crazy, rather than looking for the method to their madness. As the story of "The Old Man of the Mountain" and the Third Crusade (with inter-chapters on both Charles Manson and ISIS) makes clear, there is almost always an internal logic to any seemingly mad geopolitical interlocutor that can be followed and assessed.

3. **Gaming out "chess players."** Amidst the daily tumult of a constant barrage of information, it is easy to lose sight of the intellectual needle in the haystack: the assessment of "chess players," those geopolitical decision-makers who have stable, rational, coherent, long-term strategies in place to further their geopolitical goals. As reviewing the

history of Niccolò Machiavelli and Pope Julius II (with an inter-chapter on George Washington and Alexander Hamilton) illuminates, finding these rare geostrategic birds is well worth the effort, as once they are identified (which is difficult), their future actions can rather easily be predicted.

4. **Recognizing game-changers.** As the stirring story of John Adams in the sultry summer of 1776 makes clear, seeing the bigger picture—discerning how specific contemporaneous events fit into the larger historical pattern—is a mighty tool in geopolitical risk analysis. Separating the wheat from the chaff and intellectually drilling down on what really matters and its historical meaning (as we see both Adams and inter-chapter hero Winston Churchill doing in very different historical contexts) allows the geopolitical risk analyst as well as the foreign policy practitioner to see the world as it actually is.

5. **Balance is the key to foreign policy.** Having discovered the secrets of one major driver of geopolitics—be it macroeconomics, geopolitics, or cultural power—far too often analysts quickly forget that there are others and that it is the mix that explains everything. The twin stories of a beleaguered Venetian Republic and a seemingly all-conquering Napoleon in 1797 allow a dual critique of both economics-only and overly militaristic policies and the doom to which both one-sided initiatives inevitably lead.

6. **If you are digging yourself a hole in foreign policy—stop.** The "losing gambler in Vegas" syndrome affects both policy-makers and analysts. As the legendary Robert E. Lee found to his supreme peril at Gettysburg (and also "the best and the brightest" of the Kennedy and Johnson administrations as they met their nemesis in Indochina), pushing ahead with an already failed policy in a desperate effort to recoup past losses leads to calamity.

7. **Know your country's place in the world.** The singular case of the late Victorian titan Lord Salisbury—who bravely and correctly righted Britain's foreign policy to fit the paradox of its relatively declining but still dominant place in the world of the 1890s—highlights this vital requirement for both policy-makers and analysts alike. Only by bravely and correctly assessing your country's true geopolitical place in the world (as the inter-chapter on the *Genrō* of Japan makes clear happened across the globe from Salisbury a generation earlier) can you pursue a successful foreign policy.

8. **Do not put all your eggs in one strategic basket.** Distantly related to the "losing gambler in Vegas" syndrome, the "promised land" fallacy besets decision-makers who ruinously rely on one overall strategy to magically attempt to alter their country's overall geopolitical position in the world. In the case of Wilhelmine Germany, Admiral Von Tirpitz's disastrous plan to challenge British naval might (echoing the inter-chapter on Soviet leader Nikita Khrushchev's equally ruinous "wars of national liberation" gambit) helped lead to the Great War and Germany's destruction.

9. **Know the nature of the system you are living in.** The trials and tribulations of Beatle George Harrison (with the inter-chapter focusing on the diametrically opposed case of the fall of Brian Jones and the rise of the Rolling Stones) and the stunning, lightning-quick dismemberment of his band dramatically underline that successful systems can collapse in the blink of an eye if their underlying power realities change, failing to any longer reflect the systemic power facts on the ground that created such a system in the first place. Policy-makers as well as geopolitical risk analysts must know both the nature of the global system they are living in (is it characterized by one great power, two, or many?) as well as if that system is durable, fragile, or evolving.

10. Prepare for the "butterfly effect." The telling present-day case of Deng Xiaoping and the colossal success he made of both Chinese foreign and economic policy must not obscure the reality that East Asia today sits on a powder keg, a single seemingly random event away from 1914; just one drunken Chinese sea captain could quite plausibly upset the strategic equilibrium in Asia. The best policy-makers and geopolitical risk analysts (as the inter-chapter example of Harold Macmillan also makes clear) see the weaknesses in even the most successful foreign policies, having resilient initiatives at the ready to stave off seemingly unexpected disasters.

While the subsequent chapters will lay out in detail what the ancient Greeks would call the major "elements" of world-class geopolitical risk thought, the conclusion of *To Dare More Boldly* makes plain that it is surely the order in which they are applied—and their relative intellectual weighting—that matters most. Here, in her vague, obscure, but compelling way, the Pythia again provides the crucial clues as to how to proceed. To definitively answer this question of questions, we must go back to the gloomy confines of her lair.

For the three aphorisms carved in the Pythia's stronghold, deep in the crevices underneath Mount Parnassus, provide the keys to unlocking the secrets of geopolitical risk analysis. The first—the most important and the trunk of the tree for all advanced geopolitical risk thinking—is perhaps the Greeks' greatest philosophical contribution to Western thought itself, the simple but overwhelming imperative to "know thyself." In the context of geopolitical risk analysis, this means knowing in precise detail the sort of world in which we find ourselves, in terms of its global power structure and, more specifically, the place of one's own country in that world. This, then, is the trunk of the tree for geopolitical risk analysis, the one key insight upon which everything else rests.

To live up to this call to Drakean boldness, any successful political risk analysis must correctly assess the broad power structure of the world as well as its polarity—the major centers of power that characterize global politics at any given time. Whether you are studying the unipolar Mediterranean world of the *Pax Romana*, the complex multipolarity of post-Napoleonic Europe, or the bipolar US-Soviet competition of the Cold War, getting this overarching structure right is absolutely necessary for any incisive analysis that might follow. This is because the power structure of the world sets the rules and parameters for every state's actions within it, allowing the analyst to game out likely outcomes.

The second philosophical imperative found in the Pythia's dank lair—one of the two intellectual branches supported by the "know thyself" tree trunk of geopolitical risk analysis—is "nothing in excess." However clever or compelling an idea or insight is, without the Greek notion of balance being ever present, such monomania is bound to lead to overwhelming analytical failure. We will encounter the failure to abide by this precept over and over again in our historical journey, seeing that willful blindness to heed the Pythia's sage warning almost always leads to analytical and geopolitical disaster.

The final inscription on the Pythia's bleak walls was "Make a pledge and mischief is nigh." Roughly translated into modern foreign policy-speak, this means that analysts, however formidable, must never be too sure of their effectiveness. Instead of indulging in the ancient Greek sin of *hubris*, they should constantly check and re-check what they have assessed against the never-ending forward movement of events, of time altering preconceived notions. This second major intellectual branch of thinking off the "know thyself" trunk (the other being "nothing in excess") rounds out geopolitical risk analysis. These three clues left to us by the inscrutable Pythia, examples of which we will encounter time and again throughout our historical journey, serve as the headline categories this book will deepen and delineate with our chapter commandment examples. At the end of our intellectual travels, the result will be a clear typological outline, a ten commandments of geopolitical risk.

We can now leave the Pythia's terrible presence only to return to Mount Parnassus—as Odysseus finally made it back to Ithaca from Troy in *The Odyssey*—at the end of our long intellectual journey. Let us now set sail for a fascinating, storm-tossed ride through the history of geopolitical risk analysis. It is only proper that, having started with the ancient Greeks, we move on to the Roman Empire, where we will see what a terrible time risk analysts have in evaluating dangers that are home-grown.

The Ten Commandments of Political Risk

Know Thyself

1. Know the nature of the world you live in.
2. Know your country's place in that world.
3. Know when you are the geopolitical risk.
4. Know when game-changers occur.

Nothing in Excess

5. Balance is the key to foreign policy.
6. Game out lunatics.
7. Game out chess players.

Make a Pledge and Mischief Is Nigh

8. Avoid the losing gambler in Vegas syndrome.
9. Avoid the promised land fallacy.
10. Prepare for the butterfly effect.

CHAPTER TWO

31 AD: We Are the Risk

THE DECLINE AND FALL OF THE ROMAN EMPIRE

Edward Gibbon and How Political Risk
Analysts Think

Between 1776 and 1789, the peerless eighteenth-century Enlightenment historian (and sometime lackluster British Whig MP) Edward Gibbon set about remaking his profession. Gibbon's masterpiece, *The History of the Decline and Fall of the Roman Empire*, fastened upon an analytical conclusion that has not only proven invaluable to historians since but lays down an incredibly challenging gauntlet for political risk analysts in particular. For Gibbon's writing provides students of political risk with nothing less than our first primary element of what geopolitical risk analysis amounts to—a piece of the puzzle as to what geopolitical risk essentially is.

Better still, Gibbon's historical method more broadly is the basis for how today's political risk analysts think. For he showed the way by restlessly roaming across intellectual disciplines, regions, and topics, taking in the view from both the sky and the weeds, always striving to arrive at a holistic analysis. Gibbon was the grand generalist, interested in everything, constantly looking to make creative intellectual connections across artificial academic boundaries to arrive at a formidable, rounded analysis that explains in total why the ancient Roman world was the way it was.

This unique intellectual approach has been copied by all geopolitical risk analysts since, whether they know it or not.

It allows them to see the big picture of their subject while tracing the political trajectories of the specific country they are studying—whether it is rising or falling, and why. It is not too much to say that geopolitical risk analysts are all the children of Gibbon.

Gibbon managed to conjure up quite clearly through his life's work (six volumes of the book were produced between 1776 and 1789) a novel, cutting-edge answer to one of the most important historical questions of all time: why did the Roman Empire, in many ways the most powerful and most durable political construct ever created, finally disintegrate? Gibbon clearly argues that, while on the surface it was barbarian invasions that brought it to an end, this was only the final symptom of the Roman malaise, not the root cause of the disease. For Gibbon, Rome fell not primarily because of outside pressures, but rather owing to an internal and gradual loss of civic virtue amongst its citizens.

In other words, Rome was destroyed from within. Gibbon creatively saw that the political risk that overwhelmed the greatest of empires came about due to a failure to recognize and combat home-grown problems. Political risk analysts have grappled with Gibbon's incisive analysis ever since, as there is almost nothing harder for humans than to look in the mirror and honestly say, "We are the problem." The ability to analytically master this all-too human failing is our first element of geopolitical risk analysis as a way of thinking about the world.

In well over 1,000 pages, Gibbon masterfully makes his colossal subject accessible through wonderful, entertaining writing and his Enlightenment-driven ability to master many sub-fields (sociology, history, political science) at once. But despite the unprecedented scope of the work, the narrative content is held together by only a few basic but profound analytical insights that give unique form and balance to what by rights ought to have been an unholy mess.

It is striking that one of these themes was the micro notion that the overall decline of the greatest empire the world has ever known was the result of the individual, personal failings of its citizens. Gibbon was prescient in realizing that countries are almost always destroyed from within, and that decadence—specifically defined as a society's loss of ability to deal with its problems, coupled over time with a long-term abdication of responsibility for them—becomes the means of societal suicide.

Gibbon describes Roman decline as a problem characterized by personal passivity and a lack of creative energy and originality. It is at this very personal psychological and moral level that Gibbon sensed things began to go awry for the Romans.

This manifested itself in a policy to outsource the vital defense of the realm to barbarian mercenaries, who themselves took over the Empire from within. Specifically, Gibbon alleges that the Praetorian Guard—created by the Emperor Augustus to personally protect the imperial family—drove this process, both through periodic assassinations of emperors it did not like (the deranged Emperor Caligula being the most famous example) and by making never-ending demands on the imperial treasury for pay increases. The political instability—and geopolitical risk—this caused so weakened Rome that it eventually was hollowed out from within.

Controversially, Gibbon blames Christianity for speeding the Roman loss of *esprit de corps*. He argues that the insistence of Christian doctrine that a better life will come about after death sapped Roman believers of their desire to make sacrifices for the greater good of the Empire, or any other larger purpose on earth. Gibbon also believes that

Christianity's pacifist leanings hampered the continuation of the traditional Roman martial ethos, compelling emperors to turn to far less loyal barbarians instead to buttress an empire about which its citizens increasingly came to care less and less. As he puts it, "The last remains of military spirit were buried in the cloister."[1]

What makes internal decay as a form of geopolitical risk so devilishly hard to diagnose is that it involves looking critically inward rather than outward—not something human beings are particularly adept at. It is always easier to identify what is wrong with other countries and other peoples rather than going through the discomfort of an accurate look in the mirror. For too many mediocre modern-day geopolitical risk analysts, the discipline is merely the study of other people.

Once when I attended a meeting of the prestigious Council on Foreign Relations during America's brief unipolar moment, the members were tasked with coming up with the world's top ten political risks. When I had the audacity to mention that American political sclerosis ought to be on the list, the great and the good literally laughed in my face, as it was beyond comprehension that home-grown problems in the United States itself might pose real risks for the world in general.

I was literally (and rather haughtily) told that we were there to evaluate the rest of the world, not the United States, as though our own country were somehow historically immune from serious analysis. Gibbon's genius is to remind us that geopolitical risk analysis in general is inherently hobbled by such a lack of introspection. Gibbon does nothing less than present to us the intellectual challenge of this first primary element of geopolitical risk analysis.

[1] Edward Gibbon, *The History of the Decline and Fall of the Roman Empire* (London: T. Cadell, 1837), p. 611.

The Rise of Sejanus and the Fall of the Roman Empire

If Gibbon's theory holds true, then Sejanus, more than any other single Roman, is unwittingly most to blame for the decline and fall of the Empire. Born in 20 BC, Sejanus's family came from the knightly ranks of Roman society; his father Strabo served the Emperor Augustus with distinction. Strabo was one of two Praetorian prefects, commanders of the Praetorian Guard, a military unit formed by the emperor in 27 BC to personally protect the imperial family from security threats.

However, once Sejanus joined his father as a Praetorian prefect in 14 AD, during the reign of Tiberius, what had begun as a Secret Service soon morphed into something far more powerful and far more malevolent. Equal parts capable and ruthless, Sejanus set about fundamentally reforming the guard, making it an unaccountable domestic intelligence and paramilitary service.

Between 14 AD and 31 AD, Sejanus centralized the Praetorian Guard's administration. Overturning Augustus's wise decision to keep the guard dispersed throughout Rome in multiple garrisons and to always have two guard commanders (both measures designed to keep it in check), Sejanus increased the size of the guard to 12,000, concentrated it in a single, massive compound, and saw to it that it had but one commander—he himself. Sejanus had done nothing less than to create an important new source of political power within the Empire, one that was largely beyond anyone's control. For if the emperor could sometimes use the Praetorian Guard to enforce his will, they in turn, over time, held more than one emperor hostage to their desires.

Sejanus rose steadily, becoming a friend and confidant of Tiberius and eventually the second most important man in the Empire. When the unpopular Tiberius wearied of life in the palace and moved his entourage to the island of Capri in 26 AD, Sejanus stayed in Rome and became the de facto prime minister, in control of day-to-day administration.

In typical Roman fashion, near-absolute power corrupted Sejanus absolutely. It is likely that Sejanus personally murdered the emperor's son, Drusus the Younger, his great rival. Drusus, whom Tiberius was grooming as his heir, deeply resented Sejanus's favored position with his father and decried his tyrannical impulses. The Roman historian Tacitus records that by 23 AD the rivalry between the two reached its climax, with Drusus striking the proud Sejanus with his fist during one particularly heated argument.[2]

Sejanus was by then actively plotting against Drusus, seducing his wife Livilla along the way. With her connivance, Drusus was slowly poisoned to death by the pair; he died that same year, in September. With no rivals left to stop him, and with Tiberius far away in Capri (Sejanus controlled all information passing between the out-of-the-loop emperor and Rome), Sejanus's rise to absolute power seemed merely a matter of time.[3]

Backed by the unquestioning loyalty and power of the Praetorian Guard, Sejanus instituted a reign of terror in Rome, beginning a series of Stalin-like show trials of opposition senators. Caligula, the new heir to the throne, only survived the purge by moving to Capri to shelter under Tiberius's personal protection.[4]

In 31 AD, Sejanus reached the apogee of his power, sharing a consulship with the emperor himself and finally becoming betrothed to his partner in crime, Livilla. But dramatically to-

[2]See Tacitus, *The Annals of Imperial Rome*, vol. 4, chap. 3 (London: Penguin Classics, 2003).
[3]Ibid., vol. 4, chap. 41.
[4]Ibid., vol. 6, chap. 3.

ward the end of that year, Sejanus fell as rapidly as he had risen, for reasons that still continue to baffle modern historians.

The exact cause of Sejanus's demise is maddeningly unclear, as the critical record of Tacitus's *Annals* has been lost to time for this specific historical period. However, a preponderance of modern historical thinking has it that when Tiberius finally heard in Capri the extent to which Sejanus had already usurped his authority in Rome, and sensing the danger to himself and the imperial family, he at last took drastic steps to swiftly remove Sejanus from power.

Sejanus was dramatically arrested, led from prison, and strangled without trial, after being condemned to death by an emboldened Senate. His body was unceremoniously dumped down the Gemonian Steps in Rome, where the Roman people desecrated it. Sejanus may have been gone, but the internal decay he set in motion would contribute, centuries later, to the end of perhaps the most powerful and enduring political entity the world has ever known.

In the spirit of the greatest historian of the eighteenth century, we must use this very old idea regarding destruction from within to assess in geopolitical risk terms the very new story of the absolute decline of Europe in the twenty-first century. For while many others have followed Gibbon, on the whole no historian has improved upon his hypothesis that ancient Rome came to an end primarily because its society atrophied as a result of personal failings that accumulated over time. Geopolitical risk analysts must follow in his grand footsteps, seeing his notion of decadence as the ideational key to unlocking the riddle of the current cause of European decline. But to see this, Western geopolitical risk analysts will have to bravely look at our own society, warts and all.

The far-away Romans are not the only people who historically have had a hard time with introspection. Presently,

Europe has proven itself almost comically incapable of exercising this necessary analytical gift of self-awareness. Without being able to look at our own society as it is—rather than as we would wish it to be—any effort to construct a coherent geopolitical risk assessment of the wider world is doomed to failure.

An Avoidable Tragedy in France and the Root Cause of Europe's Decline

In early August 2003, the blood-red sun rose implacably over the city of Paris. It was the hottest summer on record in Europe since at least 1540. Temperatures were regularly hovering at a sweltering 40 degrees Celsius, or a blistering 104 degrees Fahrenheit. As the heat rose to wholly unaccustomed levels, many people—particularly the elderly—started dying. According to the French National Institute of Health, in France alone 14,802 people died of heat-related complications that sunbaked August, with more than 70,000 perishing across the continent.

Curiously, most of those who died in France that summer were relatively healthy older people living alone without immediate family, not the elderly requiring constant medical care. Those cut off from what the British thinker and Parliamentarian Edmund Burke would have termed "society" fared far worse than the obviously feeble. As Stephane Mantion, a French Red Cross official, put it, "The French family structure is more dislocated than elsewhere in Europe, and prevailing social attitudes hold that once older people are closed behind their apartment doors or in nursing homes, they are someone else's problem."[5]

[5]"Elder Careless," *Time*, September 24, 2003.

And indeed, as is the case with most catastrophes, there was plenty of blame to go around. Who had really let these doomed, neglected people down? There were many reasons for the carnage. Europe itself was wholly unused to such scorching conditions; people did not know how to react and were particularly ignorant about the imperative need to quickly re-hydrate. Most homes built in France over the past fifty years have no air conditioning, as excessive heat is rarely considered a major health hazard to worry about.

Beyond these technical explanations, there was obvious political and social fallout, as the Chirac-led government and the doctors' union predictably passed around the blame for the catastrophe as if it were a hot potato. The president and his prime minister, Jean-Pierre Raffarin, blamed French families for not taking proper care of their elderly relatives.

Family doctors also came in for criticism: their leisurely response to this flash crisis was felt to have not been sufficiently urgent. The health minister, Jean-François Mattei, was seen as particularly sluggish and would be swiftly dispatched in an ensuing March 2004 cabinet reshuffle. And that was about it. After all the immediate sound and fury, life in Paris went on much as usual, the incident disappearing from public consciousness as quickly as it had arisen.

But it shouldn't be forgotten. This is not just because of the obvious moral imperative to take responsibility for an entirely avoidable tragedy caused, at some level, by systemic neglect. That is too easy. Instead, let us go through the looking glass and see what was really going on in Paris that summer. What we see there will provide a seminal clue as to why European civilization itself is presently enduring such an existential crisis.

One basic overriding thread connects all the culprits behind this August 2003 tragedy: the absolute and ridiculous sanctity of the French summer vacation. In the place of religion or ethics, many Europeans have come to worship their comfortable (if economically unsustainable) way of life as the paramount goal of being, to the exclusion of all else.

At the time of the early August heat wave, President Jacques Chirac was on holiday in Canada. He remained there for the duration of the crisis. Likewise, Prime Minister Raffarin refused to return from his Alpine vacation until August 14, the day before temperatures at last began to cool. Health Minister Mattei also exhibited highly dubious priorities, refusing to come back to a sweltering Paris when he was most needed. Instead, his junior aides blocked emergency measures—including the state recalling doctors from their holidays—to attend to the afflicted.

But even this is too simple. Do French doctors really need to be told by the government that it is their duty to come back and deal with an obvious medical emergency? Do French families really need the state to instruct them that they must cut short their time at the beach to minister to the endangered elderly relatives they have left behind?

This was a society-wide conspiracy, in that no one was responsible because everyone was responsible. As Gibbon would have appreciated, thousands of individual, personal decisions—on their own merely dots in the national painting—all pointed in the same incredible, indefensible direction. Nothing must be allowed to get in the way of *les vacances*.

Surely the moral imperative here ought to have been obvious; heartbreakingly, it wasn't. The fact that these questions were not asked—or were quickly brushed aside—reveals the core problem that ails Europe. It is rotting from within. The geopolitical risk peril comes from its decadent culture, which cannot solve its problems (be they the euro crisis, Russian gambits in Ukraine, or the refugee crisis) and is increasingly abdicating responsibility for them.

But even if Europe had managed to muster the courage to draw the Gibbonian lessons from the heat wave tragedy, could it have managed to act on this painfully acquired knowledge? For to see what needs doing is only the first step in getting to the true reforms that could save Europe. What the ancient Greeks called *praxis*—the unity of thought and action—is the vital ingredient in regeneration. The element of geopolitical risk identified by Gibbon—analysts having the bravery to look in the mirror—must lead to policy action if it is to mean anything.

If geopolitical risk is to be ameliorated in Europe, and if it is to avoid the fate of the Roman Empire, the continent must summon the will to make the real, immediate sacrifices necessary to arrest a decline already in motion. Eschewing some of the lifestyle of today to safeguard the overall way of life for tomorrow is a sacrifice whose necessity few are ready to acknowledge, and even fewer are prepared to act on.

Everyone in France that dreadful August knew that something terribly wrong was happening back in Paris. Few had the will to give up their overly precious vacations and do anything about it. Gibbon's old concept of decadence plainly emerges as the primary roadblock—and the chief source of contemporary geopolitical risk—that not only obscures the knowledge necessary to save Europe but saps the will to act itself. Moreover, Gibbon would understand that the deadly consequences of decadence are as organic as they are ignored.

Europe's Ticking Demographic Time Bomb

This internal, societal malaise has direct economic consequences. For Europe's part, and in marked contrast to the rising powers, the post–Lehman Brothers economic crisis has discredited capitalism itself in many quarters, without putting any other sustainable economic system in its place. Given their growth rates of the past decade, it is not necessary to lecture either the Chinese or Indian leaderships about the merits of the capitalistic system, for all its flaws, as the primary engine of growth and power. The same is not true for many Europeans.

Having wholly disregarded the linked ideas of work and benefits, Europe (in Peter Hitchens's damning view) lives in a world where "the very idea that people should provide for themselves has become a horrible heresy, a barbaric view that no civilized person can hold."[6] The cynical conspiracy between an electorate who do not wish to hear that their lifestyle is simply no longer affordable and a political elite who fear even mentioning tough choices has anesthetized Europeans from the realities of the world.

According to PriceWaterhouseCoopers, in 2000 the EU accounted for 25 percent of all global product, trailed closely by the United States at 23 percent, with China bringing up the rear at 7 percent. By 2030—a blink of the eye in historical terms—these numbers are set to be dramatically reversed, with China accounting for 19 percent of global product, the United States for 16 percent, the EU countries for 15 percent, and India (up to now a blip on the global economic screen) for 9 percent.

While the lightning bolt of the global economic crisis illuminated this trend of power ebbing away from the West and migrating toward Asia, the pattern was established long before, harkening back to Chinese paramount leader Deng Xiaoping's opening of China in December 1978 and to then Indian Finance Minister V. P. Singh's liberalizing efforts in the mid-1980s. From an admittedly low base, China and

---

[6]Peter Hitchens, "Britain Can No Longer Afford to Pay the Extortionate Cost of the Welfare State," *DailyMail.com*, January 12, 2013.

India have experienced an unprecedented two-decade economic boom.

Even before the global economic crisis hit in 2008, China and India together accounted for more than one-half of all new global economic growth generated. Whether the West is prepared or not (and it is not), the world is clearly on course for a radical change in the distribution of both global economic and political power; the decline of the West will undoubtedly be the historical headline of our own age, much as the collapse of Roman hegemony was in Gibbon's magisterial narrative.

Meanwhile, Europe, like doomed passengers on the *Titanic*, has spotted the economic iceberg dead ahead but made precious little effort to right the ship of state's course. The demographic problem is especially stark. The worsening old-age dependency ratio—the relationship between the number of pensioners in a society versus the size of the working-age population—cannot simply be wished away. In 2013, it stood at an already uncomfortable 32 percent; by 2030, it is on track to leap to 45 percent. At the exact moment when its share of world GDP is set to shrink substantially between now and 2025 (from 26 percent to 15 percent), Europe's demographic bill is coming due.

The numbers are even worse in Germany, which is the undisputed economic motor of the European project. The old-age dependency ratio was 34 percent in 2013 and will rise to an economically crippling 52 percent by 2030. Over this period of time, the number of pensioners in Germany will skyrocket by five million, even as the number of workers declines by six million. Who is going to pay for those endless vacations and for the overly generous social safety net?

The broad policy responses are as simple as they are unpalatable: raise taxes (hardly possible), lower benefits and raise the retirement age (hardly popular), or take in significantly greater numbers of immigrants (given the strains exposed by the current refugee crisis, hardly likely). Instead, a *fin de siècle* sunset is descending on the continent.

And the bill is already ruining all efforts to emerge from the post–Lehman Brothers wreckage, leaving Europe economically stagnant. In 2015, the euro zone grew at an anemic 1.5 percent, well below the 2 percent threshold that geopolitical risk analysts tend to set in determining whether an advanced economy is buoyant. And worst of all, such a paltry rate of growth amounts to the best year the continent has had since the onset of economic crisis in 2008.

The very means to provide part of the answer to Europe's systemic economic problems—greater liberalization and labor market reforms leading to higher systemic growth rates—have been severely intellectually discredited. But without the motor of the market driving economic innovation, it is very hard to see how Europe can successfully slay the demographic dragon it confronts.

The seemingly never-ending euro crisis perfectly illustrates the continent's haplessness in the face of reality. The never-discussed economics lurking beneath it all bears concerted thought for a moment: EU countries comprise 8 to 9 percent of the world's population, account for 25 percent of global GDP, but consume a staggering 50 percent of the planet's social spending. However many mind-numbing summits Europe's leaders foist upon the rest of us, however often they repeat the comforting mantra that "More Europe" will save the continent from the dangers that lurk all around them, the bleak truth is that these numbers are simply unsustainable. Europe is not going through some little local difficulty; the way of life it knew and enjoyed from 1950 to the Lehman Brothers crash will never return.

Rather, as Europe has slipped into an economic coma with negligible growth, its lavish rates of public spending have continued on as if nothing had changed. A system created during the specific, very favorable economic circumstances of the post–World War II boom has gone heedlessly on, even though we live in a very different time. But free markets on the continent simply can no longer provide enough wealth to pay for the entitlement largesse that European general publics have been led to expect is their birthright. Decadence is an intractable economic, psychological, and, above all, moral problem, one that Gibbon honed in on so many years ago.

This is because, despite the economic data being available to all, no European statesman in their right mind would tell their constituencies the inconvenient truth that over time benefits reflect a country's economic success and are not a God-given right. To do so would be political suicide. Not to do so is to enable the European electorate to live in its current fantasy world, where the link between growth and what a state can actually afford to provide has been irretrievably broken.

Karl-Theodor zu Guttenberg and Germany's Distrust of Success

At base, this is as much an intellectual and moral problem as anything else. The abetting sin of modern Germany is summed up in the word *schadenfreude*, a delightful notion that roughly translated means to take enjoyment from the misfortune of others. When the others are wealthy or famous, a very unsavory, barely concealed German glee is often the response. For the German pathology is social envy, a jealousy of the successful. The problem is that Germans—despite being what's left of the economic motor of Europe—tend to agree with the anarchist Pierre-Joseph Proudhon that all property is a crime, that all wealth is based on some unfair maneuvering. To put it mildly, this makes it very hard to run a capitalistic society.

A prime example is a scandal that had all of Germany talking in 2011: the fact that the high-flying, young, dashing, aristocratic minister for defense, Karl-Theodor zu Guttenberg, had been sloppy with the footnotes of his PhD thesis and plagiarized portions of his submission. This story—allowing Germans to wallow in the trivial rather than engaging with important matters relating to being on the hook for Greek debt—dominated weeks of the country's attention.

To be transparent, let me say that zu Guttenberg is a personal friend of mine and a valued colleague who has worked with me over the years on matters as far afield as US-European relations as well as the Iran crisis. I find him by far the best foreign policy mind amongst young German policy-makers I have met in the eighteen years I have been involved in transatlantic relations. Of course what he did was wrong. Of course he should not be given a PhD for such moral and practical mistakes. And I accept the view that resignation from his position should have happened, given his lapse.

Saying all this, "PhDgate" hardly makes zu Guttenberg Charles Manson. You would not know that to hear the commentary in the German press—equal parts joyous and censorious—where the consensus view was that zu Guttenberg must be "punished." Typical was the comment of the well-respected intellectual Ernst-Ludwig Winnacker that what zu Guttenberg had done was "unforgivable" in academia.[7] True, but zu Guttenberg was German minister of defense at the time, not angling for a full professorship. Listening to this shrill and all-encompassing roar from the commentariat for weeks at a time (with Fukushima, the Greek crisis, and the

[7]"The Guttenberg Plagiarism Scandal: German Society Is Applying a Double Standard," *Spiegel online*, February 28, 2011.

future of the EU all being eclipsed), it became pretty obvious what was going on here.

Good-looking, extremely wealthy, talented, well-married (zu Guttenberg's wife is a direct descendant of Otto von Bismarck and beautiful to boot), zu Guttenberg was getting his comeuppance from people who didn't hate what he did. Instead, they hated what he was. Rather than his departure being seen as a tragedy for a country desperately in need of talented young leaders, his downfall became an orgy of joyful recrimination. Such a response is as telling as it is dangerous. Only the talented can save Europe from its peril. Perhaps they should not be run out of town on a rail.

The telling example of the zu Guttenberg scandal shows what Europe is rooting against. For Europeans, success itself is widely distrusted, being seen across much of the continent as a confidence trick leading to ill-gotten gains, rather than as a symbol of excellence. There is a reason that Bill Gates, Thomas Edison, Steve Jobs, and Henry Ford all emerged and prospered in America, and that precious few counterparts can be pointed to in Europe. Neither risk-taking as an input nor monumental success as an output is much admired on a continent where doing well is rather frowned upon.

Ford, Gates, and Jobs do not matter all that much for themselves. Rather, they are important for creating and revolutionizing products that made life in the world better for millions, as well as directly benefiting hundreds of thousands through providing skilled, high-paying employment. If excellence is to be taken off the table as a dirty word, the benefits of capitalism will not magically occur.

A France where the successful briefly had to pay a 75 percent rate of tax is not a place likely to retain that elite for long. As Lenin might put it, they will vote with their feet, becoming citizens of Belgium (or even in the bizarre case of film star Gérard Depardieu, Russia), or most likely denizens of London—anyplace where success is not so obviously punished.

In other words, the German commentariat may feel personally very good about the exiling of the undeniably talented zu Guttenberg, just as the failed, outgoing French president, François Hollande, admits to not liking the rich, all the while enacting punitive taxes to "keep them in their place." But without the talented (and let's face it, not all the rich are chinless wonders, unworthy inheritors of their wealth) and the risk-takers, capitalist societies will not do very well, certainly compared with a rising world so eager to promote these very values. In fact, it is only through nurturing far more innovation that Europe can possibly hope to survive and thrive in this increasingly competitive new era. Scaring off talent is a very bad idea.

The Sudden End of Europe's Sunny Way of Life

So the policy path for avoiding Gibbon's road to self-ruin in Europe is relatively clear in the medium-term. The overly generous safety net must be cut back in line with the new economic realities. Retirement must come much later (contrary to the fantasies of the French), benefits must be means-tested and scaled back, government-funded health care must be topped up with individual insurance, and pensions must be largely privatized.

While the pump may need to be primed in the short run, over time there will be a general need for both tax increases and spending cuts, optimally at a ratio of three-to-one in favor of cuts, significantly decreasing the size of the bloated state, if the continent is not to drown in excess public spending. Overall public debt in the euro-zone countries stood at over

90 percent as of 2016, explosively above the 70 percent level it was at as recently as early 2010.

All this is straightforwardly obvious. Today's major political risk firms deal with European leaders in both the debtor camp (Italy, Spain, Greece) as well as the creditor camp (Germany, the Netherlands). Privately, a majority on both sides would easily agree to what I have just proposed in abstract policy terms. But in the honest and telling wail of Jean-Claude Juncker, then prime minister of Luxembourg and now European Commission president, "We all know what needs to be done, we just don't know how to get re-elected after we've done it."[8]

European governments can demonstrably no longer fulfill the many promises they have made to their various constituencies. These promises must be scaled back if the lifestyle so many on the continent cherish is to be preserved at all. It is a glaring sign of how far Europe has truly gone down Gibbon's road to ruin that what needs to be done is blatantly obvious in policy terms, but such suggestions dare not be attempted, or indeed even mentioned. This is advanced-stage decadence.

The inability of European society to master Gibbon's geopolitical risk element of self-reflection forces the vast majority of its politicians to dissemble. Austerity becomes something other people must do. Taxing the top 1 percent will magically alleviate the need for government spending cuts for the rest. Modern life, however, is not the tale of Robin Hood.

In Europe, the narcotic is indolence. While Europeans remain the most productive people in the world per hour worked, this matters little if they work one-third fewer hours than their American competitors (and are positively slothful compared to the work ethic of rising Asia). No amount of

---

[8]"Jean-Claude Juncker's Most Outrageous Political Quotations," *The (London) Daily Telegraph*, July 15, 2014.

whistling past the graveyard can make such a ruinous course of action sustainable. But having bought into the cult of time off as an inalienable right, it is devilishly hard to row back from this primary sign of decadence.

In Europe, what is truly going on is the end of economic life as it has been known. Europeans simply can no longer afford the serene, cosseted, not overly strenuous, and very attractive way of life they have grown used to; government in European countries has grown simply unaffordable. But almost no one wants to hear this, much less do anything about it, as to do so would require a very painful, immediate retrenchment for millions. That is human and understandable, but it is also fatal. For it means that at present democratic politics in Europe is being conducted based on lies.

The Political Naïveté of Lying about Europe's Gloomy Future

Lying—beyond the immorality of it—is a very poor basis for making sustainable policy, at least in any open society. As such, what started as a debt and banking crisis has morphed into Europe's greatest political crisis since the Second World War. European Economic and Monetary Union (EMU) as constructed is itself the problem, with around a 20 percent currency misalignment blotting economic ties between the north and the south of the continent.

Worst of all, for all the three bailouts of Greece and the bailouts of Ireland, Portugal, and Spain, despite all the recent happy talk on both sides of the Atlantic that Europe has saved itself, the bleeding has not stopped, given the economic wobbles in Italy above all, but also in France. For it is merely a case of plates being thrown in the air; nothing has been rectified. Likewise, at the equally unsustainable microeconomic level, reality continues to be ignored, but only by keeping unsustainable borrowing going. Europe itself is on a drip feed, but the patient is certainly not getting well as the debt numbers explode.

Germany is the primary example of the present dissembling being the hallmark of policy owing to the willful ignorance of its society. Contrary to all that Chancellor Angela Merkel has said up until now, German taxpayers *will* be on the hook for a good portion of the bailout money that Germany has been forced to give to its ailing fellow euro-zone members. The idea that the rest of Europe could go through what amounts to a Depression while Germany somehow stays above the fray certainly appeals to the country's desperate desire to avoid all this; it isn't for a moment a realistic possibility.

The chancellor surely knows this, as well as the fact that in the end—for all the intricate complexity of the crisis—the euro zone will stand or fall based on a simple policy decision made in Berlin: if the euro is to survive, there will need to be far greater fiscal union, with tax and spending decisions taken by a treasury minister in Brussels with national states relinquishing basic control over their economies.

In essence, the euro zone will move toward true federation, becoming a debt union complete with fiscal transfers (all done on largely German terms), or the euro will cease to exist. As such, Berlin will be the primary paymaster for such a new political constellation. As none of this appeals to much of anyone in Germany, best not to talk about it. And so Chancellor Merkel does not. She has chosen not to let her people in on the tragic truth articulated so well in Lampedusa's masterpiece *The Leopard*: "If we want things to stay as they are, things will have to change."[9]

---

[9] See Giuseppe Tomasi Di Lampedusa, *The Leopard* (London: Vintage Books, 2007), p. 19.

At some point, Berlin will have to endorse an official (read taxpayer-funded) write-down of Athens's staggering 340-billion-euro debt, which as of today amounts to 180 percent of its GDP. The best guess is that to ultimately leave Greece with a fighting chance of sustainability, a full 50 percent of this debt must be written off. Of this 170 billion euros, Germany will have to forfeit the largest national share. Until then, the less said the better. As one German official made clear in decidedly un-Jeffersonian tones, "How do you expect us to sell the idea of more Greek bailout money [which may very well be needed] to German voters if they see that public money already lent is being written off?"[10]

It is at this point that even the sleepiest German citizen will wake up, howling. It is also here that not leveling with one's own people becomes as poor a strategy as it is immoral. For by not making clear what is really going on here, Merkel has been able for quite a long while to put off an awful lot of unpleasantness. But to imagine for a moment that the German people won't feel fundamentally lied to once the check for this Kafkaesque party comes due is not to be Machiavellian. Rather, it is to be hopelessly naive.

No policy requiring the coming sacrifices—for whatever Germany decides to ultimately do, there will have to be sacrifices—that is not buttressed by public support stands any chance of success. Lying as a way to avoid the democratic deficit over the European crisis is not clever. Rather, it is just a primary example of what happens, as Gibbon described it, when internal problems overwhelm formerly great societies.

For Europe—despite the arrogant and false narrative of it producing a more just and more nurturing form of capitalism

---

[10]Jeremy Warner, op-ed, *The (London) Daily Telegraph*, November 17, 2012.

than that of its American cousins—the problem of vested interests is killing it from within. Youth unemployment rates of a sickening 40 percent plus in afflicted Greece and Spain have led to an entire generation's dreams being written off. This is just the tip of a generational divide that could well produce violence before long.

Due to its societies' insistence that employment security is sacrosanct, Europe has unwittingly created a two-tier caste system, with older workers with jobs for life voting their pocketbooks. Europe's lucky older generation is standing in the way of needed liberalization and electing social reactionaries like the French Socialist Hollande, who promise above all to protect their cosseted and easy lives, whatever such a pledge is doing to the next generation in particular, as well as to French society in general.

This younger underclass—often working for free in an endless series of internships that lead nowhere—amounts to nothing less than the nitroglycerin that may soon send the whole flawed European social model sky high. It should come as no surprise that populist Marine Le Pen—intent on overthrowing the French establishment—is winning a disproportionately high percentage of young voters, with her siren song that she can somehow shield France from the rigors of global competition. The fundamental unfairness of this system is locked in place by the vested interests that benefit from it, making salvation almost impossible.

It is these vested interests that have grown up over decades—fueled and sustained by well-meaning people agreeing that cuts should be made, but not to the things they personally feel are important—that, not in some conspiracy-laden manner, are proving to be the primary, gargantuan obstacles to steering clear of fiscal catastrophe. This is a major reason today's problems are proving so terribly intractable, and why Gibbon is still so worth reading.

Rome Dies from Within

For the story of internal decay, of societies being unable to see themselves clearly, has an ancient lineage. In spite of his own grisly end, Sejanus's creation, the Praetorian Guard, came to live on and on, becoming the Frankenstein's monster of the Roman Empire. Retaining its power despite its prefect's fall from political grace, the guard came to play an increasingly important and bloody role in the Empire's history, serving as the primary source of its internal political destabilization.

In 41 AD, conspirators centered in the guard and the Senate killed the mad Caligula. The Praetorians themselves placed the supposed idiot (he was hardly that) Claudius on the vacant throne after Caligula's assassination, feeling they could use him as a puppet to further their ends. Tradition has it that they found him cowering behind a drape, fearing that the guard would finish him off next, when the Praetorians offered him the throne.

The guard's destabilizing influence became endemic; proving to be a domestic political force capable of causing great chaos, it gravely weakened the Roman Empire from within. After the suicide of the last Julio-Claudian emperor, Nero, in 68 AD, the guard prefect Gaius Nymphidius Sabinus failed in an effort to make himself the founder of a new dynasty. Just a year later, the guard assassinated the Emperor Galba after he refused to give them yet another pay raise.

In 193, in one of the most remarkable acts in Roman history, Didius Julianus actually purchased the Empire from the guard—which the Praetorians were auctioning off following their killing of the Emperor Pertinax—for an astronomical sum of money. In the early third century, the Emperor Caracalla was murdered and replaced on the throne by the Praetorian prefect Marcus Opellius Macrinus. It had come to this. The guard had finally made one of their own ruler over all the Empire.

Throughout all this time, the Praetorian Guard remained steadfastly fixed upon its own specific and narrow interests, endlessly agitating for pay raises and zealously tending to its power base; the overall interests of Rome were rarely its concern. Gibbon speculates that as its membership was not drawn from Rome itself—the ranks of the guard were instead enrolled from the provinces—a powerful, disruptive, and foreign presence slowly poisoned Roman domestic political life.

Finally, in the fourth century, the able Emperor Constantine had the good sense to abolish the Praetorian Guard. But by then, as Gibbon so majestically records, the damage had been done. The guard had disrupted the organic development of Roman domestic political life for centuries. It was this home-grown weakness, directly springing out of Sejanus's reforms, that led to the downfall of Rome and nothing less than the eclipse for centuries of Western civilization.

Of course, through these hundreds of years many Romans bewailed what was going on with their society, condemned what the Praetorian Guard was doing, and bemoaned the endemic domestic political strife and chaos that the guard was engendering. They complained, but they did nothing. Worse still, they did not clearly see the vital geopolitical risk link between domestic decay and the ultimate weakening of the Roman state itself, which seemed at the time (as all dominant powers do) as if it would last forever. They were unable or unwilling to look clearly in the mirror, and it was their doom.

But this is not some archaic, ancient problem, having no bearing on the world that we live in today. For Gibbon has presented modern geopolitical risk analysts with an essential piece of the puzzle as to what it takes to be an expert in the field, an invaluable first overall commandment as to the rules of the road for mastering geopolitical risk. To begin to dare to see the future clearly, geopolitical risk analysts must be able to calmly and unemotionally assess the very society they find themselves in, to see it for what it is, warts and all, and to evaluate its strengths and, particularly, its weaknesses. For as was true of Rome, so it is true of the West of today: we are the geopolitical risk.

Now that we know who political risk analysts are today, and how they generally think, the rest of this book will look in detail at the history of the ideas—or elements—that are at the center of the geopolitical risk business and form the rules of the game for mastering geopolitical risk across the ages. Following on from ancient Greece and Rome, our next historical stop will be the war-torn (then as now) Middle East during the Third Crusade. There, despite daunting odds, a supposed lunatic, through an able understanding of his many Western enemies, managed to best them all.

CHAPTER THREE

1192 AD: Gaming Out Lunatics

THE ASSASSINS AND THE OLD MAN
OF THE MOUNTAIN

The Old Man of the Mountain Demonstrates
What Power Actually Is

Legend has it that at the height of the Third Crusade (1189–1192), Count Henry of Champagne spoke at length with the mysterious, charismatic "Old Man of the Mountain," Rashid ad-Din Sinan.[1] The haughty Crusader claimed that he, and not Sinan, had the most powerful army in the Middle East, one that could at any moment defeat the *Hashashin*, the Old Man's threadbare cohort of adherents. Count Henry went on, pointing out that his force was at least ten times as large as that of Sinan.

Unimpressed, the Old Man calmly replied that the count was mistaken, and that his unremarkable-looking rabble constituted the most powerful army then fighting. To prove his point, he beckoned one of his men over to him and casually told him to jump off the top of the Masyaf mountaintop fortress in which they were staying at al-Kahf castle. Without hesitating, the man did so.[2]

Through the many centuries that separate us from Count Henry, the myriad twists and turns of Western politics, culture, and life that come between us, there is absolutely no

---

[1]The term is one of respect, conveying that Sinan was an elder of the Ismaili religious sect of Shia Islam.

[2]See Bernard Lewis, *The Assassins: A Radical Sect in Islam* (Oxford: Oxford University Press, 1967), p. 25.

doubt at all that Westerners today would share his horrified reaction to what the Old Man of the Mountain had demonstrated for him.

"This guy is totally nuts."

Geopolitical risk analysts have always had a very hard time getting past this wholly understandable first reaction. Yet it is imperative that they do so. Whereas the first element in mastering geopolitical risk ("we are the political risk"), provided to us by Gibbon and Sejanus, fits snugly at the base of the geopolitical risk typology tree (under the Pythia's heading "know thyself"), gaming out seemingly irrational behavior is organically a commandment in the "nothing in excess" sub-heading branch.

At the highest level, both effective statecraft and analysis require a hard-headed assessment of geopolitical risk. Yet all too often, analysts throughout time have written off those with radically different belief systems from their own, meekly giving in and assuming that such people and organizations are simply unknowable. The reason for this is that it is all too easy for geopolitical risk analysts to write off "lunatics," lazily saying to themselves that the irrational, the strange, the crazy, simply cannot be understood.

As the examples of Sinan, Charles Manson, and ISIS make clear, this is a fundamental analytical mistake. For while many of the goals of each group may be otherworldly, wicked, and unattainable, an understanding of their strategic objectives is nonetheless very necessary. For once these "irrational" objectives are taken seriously, the tactics to reach them all too often can be gamed out, a process that makes "lunatics" suddenly explicable. As all these cases will show, the excess often lies in the analysts' lack of curiosity, mesmerized as they are by the "madness" of their subjects. The proper gaming out of seemingly irrational behavior is a vital element in the geopolitical risk intellectual toolbox.

Rashid ad-Din Sinan and the Benefits
of Being Seen as Crazy

Rashid ad-Din Sinan, the mastermind behind the Assassin network in Syria at the time of the Third Crusade, was born in either 1132 or 1135 in Basra, in today's southern Iraq. As a youth, Rashid came to Alamut (in present-day Iran), the center of the burgeoning *Hashashin* movement, and was inducted into the mysteries of this secretive religious sect. Specifically, the *Hashashin*, or the Assassins, were Nizari Ismailis, an offshoot of Shia Islam, a movement that originated in the late eleventh century.

In 1162, the sect's overall leader, Hassan Ala Dhikrihi Salam, sent Sinan to Syria to assume control of the group's affairs there. Sinan quickly proved himself a born leader, establishing what amounted to a largely independent operation, with little control being exercised from far-away Alamut. Over time Sinan forged his *fidai* followers, who came to believe he had semi-divine status, into a wholly new sort of military force, shock troops willing and able to carry out his every whim. Based in the Nizari mountain stronghold of Masyaf, Sinan came to control much of eastern Syria.

The single-minded fervor of the *Hashashin*—their intensity, morale, and absolute commitment to Sinan rather than to the Western value of the sanctity of life—terrified the Crusaders at the time and continues to fascinate us in the West to this day.

Operating in what is today Syria and Iran, the Assassins were a secret order determined to protect the relatively new sect, from both the predominantly Sunni Muslim overlords of the time (personified by Saladin, ruler of Egypt and much of Syria and the Holy Land) as well as the invading Western Crusaders (personified by Richard the Lion-Heart). While the Assassins, on paper, were far fewer in number than either group, in promulgating the cult of the Assassin, Sinan found a way around his basic political problem, using terror and strategic assassinations as weapons to compensate for what he lacked in numbers.

In practice, only a class of Sinan's believers known as the *fidai*—which in Arabic means "one who sacrifices himself in the name of a faith or an idea"—actually carried out the assassinations. That they usually attempted to murder their political enemies in public places created an air of invincibility surrounding the Assassins, sowing the seeds of great fear amongst Sinan's surviving foes.

Assassinations were often carried out with a dagger, which was sometimes dipped in poison. Horrifyingly, to Western standards, after completing an assassination, the *fidai* would often wait at the site of the murder to be caught, exhibiting total contempt for the consequences of their actions, instead wanting to be sure all the world knew it was the Old Man of the Mountain who had struck the decisive blow.

Another often-used tactic to terrify the Old Man's foes was to intimidate them rather than kill them. For example, by leaving a dagger with a threatening note on their enemy's pillow, the Assassins would demonstrate beyond all doubt that they could reach out and kill their enemy anytime they chose to.

The Western confusion in even naming Sinan's followers—Westerners came to call them the Assassins, supposedly derived from *Hashashin*, or "users of hashish"—conveys a real sense of the horror the sect evoked at the time. In truth, there is little evidence that it was the drug that motivated the Old Man's adherents to do anything for him, but Western minds were hard at work trying to explain what to them amounted to the inexplicable.

More likely, the term *Hashashin*, originally coined by the sect's Sunni enemies, was one of derision, meant to signify that the Old Man's followers were lowborn rabble, losers, outcasts in Islamic society. However, by the time Marco Polo heard the tale a century on, the more literal drug interpretation amounted to a much-needed explanation for Western minds as to what motivated the Assassins to kill for Sinan unquestioningly.[3]

For the legend of wild-eyed, murdering drug-takers was too good a story to let go of. Echoing the real criminal career of Charles Manson centuries on, the myth grew that after being drugged, the *fidai* would be taken to a beautiful, secluded garden, filled with gorgeous doe-eyed maidens, in which they would awaken. Believing themselves to be in paradise, the initiates would come upon the Old Man of the Mountain, who would tell them that this was just a glimpse of the life eternal to come. All they had to do to preserve their place in such a glorious, never-ending world was to follow his orders explicitly.

It's a lovely story, amounting to a clever Western effort to explain the baffling fervor of their Ismaili foes. Sadly, it's almost certainly untrue. As such, the two basic Crusader efforts at explaining the Assassins in political risk terms— either that they were crazy and no more thinking is called for, or that they were stupid, drug-addled dupes of the wily Sinan—conceal more than they reveal, for they don't begin to get at the method behind Sinan's seeming madness.

In this obtuseness the Crusaders are far from alone. Geopolitical risk analysts down the ages have had a terrible time in assessing what they might term "lunatics"—those whose behavior at first glance seems to be wholly irrational. However, more often than not, "irrational behavior" merely amounts to an ideology that may be radically different from that of the geopolitical risk analyst, but nevertheless still contains an

---

[3]See Marco Polo, *The Travels of Marco Polo* (London: J. M. Dent and Sons, 1918).

internal logic, complete with discernible and overarching strategic goals, tactical gambits, and a battle plan to achieve both.

We cannot let ourselves off the hook so easily by lazily saying that our foes are crazy and therefore don't need to be studied, because their belief systems are different from (and admittedly often wildly alien to) our own. Such a limp intellectual reaction merely deprives geopolitical risk analysts of the incentive to do what they ought to—to dig deeper in understanding what at first glance seems deceptively random.

The Elusive Madness of Charles Manson

Seven hundred and eighty years later, Vincent Bugliosi, one of modern America's foremost legal minds, found himself in an eerily similar position to that of Count Henry of Champagne.[4] He had been assigned to prosecute the Tate-LaBianca murder cases in August 1969, a series of ritualistic slayings in Los Angeles that had terrified the whole of the United States, owing to both the frenzy of the murders as well as the seeming randomness of the crimes.

Through good old-fashioned detective work, Bugliosi had rightly fastened upon Charles Manson and his hippie death-cult as the perpetrators; the so-called Family believed that their leader was the reincarnation of Jesus Christ. But there was a major practical problem with prosecuting Manson: he had not personally killed anyone. Instead, he had ordered others to do his diabolical bidding.

Why had he done so and why had the Family followed him? Bugliosi knew that if he didn't address the crucial issue

---

[4]While serving in the Los Angeles District Attorney's Office for eight years, Bugliosi successfully prosecuted 105 out of 106 felony jury trials, an almost unprecedented record of legal success.

of motive, there was simply no real case against Manson, who was the ringleader of the whole horrendous plot. The good news was that over time Bugliosi hit upon Manson's reasoning; the bad news was that it seemed—on the surface— so mind-bogglingly crazy that colleagues of the prosecutor urged him to discard it, as no normal person was likely to believe him.[5]

Indeed, when the Los Angeles police were initially made aware of Manson's philosophy of "Helter Skelter," they replied as all poor geopolitical risk analysts would: "Ah, Charlie's a madman; we're not interested in all that."[6] But they should have been. Because of their shared philosophy—no matter how far out—otherwise normal people had been motivated to savagely kill at Manson's bidding. Helter Skelter provides the crucial link explaining why the murders came about, making sense of what the ancient Greeks would describe as *praxis*: the unity of thought and action. Successfully gaming out lunatics requires that analysts suspend their own disbelief and intellectually follow others' philosophies wherever they lead. For only by doing this can *praxis* be discovered and sound analytical judgments arrived at.

For Manson, the philosophy of Helter Skelter lay behind his murderous rampage. It was to be the last war on the face of the earth, an end-times racial conflict between African Americans and whites, wherein the African American minority would rise up and eviscerate formerly dominant white society in America.

Paul Watkins, a former member of the Family who often acted as Manson's direct lieutenant, provided Bugliosi with the missing motive of Helter Skelter. The apocalyptic war

---

[5] See Vincent Bugliosi, with Curt Gentry, *Helter Skelter: The True Story of the Manson Murders* (New York: W. W. Norton and Co., 1974), p. 323.

[6] Ibid., p. 332.

would arise naturally from the deep racial tensions in late 1960s America, where ghettoes across the country had just recently been on fire, following the assassination of Martin Luther King Jr.

Weak, decadent white society would be split, in Manson's view, between liberals calling for restraint and conservatives determined to decisively prosecute the race war. This fatal division would lead African Americans over time to triumph in wiping out the whole white community in America. But Manson, an avowed racist, believed that such a fantastical outcome would redound to his own personal benefit.

The only white Americans to survive would be his Family, who by then would have moved to the inhospitable confines of Death Valley to escape the fighting. As Manson believed that African Americans were incapable of running anything, after a period of chaos, he prophesied they would turn to him to manage things, with the Family ultimately coming to rule the world. Suffice it to say, you can see why Bugliosi was hesitant to put this fantastical thinking forward as the primary motive for the crimes.

But just because something is outlandish does not mean it is unimportant. The more Bugliosi dug, the more bizarre Manson's faux religion seemed to become. Using the twin planks of the Beatles and the New Testament Book of Revelation as the pillars of his demonic thought, Manson had created a narrative that was compelling enough to allow him to orchestrate the killing of people he had never met before, or with whom he had only the slightest contact.

Looking on the Beatles as the four prophets mentioned in the Book of Revelation (chapter 9), Manson proclaimed to the Family that "The White Album" (released in December 1968) was in practice a series of coded messages from the Beatles to him, allowing for the fulfillment of a series of biblical prophecies mentioned in the New Testament.

The phrase "Helter Skelter" (a British term for an amusement park slide) was the title of a Beatles song on the album. Manson construed it to signify the coming race war, in which those on top would go down (whites) and those on the bottom would go up (African Americans). Manson believed that the Beatles were sending him another such message in the Paul McCartney song "Blackbird," also on "The White Album." Manson believed the song was nothing less than an effort by the group to get African Americans to rise up, initiating the coming race war.

But by the summer of 1969, Manson was growing impatient, as things weren't going to plan. Having proclaimed to the Family that Helter Skelter was due to start imminently, little seemed to be happening to confirm the demented prophet's predictions. Earlier, Manson had pressed his friends in the music business (for a time the cult had lived at the house of Dennis Wilson, the drummer of the Beach Boys) to allow him to record an album, which he thought would finish what the Beatles started, igniting Armageddon. Frustrated by the lack of interest in his musical talents, Manson came to believe that another more direct way had to be found to bring about Helter Skelter.

Bugliosi was convinced that it was only within this barely believable philosophical context that the murders could be assessed. The slayings were a crucial part of Manson's plan to trigger Helter Skelter. By committing a series of brutal, seemingly senseless crimes against members of white society, the cult leader became convinced that eventually radical African American movements, such as the Black Panthers, would be blamed for the outrage, which would lead to fighting in the streets. Manson confided to Watkins that he had orchestrated the murders to show African Americans that now was the time to start a race war.

Bugliosi contended that Manson ordered the murders and that his way-out philosophy directly led to the killings, as it was designed to start Helter Skelter itself. Looking soberly at the evidence today, as outlandish as it all seems, there can be no doubt that Bugliosi's analysis was correct. At the conclusion of the first set of slayings, Manson asked his proxy at the Tate killings, Charles "Tex" Watson, whether it had been Helter Skelter. After the second night of murders, Patricia Krenwinkel, one of the killers, wrote "Healter Skelter [*sic*]" in her victims' blood on their refrigerator.[7]

Manson's sick philosophy, plus his total control over the Family, made them willing participants in his homicidal rampage. Much as was true for the followers of the Old Man of the Mountain, Manson's adherents were yearning to do anything he asked, however crazy it might seem to modern Western eyes. Of all his former disciples, only Paul Watkins seems to have taken the full measure of his former god. "Charlie was always preaching love . . . Charlie had no idea what love was. Death is Charlie's trip. It really is."[8]

Because he was unafraid to follow Manson's twisted philosophy analytically wherever it took him, and because he got beyond the obvious fact that Helter Skelter was patently "crazy," Vincent Bugliosi discovered the motive that tied mass murderer Charles Manson to his crimes. Despite heavy odds, Bugliosi succeeded in convicting all the defendants of their crimes, crucially including Manson. The first-rate analytical skills of Vincent Bugliosi underline a key point for geopolitical risk analysts. Just because a warped ideology seems demented emphatically does not mean that it fails to explain an opponent's *praxis*, providing the key link between a person's thought and their actions.

---

[7] The murders occurred on August 9 and 10, 1969.
[8] Bugliosi with Gentry, *Helter Skelter*, p. 498.

The Method of ISIS's Madness

But we do not need to go back to the Swinging Sixties to find examples of seemingly insane behavior, let alone travel through the dim reaches of time to the Third Crusade. With the terrifying rise of ISIS, all we need to do is to open any newspaper.

Since bursting upon the international relations scene in the summer of 2014 like a thunderbolt, at its height ISIS managed—despite much of the world actively fighting it—to dominate territory the size of the United Kingdom: it controlled roughly one-third of Syria and one-third of Iraq. Even as ISIS's horrifying advance was halted before the gates of Baghdad and Erbil in Iraq, it held on to the territory it had conquered with a surprising tenacity; only recently has its grip over portions of Iraq and Syria been decisively loosened.

But if a terrorist state is a new philosophical innovation, radical Jihadi terrorism would seem to be old hat for the West, especially after grappling with al-Qaeda. But as any Westerner who has paid the least attention can tell you, ISIS is completely different, being a genuine throwback to some primordial period of the Dark Ages. The beheadings, mass killings, near-genocide of the Yazidi people, crucifixions, selling of children and others into sexual slavery in the marketplace of Raqqa, burying people alive, burning people alive, and other acts of barbarism, are literally beyond the pale of modern Western thinking.

But that is exactly what ISIS wants: for us to shudder (as I just did) in merely cataloging their atrocities, to give up trying to assess them, and to merely point out the obvious: this is a group of evil, insane (by my standards), homicidal maniacs. ISIS is certainly all these things, but if analysts let it go at that, any effort to assess them—to search for ways to practically defeat them—go out the window, as no one can get beyond their gleeful madness, sickeningly and slickly packaged by their media-savvy public relations department.

I for one refuse to take the easy way out and merely shrug at what ISIS mouthpieces say about their depravities, just as the Tate-LaBianca detectives did about Charles Manson's views. For to beat them, we must discover—as Shakespeare put it so wonderfully in *Hamlet*—the method to their madness.[9]

Behind its terrible bells and whistles, upon examination what ISIS wants is perfectly comprehensible, as is true of both Manson and the Old Man of the Mountain. To put it in geopolitical risk terms, ISIS cannot be defeated without first being analytically understood. This is eminently possible, but risk analysts must take the first step through the looking glass of separating themselves from the genuine feelings of absolute repugnance that are bound to bubble up. ISIS is certainly evil, and it can seem beyond crazy. But what it wants is understandable and explicable; that means a good geopolitical risk analyst can assess ISIS—just as they would any other political entity—and devise ways to defeat it.

ISIS's main strength is also its Achilles' heel; the clue is in the name. In direct intellectual contradiction to its former parent and present rival al-Qaeda, the terror group has always had aspirations of statehood—the desire to hold and control territory, setting up the longed-for caliphate that radical jihadis have up until now only dreamed of. It is to be paradise now, not put off until some future date. This has proven to be an unbelievably seductive message for jihadis throughout the world, propelling ISIS past al-Qaeda as the pre-eminent, global, radical Islamic brand.

[9]See John Hulsman, "Forget the Neocons: Lawrence of Arabia Can Help Save Iraq from Chaos," *City AM*, June 19, 2014; "How to Defeat ISIS: We Already Have a Playbook for Beating These Extremists," *City AM*, July 7, 2014; "Paris Terror Attacks: We Must Deny ISIS the Narrative It Craves," *City AM*, November 16, 2015.

Rather than talking in esoteric terms, as al-Qaeda does, about fighting far-away "Crusader Imperialists" (as you can see, the Lion-Heart and his atrocities have not been forgotten in the Middle East), ISIS has focused on the practical building up of a state, on controlling a tangible piece of territory, a caliphate that must be secured, as over time its radical doctrine spreads to the rest of the world from this new homeland. Its adherents can see the practical steps that are ongoing now as ISIS puts its words into practice in a way no terror organization ever has in the modern world.

But the problem with countries is that they must be governed. Particularly as ISIS has set such store in its statehood, this difficulty has laid bare the key weakness in its overall philosophy: its governance has proven shambolic. Besides this revelation, we have a practical, historical example of how to best ISIS, taken from the recent past.

The earliest incarnation of ISIS, al-Qaeda in Iraq (AQI), became dominant in Iraq's Anbar province in 2006–2007, riding to power on a wave of sectarian chaos (largely caused by the American invasion) and Shia chauvinism in Baghdad, directed against the Sunnis of the country's west. However, taking territory is one thing; holding it is another. AQI proved itself laughably incapable of governing, combining administrative incompetence with savage repression of the local population. This in turn led to the organic creation of a political counter-movement of local Sunni tribal leaders, who instigated the *Sahwa*, or Awakening—a rising up against their foreign oppressors.[10]

David Petraeus, the most talented American general of his generation, saw his chance. America poured arms and technical assistance into the *Sahwa* movement, as American counter-insurgency forces—crucially allied with indigenous

---

[10]The leader of AQI, the charismatic Abu Musab al Zarqaui, was a Jordanian.

Sunni tribal leaders who possessed the magic elixir of local political legitimacy—quickly routed AQI. By 2008–2009, AQI had been subdued, if not destroyed, with local Sunni tribal leaders taking de facto charge of their vast province. This playbook remains the best chance to defeat ISIS.

For the caliphate has had to prove itself capable of governing and has had a wobbly record in doing so. While fighting wars on all fronts, ISIS was forced to set up public administration, collect taxes, provide services, and create institutions on the fly, and all with an elite without nearly enough bureaucratic experience. Sensing the danger, it is little wonder that the supreme leader and *Caliph* of ISIS, Abu Bakr al-Baghdadi, issued a series of desperate calls for Islamic judges and administrators to immigrate to the new country. Without possessing true administrative competence, ISIS was always going to have a hard time holding on to its conquests.

If assessing—in geopolitical risk terms—the objective strengths and weaknesses of ISIS provides a policy plan for defeating it, so looking at the purpose of its terrorism illustrates what we in the West ought not to do. First and foremost, following on from the horror of ISIS's November 2015 terror attacks in Paris, which killed 129 innocent people and wounded upwards of 300, we must deny ISIS the narrative it so desperately craves.

The purpose of terrorism is simple enough: it is designed to terrorize, to force one's enemies in their horror to make strategic mistakes, overcome as they are with emotional revulsion for the heinous acts perpetrated against their people. A geopolitical overreaction, such as certainly occurred with the Iraq war following on from 9/11, is precisely what ISIS so hopes we in the West will succumb to. To triumph, we must deny our enemies what they want. In this case, what is that specifically?

Ideally, ISIS would like the West to commit to yet another futile, full-out war in the Middle East and slowly drown in the quagmire that is Syria. There is absolutely nothing that would so help its recruitment and financial drives as yet another Crusader foray into a ground war in the region.

Failing this (but almost as good), a greatly enhanced and strategically pointless bombing campaign is the next-best outcome. For impotent, futile Western involvement in Syria merely underlines both the great powers' weakness and their cruelty and casts ISIS in the heroic light of successfully standing up to Crusader imperialism.

Given the relative success of the Russian intervention to defend the bloodstained Assad regime in Syria, President Trump's controversial desire for better ties with Vladimir Putin could pay dividends in Syria. As the Syrian civil war shows signs of winding down, with ISIS having lost Mosul in Iraq and with Raqqa in Syria under siege, a united front is now possible. While this is militarily to the good, unless restive Sunni complaints in eastern Syria against the Alawite-dominated Assad government are heard (the Alawites are an adjunct of Shia Islam), look for a new—and possibly even more bloodthirsty—incarnation of ISIS to emerge in a few years' time, just as AQI was succeeded by ISIS itself.

If drawing the West further militarily into Syria is part of the ISIS strategy lying behind the Paris terror attacks, so Europe keeping Muslim refugees out is the other basic political goal of the atrocity. Specifically, the attack can only help the xenophobic French Front National (FN), which finds itself in a devilish symbiotic relationship with its radical Islamic foes. Hoping enraged, dispirited, frightened Europeans will conflate the huge refugee exodus from Syria (Germany took in 1.1 million refugees in 2015 alone) with terrorism, ISIS is banking on the continent shutting its doors to the needy.

If that comes to pass, then ISIS will have been given its cherished narrative. It can say to the broader (and still not radicalized) Muslim world: "The West hates us; look at what they are doing in Syria. But the West hates you as well, and all Muslims. For all their hypocritical talk, they will do nothing to alleviate our humanitarian suffering by taking Muslim refugees in. Your only home is with us." If it comes to this, ISIS could win over the long run.

But if Europe remains marginally generous to the almost biblical exodus on its doorstep—as pivotal Chancellor Angela Merkel seems to want to be—and further significant intervention in Syria is mitigated, ISIS remains, as we have seen, eminently beatable.

In Iraq, where ISIS is on the wane, the United States must politically push the well-meaning but weak government of Prime Minister Haider al-Abadi to radically decentralize the country, allowing a great deal of freedom for local Kurdish leaders in the north and for the Sunnis in the west and center of Iraq. As Lawrence of Arabia did so well, geopolitical risk analysts must now recognize that the political unit in Iraq and Syria isn't the state, but rather is ethno-religious.

In the case of Iraq, the three big political building blocks are the Sunni, the Shia, and the Kurds.[11] The only kind of political configuration that has any chance of leading to stability must reflect this organic political reality. If Shia-dominated Iraq is to remain a viable state (and the jury is certainly out as to whether this is possible; I have grave doubts), it must decentralize power so as to buttress the loyalties of the Kurds and the Sunnis, a reform that would put great pressure on ISIS, which currently fancies itself as the champion of the Iraqi Sunnis.

---

[11] See John Hulsman, *To Begin the World Over Again: Lawrence of Arabia from Damascus to Baghdad* (London: Palgrave Macmillan, 2009).

Such a geopolitical risk strategy requires patience, a knowledge of recent Middle Eastern history, and an understanding of local Iraqi and Syrian political culture—not qualities the West has in great abundance. But if we can get beyond the horror of ISIS (and in perpetrating that horror they sincerely hope that we cannot), there is a clear strategic road map to defeat them, precisely because, beyond being "crazy," there is real method to their madness, if we could but see.

Sinan Bests Saladin

That Shakespearean phrase "There's method to their madness" is the key lesson for geopolitical risk analysts to keep in mind in successfully gaming out lunatics, those whose apparently irrational behavior makes them seem at first glance patently unable to be studied and assessed. But there is almost always an internal logic to any serious foreign policy actor, however diabolical or seemingly random. Geopolitical risk analysts must first get beyond the simple immediate—and very human—impulse of writing off such players on the international scene as being incapable of assessment, study their ideology (no matter how twisted), and then treat them as they would any other player on the chessboard: what do they want, how are they prepared to get it, and what is their likely strategy?

Besides making this admittedly difficult read on seemingly irrational actors, geopolitical risk analysts must take one more intellectual step if they are to fully go through the looking glass in dealing with them. The irrational are almost always politically underrated; in their strangeness, they are too often subconsciously viewed as inherently incapable of actually succeeding on the foreign policy stage.

Yet the final portion of the story of the Old Man of the Mountain would suggest otherwise. The seemingly irrational not only have method to their madness and can be assessed much as any other foreign policy actor can be; they are also entirely capable of winning.

The Third Crusade (1189–1192) placed Sinan and his sect in an almost impossible strategic position. At the pivotal Battle of Hattin on July 3–4, 1187, the great Saladin—the Sunni Muslim ruler of Egypt and much of Syria—decisively defeated the Western-oriented Crusader Kingdom of Jerusalem, routing his foes (including capturing the reigning king, Guy of Lusignan) and securing the Holy Land for Muslim rule. It was in direct response to this cataclysmic shift in the balance of power in the Middle East that the Third Crusade was launched by the West in the first place.

As Sinan watched all this from his mountain stronghold at Masyaf, he must have been gravely concerned. The most likely coming outcome would be his personal fiefdom becoming merely the arena where two far greater powers played out their rivalry for control of the Holy Land. It looked as though Sinan and his puny sect would probably be overwhelmed by one or both of the great powers descending upon him. But Sinan had one ace left up his sleeve: the fanatical devotion of his followers and the inordinate fear that devotion struck in the hearts of his enemies. He immediately set about using this fact to his maximum advantage.

The Old Man had set upon Saladin first, well in advance of the Crusade. Even as Saladin marched against Aleppo in Syria, devastating Nizari Ismaili territory, the great sultan had twice managed to escape assassinations ordered by Sinan. In 1176, Saladin had laid siege to Masyaf itself, but had failed to break the will of Sinan and the Assassins. Instead, despite a seemingly vast numerical advantage, Saladin had quit the field. Why in the world had he done so?

The story goes that one night Saladin awoke to barely make out a dimly lit figure, stealthily retreating from the darkness of his room. Turning, he found a note pinned next to him, held in place by a poisoned dagger. It proclaimed that though he had been spared this time, the next time Saladin would be slaughtered, if he didn't withdraw his forces immediately.

A terrified Saladin came to believe that it was Sinan himself who had been the man withdrawing from his bedroom that fateful night. Whoever actually did the deed, the Assassins' demonstration of their fanatical commitment to their cause, and their ability to reach out with impunity and strike the great leader, deeply and personally terrorized Saladin, which of course was the purpose of the whole exercise. He withdrew his forces from Masyaf immediately and sought to ally himself with the Assassins from then on. Method to their madness, indeed.

Sinan Bests the Crusaders

Having secured his freedom of maneuver from Saladin, by first terrorizing him and then allying himself with the great man's empire, Sinan was not about to let a rejuvenated Western-oriented Kingdom of Jerusalem reappear on the scene. For, despite the bickering leadership of Richard the Lion-Heart, Philip Augustus of France, Guy of Lusignan, and Conrad of Montferrat, the Westerners were gaining traction in their efforts to restore Christian rule in the Holy Land.

It was the talented Conrad who had rallied Western forces, following the disaster at Hattin. An Italian nobleman brought up in the Piedmont in northern Italy, Conrad hailed from a prominent family, being the cousin of the Holy Roman Emperor, Frederick Barbarossa, Leopold V of Austria, and Louis VII of France. Strikingly handsome, intelligent, charming, and courageous, Conrad arrived in the Middle East after the defeat at Hattin and gave new spirit to the demoralized

Crusader forces, successfully defending the vital coastal city of Tyre, in today's Lebanon.

When Conrad came to the city, the Crusader remnant was negotiating its surrender to Saladin's forces. The story goes that, outraged at their weakness, Conrad threw Saladin's banners into a ditch and forced the city's elders to swear direct loyalty to him instead. After successfully holding off Saladin twice in front of the gates of Tyre, Conrad then sent Jascius, Archbishop of Tyre, westwards, in a desperate appeal to the Christian kingdoms of Europe for aid. This plea and the cataclysm at Hattin, which led Saladin to take Jerusalem, precipitated the Third Crusade.

There is no doubt at all that Conrad was as grimly determined to re-establish the Crusader kingdom as Saladin was to finish it off completely. At the time of his second siege of Tyre, Saladin placed Conrad's aging father, William V of Montferrat, who had been captured by Muslim forces at Hattin, before the walls of the city. Seductively, Saladin offered to release him and to make Conrad a very rich man, if he would only open the gates of Tyre and relinquish the city.

Displaying his own courage, William called to his son, imploring him to stand firm in the face of this overwhelming bribe. Impressively, Conrad made it known that William had benefited from a long life already, and himself aimed a crossbow at his father from the ramparts of Tyre. Saladin's bluff was called; William was released unharmed and returned to Conrad. This was the mettle of the man who from then on devoted his life to recapturing the Kingdom of Jerusalem's past glories.

However, Conrad's path to power as the new King of Jerusalem was not to be easy. In the summer of 1188, Saladin finally released the hapless king, Guy of Lusignan, who had been vanquished at Hattin. For the next few years, both he and Conrad bitterly vied for the throne, with Conrad thundering that Guy had forfeited his right to the crown owing to his battlefield ineptitude. Predictably, the Crusader kings of Europe were drawn into this power struggle, with Richard of England supporting Guy, while Philip of France and Leopold of Austria sided with their kinsman Conrad.

In April 1192, the fate of the Kingdom of Jerusalem was put to a vote. To the Lion-Heart's frustration, the barons of the kingdom unanimously elected the able Conrad as king. In compensation, Richard bought off any more internecine Western rivalry by selling Guy the island of Cyprus as a consolation prize. At last, the stage seemed set for a glorious revival of the Crusader kingdom's fortunes.

And that is exactly what it looked like to Sinan as well. The gifted Conrad made a threatening potential rival, which is the last thing that either the Old Man of the Mountain or his Sunni allies under Saladin desired. Having watched with alarm as Conrad successfully restored the Crusaders' morale after Hattin, Sinan clearly saw that the talented new king was an ideal candidate for assassination at the hands of Sinan's *Hashashin*, as whoever replaced him was bound to be less able.

Even more temptingly, the many internal feuds that had been finally stilled with Conrad's accession to the throne were bound to re-emerge with his death, divisions that could well lead to the end of the Western incursions into the Middle East. All this could be strategically achieved with the removal of just one man.

The Assassins were to succeed in besting Conrad where their mighty ally, Saladin, had failed. For Conrad, having won the coveted prize of the Kingship of Jerusalem, was never to be crowned. In the late morning of April 28, 1192, Conrad's wife—the pregnant Queen Isabella—was late in returning from the Turkish baths to dine with him. Undeterred, the new king went to eat his midday meal at the home of his kinsman and ally, Philip of Beauvais, in the Crusader stronghold of

Acre. However, Conrad found that Philip had already eaten, so he began to return to his palace.

Riding back through the city, Conrad was flanked by a pair of his guards.[12] As he turned down a narrow thoroughfare, the king saw two men loitering by the side of the road. As Conrad approached, the two strangers stood up and walked over to meet him. One of the men was holding a letter, which seemed to be some sort of official document. Conrad stretched his hand down from his horse, reaching out to grasp the parchment.

Now was the supreme moment for the *Hashashin*. Striking instantly, the man holding the letter drew a knife and stabbed upwards, its point plunging deep into Conrad's body. At the same instant, the second assassin leaped onto the back of the king's horse, stabbing him in the side. Conrad died later that same day. Though Conrad's guards killed one of the *Hashashin* and captured the other, it was all too late. He had been King of Jerusalem for less than a fortnight. The loss of this potentially remarkable king amounted to the deathblow for Western efforts to prevail in the Third Crusade.

While most assassinations do not actually alter matters of state, as policy tends to remain remarkably constant regardless of who is in charge, this was a political killing that mattered in that it altered everything.[13] For the assassination led to the end of the Third Crusade, and on Sinan and Saladin's terms. It is not too much to say that Sinan had astutely assessed what would follow from assassinating Conrad, bringing about the Muslim victory.

Not only had the Old Man of the Mountain managed to remove his most talented foe, but as Sinan forecast,

---

[12] For a gripping account of Conrad's assassination, see Dan Jones, *The Plantagenets: The Kings Who Made England* (London: William Collins, 2013), pp. 127–29.

[13] The modern-day murder of Israeli Prime Minister Yitzhak Rabin by a right-wing Jewish settler is another exception to this general political rule, unlike the assassination of John F. Kennedy.

the politics of the Kingdom of Jerusalem were once more thrown into chaos following Conrad's death. Militarily, the Third Crusade had already devolved into a stalemate, with Saladin retaining control of Jerusalem, while the Crusaders held the coastal ports of Tyre and Acre, in modern-day Israel, a balance of power that greatly frustrated many of the European kings, such as Philip Augustus of France, who yearned to return to their homelands. Western enthusiasm for the cause was waning even before Conrad's assassination; his death finished off the Crusades for the next decade.

And just as the Old Man had predicted, the surviving Crusader leadership lost no time in quarreling with one another, opening an irreparable political schism. Under torture, the surviving Assassin—undoubtedly following Sinan's orders to the last—insisted that Richard the Lion-Heart was the political force behind the killing. It did not help matters that Richard's nephew, Henry II of Champagne, married Conrad's widow, Queen Isabella, in unseemly haste just days after his death. As Richard, in contrast to the rulers of France and Austria, had supported Guy's claim to the throne rather than Conrad's, there was just enough plausibility to the charges to poison the well of Crusader unity.

A three-year truce was finally agreed on between the Muslims and the Crusaders on September 2, 1192. Saladin kept the jewel of Jerusalem, but agreed to allow a limited number of Christian pilgrims to pray at the Holy Sepulcher, the site Christians recognize as the tomb of Jesus. The Crusaders kept the cities they held on the coastline, from Jaffa to Tyre. In October 1192, the Lion-Heart himself sailed away, never to return, having failed to fulfil his vow of re-taking Jerusalem for Christianity. The Assassins had overcome one of the greatest generals in history and won the Third Crusade. The "madman" had triumphed.

Getting beyond the over-the-top fervor of Sinan's *Hashashin* proved an impossibility for the Crusader mindset. However, such an analytical effort would have been worth it. Far from being irrational, the Old Man of the Mountain emerges—even compared with his legendary contemporaries Saladin and Richard—as by far the most astute strategic thinker of the Third Crusade. By personally terrorizing Saladin with the proven threat of assassination, Sinan made an ally of him, succeeding in defending his fortress Masyaf, and successfully fending off Saladin's efforts to wholly dominate Syria.

Faced with a second existential threat to his power, the Old Man of the Mountain succeeded in eliminating the one Crusader leader, Conrad of Montferrat, who posed a long-term danger to his security. Better still, in successfully assessing the political schisms that plagued his Crusader opponents, Sinan set in motion the events that led to their dispirited end, once again securing his own power base and the future of his sect. If this amounts to craziness, I only can wish that Sinan were around to bite some of my geopolitical risk analysts.

Sinan did not have long to savor his improbable victory. He died at Al-Kahf castle in Masyaf in Syria in 1192. Following his death, the Nizari Ismaili central order in Iran—situated at Alamut—regained closer control of the Syrian branch of their sect. But Sinan must never be forgotten by modern-day geopolitical risk analysts, as his against-the-odds successful career underlines the vital need to game out lunatics. Not only is there almost always method to their madness. Sometimes they actually win.

CHAPTER FOUR

1503 AD: Gaming Out Chess Players

MACHIAVELLI, CESARE BORGIA, AND POPE JULIUS II

Machiavelli Attempts a Comeback

The mirror opposite of gaming out lunatics is the imperative for geopolitical risk analysts to accurately assess chess players—the foreign policy actors playing the long game, possessing fixed, long-term strategic goals, even as they use whatever tactical means that come to hand to achieve them. Patient, low-key, but implacable, chess players do that rarest of things: they actually think ahead and are not prisoners of short-term day-to-day events, conditioning all that they do in furtherance of their long-term strategy.

President Vladimir Putin of Russia is a perfect modern-day example of a chess player, as all the many devious tactics he pursues ultimately amount to a very single-minded effort to restore Russian greatness, often by blunting the West's drives into what he sees as Russia's sphere of influence in the countries surrounding it. As such, Putin's behavior is eminently explicable, rational, and is easy to assess, but only if the analyst starts at the strategic end goal and works backwards.

Gaming out chess players is another major commandment in mastering geopolitical risk analysis, grouped with its twin of gaming out lunatics under the "nothing in excess" typological sub-heading. Geopolitical risk analysis is founded on the search for the very real long-term strategic patterns that explain and largely determine seemingly random daily tactical behavior in foreign policy. While very hard to spot, the reward for gaming out chess players is as great as is the difficulty in finding them. For if the ultimate goals of a chess player can be determined, all that they do to achieve them along the way makes eminent sense and can be foreseen.

Following on from the Crusades, the Western world entered a period of cultural and political regeneration we now call the Renaissance. As is true for most eras, it was more politically chaotic, brutal, and bloody than it seems in retrospect. In the confusing, uncertain milieu of early-sixteenth-century northern Italy, a man arose who fit the tenor of his times.

The year 1513 found Niccolò Machiavelli in desperate straits. True, the Italian Renaissance historian, philosopher, humanist, dramatist, and writer had just about escaped execution following his deposition from a major position of authority in the Florentine Republic. But beyond all the sidelights that decked out his glittering CV, Machiavelli's day job was beyond question as a politician and diplomat. And while he still had his life, he had just been unceremoniously bounced into enforced retirement at his country estate of Saint Andrea outside of Florence, following the disastrous August 1512 defeat of the Florentines at the Battle of Prato at the hands of the Medici family (erstwhile rulers of the city-state) and their Spanish allies, with the backing of Pope Julius II.

Following the cataclysmic setback, the Republic was disbanded as the Medici were returned to power, and Machiavelli was consequently put out to pasture. For a man used to being "in the thick of it," as we would put it today, this premature ending of what had been a bejeweled career rankled his very soul.

Machiavelli responded to this huge setback in a surprisingly modern way: he decided to write a book, detailing all that he had learned about politics through the great tumult of the Renaissance, an age in which alliances kaleidoscopically changed as fragile governments rose and fell with startling speed. In such a violent and unsure world, Machiavelli's teachings in *The Prince* were baldly conditioned to reflect nothing more and nothing less than the acquisition and retention of power—no small feat in the chaotic northern Italian world of the sixteenth century. For him, only those with a coherent long-term strategy—and the will to follow it through tactically, whatever the cost—were likely to survive and thrive in those cutthroat days.

However, *The Prince* is about far more than political theory. Practically, it was an exercise in marketing, a way to keep Machiavelli's name before the educated public of his time and more importantly to get the attention of the new masters of northern Italy. In essence, *The Prince* amounts to a high-brow job application. It was with these very self-interested goals in mind that Machiavelli sat down to write *The Prince*, which has become the bible of *realpolitik*, supposedly detailing how the world really works, as opposed to how we might like it to.

In the end, Machiavelli utterly failed in his personal desire to make himself a player in Italian politics again; despite the publication of *The Prince*, he never again managed to really escape his imposed exile and secure a major political role on the Renaissance stage. However, in *The Prince*, he did manage to gain something more: immortality as a great political thinker. He particularly won the admiration of those who methodically go about securing their political goals; for these chess players, Machiavelli's *Prince* has become the ur-text where all true thinking about modern-day politics begins.

There is only one real problem with this conventional narrative of the supposedly great Italian thinker: in his own time and own place, Machiavelli personally proved to be not much of a chess player at all. For when it came to evaluating who the greatest statesman/chess player was of his own age, he analytically got things entirely wrong.

Beguiled by the dark glamor of the diabolical Cesare Borgia, the Bond villain of Renaissance Italy, Machiavelli saw this attractively evil charmer as the man of the moment, as all the while the real chess player of his time, Pope Julius II, sat disregarded in front of his nose. The supposedly great manipulator utterly failed to make the correct geopolitical risk analysis call in his own time, echoing our contemporary problems assessing chess players—those who possess stable, long-term strategic goals, using varied tactics to flexibly attain them.

For if overly bizarre actors have thrown geopolitical risk analysts since time began, as we just saw in the preceding chapter, the other extreme—ignoring long-term, well-ordered strategies and strategists—is the mirror-image sin. Too often, we view such chess players as something less, allowing the day-to-day noise of the world to obscure long-held and highly rational patterns of thought and the goals of these highly disciplined political actors. Spotting chess players early on gives the geopolitical risk analyst a huge advantage in gleaning what the future holds. But as proved the case for the supposedly wily Machiavelli, assessing chess players is a daunting task.

Machiavelli Backs the Wrong Horse

Niccolò Machiavelli was born in Florence in 1469, the third child and first son of a prosperous attorney. Relatively early on, his intellectual gifts were recognized by the city-state; in the decade between 1500 and 1510, he served as a senior Florentine diplomatic emissary on missions to the Papacy in Rome, the French court of Louis XII, and the powerful Spanish king. Closer to home, from 1503 to 1506, he was responsible for raising and training Florence's militia; he believed that the city-state must be defended by an army of its own citizens, rather than risk protection from unreliable mercenaries. A high point of his career came in 1509, when Florentine troops under his command defeated the rival city-state of Pisa.

However, his triumph proved to be short-lived. With the coming of the disastrous and decisive Battle of Prato in 1512, the Florentine Republic—to which Machiavelli had given his best years of service—was no more. Following their resumption of power, the victorious Medici family accused Machiavelli in 1513 of conspiracy and had him imprisoned. During his incarceration—as was the custom of the time—he was tortured by being hanged from his wrists, a process that dislocated his shoulders. However, despite the excruciating pain, Machiavelli continued to deny his crime, and after three weeks he was released from prison and allowed to return to his country estate outside of Florence. But you cannot keep a good Renaissance man down. It was from here that he almost immediately began to plot his political comeback, with *The Prince* serving as a central part of his strategy.

I am somewhat embarrassed to admit that, while I am a rather well-known card-carrying member of the realist club, I find *The Prince*—the oft-quoted key text underpinning my school of thought—to be a highly disappointing work. The aphorisms passing for political theory in the book strike me not as scandalous, as so many others have perceived them, but worse, as terribly obvious, and the text itself is poorly written. It is only when the supposed grand master of chess players uses examples from his own storied time to buttress his points that the book comes vividly to life. *The Prince* is one of those books that is honored in the breach, quoted extensively, but not really read very much. Given the genuine as opposed to the reputed quality of the work, that may be for the best.

As a result of the political chaos that raged all around him, it is little wonder that Machiavelli focused in *The Prince* on the immeasurable political benefits of security and stability. The whole of the work merely serves as a handbook as to how these ultimate political goals can be achieved, using various tactical strategies depending on differing political circumstances. For example, Machiavelli counsels that newly enthroned princes (and most modern-day Western politicians) must first stabilize their power base if they are ultimately to build an enduring political structure. As we shall see, this is a point of view that has been adopted by chess players as disparate as George Washington and Julius II as a central focus of their strategy.

In true realist, chess player fashion, Machiavelli is agnostic about the tactics that must be used by a prince to stabilize power in his new realm. To put it in today's terms, it is not a question of relying on mantras, such as "always use force first" (favored by the neo-conservatives in America) or "always use diplomacy first" (a central American Wilsonian adage). Rather, Machiavelli and most realists, saying that "it depends on the circumstances," consider force and diplomacy, not ends in themselves, but merely supple tactics that are both to be employed to further the ultimate goal of political stability.

It is due to this agnosticism about means, shocking for reasons that pass my understanding, that Machiavelli has horrified his critics for centuries. He has been vilified as teaching evil and, worse still, propounding evil policy recommendations to tyrants throughout history, enabling them to maintain their wicked positions. The phrase "Machiavellian" has entered English usage as a highly pejorative term, connoting one at ease with political deceit, deviousness, and amoral *realpolitik*, a person having few moral scruples in attaining the nirvana of political or personal success.

But this ghost story simplification makes a cartoon of what the man truly thought, dismissing the chess player's credo that to attain the magical, maddeningly elusive strategic end of stability, the means must be varied and often harsh. And while it is true that unutterably evil men such as Stalin have been attracted to Machiavelli, so too have highly decent, moral statesmen such as George Washington and Alexander Hamilton, who used chess player precepts to forge the success of the fledgling American Republic.[1] *The Prince* is not immoral; instead, it is the nature of the leader reading it—rather than the text itself—that determines whether good or evil outcomes will flow from its amoral attempt to illuminate how the world of politics really works.

The only major idea behind such chess playing—and it is certainly an important one—is the acquisition and retention of political power. While modern-day American Wilsonians and neo-conservatives have more in common with the "lunatics" we sketched out in the prior chapter—believing that a set of extra-worldly ideas should and do govern political action—realist chess players refute Plato, insisting that an imaginary ideal society founded on such ethereal principles is simply not a model by which a leader in the real world should attempt to guide his reign.

Chess players wearily (if not altogether happily) accept that human nature is largely immutable, and that in practice human beings are driven by passions as much as by reason. While they may bemoan this reality, crucially they do not think they can change it; such an idea is often the political bane of supposedly more "moral" political creeds that are endlessly doomed to failure because of this fundamental misreading of what human beings are actually like.

---

[1] See Robert Service, *Stalin: A Biography* (Cambridge, MA: Belknap Press of Harvard University Press, 2006).

No, it is not for its brave bleakness that I am critical of *The Prince*; actually that is the quality of it that I admire. It is rather that, in his own time, Machiavelli—like so many of his detractors through the ages—confused evil with effectiveness, seeing the charismatically dysfunctional Cesare Borgia as his ideal model prince rather than the far less morally grotesque (and far more politically successful) Pope Julius II as the true exemplar of the chess-playing creed.

For chess playing is not ultimately about pantomime villainy, but rather about effectiveness in attaining and retaining political power over the long-term. Instead, Machiavelli was as much an emotional sort as the many he disparaged; enamored of the dark side of Cesare Borgia's glamor, he neglected to look dispassionately at the political record on the ground in Renaissance Italy. In essence, for all his bombast, the father of modern political thought proved himself a dreadful geopolitical risk analyst.

Cesare Borgia's Overrated Bond Villain Luster

Cesare Borgia was an Italian nobleman, politician, and one-time cardinal in the late fifteenth and early sixteenth centuries. His picaresque, swashbuckling struggle for power served as a primary inspiration for *The Prince*; indeed, Machiavelli first planned to dedicate the work to his idol, somehow seeing in all his attractive villainy the ideal exemplar of his views. While serving on a diplomatic mission for Florence from October 1502 to January 1503, Machiavelli came to know Borgia, then at the height of his power.

His dark, if compelling, reputation made Cesare a legend of sorts, even in his own time. Contemporaneously, he was accused by his enemies of adultery, incest, simony (selling church offices), theft, bribery, and murder, probably being guilty of most of these lurid crimes. Even for a violent time when almost anything went, Cesare Borgia stands out as a symbol of the darker side of humanity. Coupled with his undeniable talents and charm, he cuts a compelling figure across the centuries. It is easy to see why Machiavelli fell for him—easy, but wrong.

Born in Rome in 1475 or 1476, Borgia was the illegitimate son of Pope Alexander VI, who reigned as pontiff from 1492 to 1503. Alexander was the first pope to openly recognize his progeny, though they were born out of wedlock. In his ceaseless efforts to promote the position of his children (he had several) and his family, Alexander had Cesare made an improbable cardinal at the tender age of eighteen, after his own election to the Papacy.

At the same time as Cesare was made a prince of the church, his older brother, Giovanni, was made captain general of the military forces of the Papacy, an appointment his younger brother viewed with great envy and resentment. Giovanni was mysteriously assassinated in 1497; Cesare may well have had him killed for multiple reasons, both personal and professional.

Chafing at a life in the church, Cesare had always been more desirous of a career in the military. With Giovanni out of the way, such a road became open to him. Also, Giovanni and Cesare shared a long-time mistress, Sancha of Aragon, scandalously the wife of their younger brother Gioffre. As such, with the demise of Giovanni, Cesare had at one stroke seen his primary professional and personal rival removed from his life. Following these murky events, in August 1498 he became the first person in history to resign a cardinalcy as his attention turned to earthlier forms of power.

His adoring father established Cesare as a prince in his own right, with territory carved out of the papal states that dominated the politics of central Italy. In such a capacity, Cesare briefly reigned from 1498 to 1503. He was appointed commander of the papal armies in the place of his deceased brother and was also sent a significant detachment of Swiss mercenaries by the king of France to secure his new possessions. Cesare made an advantageous marriage to a French princess, Charlotte d'Albret, in order to cement continuing French support for his military campaigns.

However, Cesare's reign—try as he might to change this basic political reality—remained dependent on his father's ability as pope to distribute patronage and on his family's shaky alliance with France, which invaded Italy in 1499. Cesare never acquired the magic elixir of local political legitimacy for his rule. This was palpably not the basis for long-term political stability, the lodestone for all chess players.

What he lacked in legitimacy, Cesare tried to make up for in cruelty. His military generals (or captains, as they were then called), fearing his rages, began plotting his removal. Using his considerable guile and charm, Cesare publicly reconciled with his feckless captains, only to deceive them; turning about, he imprisoned and then executed them. Such blood-soaked actions managed to keep Cesare in power, but conversely made it clear that his hold on his newly founded principality was highly precarious.

But Cesare was certainly more than merely an out-and-out villain (though he was surely that as well). A capable general and diplomat in an age that demanded it, his many gifts were simply not enough to keep his artificial domains together. Machiavelli, though looking at Cesare through rose-colored glasses, does make clear in *The Prince* that his continued, fundamental dependence on the goodwill of the papacy under the control of his father was the principal drawback of his reign.

And it was over this key political weakness that Cesare met his doom, proving himself anything but a first-rate chess player. Alexander's immediate successor as pope, Pius III, died after a reign of only twenty-six days. Almost immediately, a new papal conclave was necessary. Into the void stepped Giuliano Della Rovere, who—unlike the stylish Cesare—actually knew how to get his way in the shark tank of Italian Renaissance politics. This true chess player was more than a match for Machiavelli's tin idol.

Above all, Borgia was looking for a new pope who wouldn't threaten his fragile principality in central Italy. Luckily for him, given his father's patronage network and the geographical proximity of his power base to Rome, Borgia assumed a critical role in anointing the new pope. However, it was over this crucial point that he fatally bungled things in a most inexpert manner.

Ahead of the papal conclave of October 1503, Della Rovere succeeded in duping Cesare into actually supporting his bid to be the new pontiff by offering him a much-needed bribe, assuring Borgia he could maintain command of the papal army, and solemnly vowing to continue Rome's backing for Borgia policies in central Italy. Cesare, for once, proved as good as his word, delivering the crucial support of all eleven Spanish cardinals for Della Rovere.[2] The conclave lasted only ten hours—the shortest in history—before Della Rovere was almost unanimously named Pope Julius II.

But what Cesare could not see—a central point that Della Rovere perceived all too clearly—was that once his vital support had elevated Julius to the papacy, his rival's goal of attaining power had been realized. From that new perch, maintaining power would be the new fixed strategic compass point for all of the new pope's subsequent plans. As such, Cesare, who had proven so vital in elevating Della Rovere to

[2] Frederic J. Baumgartner, *Behind Locked Doors: A History of Papal Elections* (London: Palgrave Macmillan, 2003), p. 89.

the position as the new pope in the first place, now became an extreme liability in allowing Julius to sustain his newly won power.

So Julius did what any good chess player would have done, a fact which somehow managed to elude the analysis of Machiavelli himself: he pocketed the advantages of Cesare's alliance up front, and then immediately repudiated his agreement upon his accession, becoming Borgia's greatest enemy. Cesare never recovered from Julius's political betrayal, losing his control over central Italy by the end of 1503.

Without papal support, Cesare's rule on his own lasted merely a matter of months, with his lands reverting to Julius and the Papacy itself, thereby securing the stability of the new pope's reign. After this decisive betrayal, Borgia never managed to undo the damage that Julius's treachery did to his political chances. He eventually escaped to Spain, where he farmed himself out as a mercenary captain, meeting his demise there in battle in 1507. In the end, it is clear from this tale—in a way the gormless Machiavelli entirely missed—who the real chess player in early-sixteenth-century Italy actually was.

Washington and Hamilton as Chess Players

Contrary to Machiavelli's dark fixation on Cesare Borgia, far more moral men and far more decent causes have been blessed with the long-term insights of chess players. Nowhere has this been more the case than with the birth and success of the American Republic, where beneath all the tumult, the basic foreign policy outlined by George Washington held in place for a full century, paving the way for America's emergence as a global power. It is hard to think of a better example of chess playing: almost wholly undetected by analysts, a long-term policy was established and successfully acted upon for the better part of 100 years.

The highly contentious 1794 Jay Treaty, negotiated between the fledgling American Republic and all-powerful Great Britain, was the seminal event that sent Washington's foreign policy chess playing into motion. As tensions rose between great powers London and Paris with the advent of the French Revolutionary era, Americans in general were broadly inclined to support the French position.

The reasons for this were both emotional and ideological. France had been the invaluable ally of the American Revolution, supplying the hard-pressed colonies with troops, vital naval support (which helped win the critical Battle of Yorktown), and most of all, the money to keep the rebellion going. Many Americans, including Francophiles Thomas Jefferson and James Madison, felt an immense debt of gratitude to the country for all that it had done for the American cause.

Then there was the fact that the French Revolution—bloody as it so quickly became—was at least founded on the same universalist principles of liberty, equality, and fraternity that had guided the American revolutionaries so recently. It would have taken hearts of stone for the American Founders not to have felt a genuine kinship with the French for what they were attempting to accomplish—following on from the American example—with their own revolution. By contrast, conservative, monarchist, elitist Britain served for many such as Jefferson as the glaring counter-example of what their new country must avoid degenerating into at all costs.

Fortunately, Alexander Hamilton—secretary of the treasury and the dominant figure in Washington's administration—had a head as well as a heart. In many ways, the careers of both Washington and his headstrong, brilliant protégé amount to being curious political throwbacks, as both served as bridge figures linking the recent, staid, American colonial past to the country's future as a rough-and-tumble Republic.

In a lot of ways, Washington effectively served as America's last king, with Hamilton playing the recognizable role of prime minister, his influence venturing far afield from his specific purview as treasury secretary. Fascinatingly, their great success as chess players in both winning and then crucially maintaining the viability of the Republic they created made the need for the two founding giants fleeting, as in the future it would be institutions and not great men that would make the country secure. But to give the national institutions brought into being by the constitution time to organically take root, it was absolutely essential that America hew to a foreign policy that would not upend its promising experiment in self-government.

For Alexander Hamilton, this meant above all that tensions with Britain—the superpower of the age—had to be cooled, to avoid the chaos and tumult of another war on North American soil, one the Republic might well lose this time. With this mandate, Supreme Court Chief Justice John Jay was sent to London to bargain with the court of George III, resolving the issues left unsolved by the Treaty of Paris of 1783, which had ended the Revolutionary War.

At first glance, the specific provisions of the Jay Treaty seem to greatly favor the Court of St. James.[3] The new accord failed to end impressment, the odious British practice of kidnapping American sailors on the high seas, forcibly recruiting them into the Royal Navy. Economically, Britain was given most-favored-nation trading status for its imports to America, without the same advantage being reciprocated for US goods. Jay also failed to win British compensation for slaves who had been taken by the United Kingdom at

[3] See Ron Chernow, *Washington: A Life* (New York: Penguin Books, 2010), p. 729.

the end of the war, a fact that riled Southerners against the treaty in general.

For all that, the Jay Treaty was an undeniable diplomatic success for America. England finally consented to evacuating the forts it still held in northwestern America (today's Michigan, Indiana, and Ohio); their continued occupation had greatly impeded American immigration there. In terms of trade, London did consent to open the lucrative British West Indies to small American ships. American merchants were also compensated for their goods confiscated by the British navy on the high seas.

But beyond this mixed record of haggling over tactical provisions of the deal, one great strategic point loomed, which informed Hamilton's passionate defense of the deeply unpopular treaty: The accord arrested a possibly fatal drift of the two countries towards war, as the weight of these myriad unresolved issues could well have lit a spark that would have plunged the new Republic into chaos. For that strategic, chess-playing reason above all, the Federalist administration decided to back the accord.

It took all of Washington's unparalleled prestige and credibility with his countrymen to see the treaty through the Senate, which debated it in secret in June 1795. In the end, the treaty was ratified by the necessary two-thirds Senate majority in August 1795, 20–10, without a vote to spare.

However, as the constitutional process moved along, the specific terms of the Jay Treaty were leaked to a furious public in early July 1795. As the gloomy Jay remarked, such was the displeasure of his countrymen with the accord that by July 4th, 1795, he had been burned in effigy in so many towns that he could have traversed the entire length of America by the glow of his own flaming figure.[4] Things got so bad in terms

[4]Ibid., p. 731.

of public opinion that pro-French protesters hurled stones at Hamilton while he attended a pro-treaty rally in New York.

Unsure of what to do, even questioning whether he should sign the accord in the firestorm of condemnation that shook America following the publication of the treaty's details, Washington called on Hamilton (now having returned to his law practice in New York) for advice, asking him what he thought of the treaty. In his typical fashion, Hamilton replied with a masterful fifty-three-page geopolitical risk assessment, urging the wavering president to sign the imperfect but vital agreement.

Washington kept his nerve, focusing on the key chess player rationale that he wasn't about to risk the fruits of the revolution on a second war with Britain; he was also thinking that the Jay Treaty would prevent a harmful deterioration in trade with the United Kingdom, on which the United States was entirely economically dependent, as it was by far America's largest single commercial partner.

Washington duly signed the Jay Treaty in August 1795, with its provisions coming into effect on February 29, 1796. The president made it clear that in terms of America's long-term foreign policy, the United States must—for its own long-term stability—remain neutral in the face of Europe's great revolutionary wars.

The domestic political consequences of the controversy arising over the Jay Treaty were long-lasting, leading directly to the first party system in the United States. The treaty became the core dividing issue separating the two nascent political parties. Both the Federalists (who supported the Jay Treaty) and the Jeffersonians (who opposed it) became far more organized after the tumultuous days surrounding the treaty's ratification, and then remained so. The Federalists were seen as being broadly pro-British, with the Jeffersonians strongly inclining to a more pro-French foreign policy position. Never again would the Republic operate without two broadly opposed and organized parties endlessly battling to secure political power; the Jay Treaty was that seminal a domestic political event.

In practical policy terms, there is little doubt that the Jay Treaty proved a success for the American Republic. Even its arch-foe Thomas Jefferson did not repudiate the agreement when he became president in 1801, a sure sign of its efficacy. In terms of strategic chess playing, it was an unmitigated success, buying America a decade of peace and ever-increasing commerce with Great Britain in the midst of the French Revolutionary Wars and the rise of Napoleon. As Joseph Ellis astutely notes, the Jay Treaty "bet, in effect, on England rather than France as the hegemonic European power of the future, which proved prophetic."[5]

In the end, Washington and Hamilton's insistence on cool, sober chess playing, even when it ran directly counter to American passions and ideological proclivities, carried the day. It is safe to say that the Republic itself was the great benefactor. As Chernow states, "With the Jay Treaty, Washington had made good on his solemn oath to maintain peace and prosperity during his presidency," a state of affairs that made possible the steady rise of America to the position of the greatest global power.[6]

Washington's Farewell Address as Geopolitical Strategy

But America's first president remained deeply troubled by the personal attacks that befell him as a result of the Jay

---

[5] Joseph Ellis, *Founding Brothers: The Revolutionary Generation* (New York: Vintage Books, 2000), pp. 136–37.

[6] Chernow, *Washington*, p. 743.

Treaty, easily the most sensitive crisis of his highly successful presidency. Things had gotten so bad that Jeffersonians now openly (and for the first time) stopped drinking the customary toast to the president's health after dinner. As his presidency entered its twilight days, for one final time, Washington felt the need to explain himself to the American public. The result was his Farewell Address, a magnificently straightforward defense of his sublime chess-playing strategy.

On its surface, the address amounts to an open letter written by Washington to the people of the United States near the end of his second term, before heading into a final retirement on his Mount Vernon estate. However, the address—originally published in the *American Daily Advertiser* on September 19, 1796—functions as something far more: it gives a glimpse into the chess-playing credo that had steadily guided all of Washington's actions during his presidency. As was so often the case, Washington turned to Hamilton, his long-time intellectual collaborator, to craft the address, even as its themes remained distinctly his own.

But Hamilton would also play a central role in the address's success. He began work on the address with a series of notes Washington had given to him that sounded petulant, almost defensive, of the criticisms he had endured. Hamilton's draft erased this off-putting tone; instead, he wrote a letter that reads as a coolly statesmanlike document, the final utterances of a self-assured man speaking for a last time to posterity.

The address opens with Washington informing his countrymen that he will not run for a third term as president (despite the fact that he almost certainly would have won such a prize). The president sketches out broad, strategic vistas, imagining America's grand future. To secure the country's long-term political stability—his chess-playing goal—Washington argues that a series of dangers must still be overcome: America's national identity must come to override sectional attachments, law and order must be maintained, and something must be done about political parties, which he rails against and sees—incorrectly, in history's verdict—as a sign of domestic decay.

But beyond all this, Washington stresses that America's western territories—the almost limitless geographical patrimony that ensured America's future peerless position in the world—must be kept free at all costs from foreign encroachments. In other words, America must not become a carbon copy of Europe, an area of limited space endlessly fought over by a large number of powers, all of whom remain permanently unable to exercise political dominance. America had been blessed with a continent where eventually only it would hold sway. Such an unbelievable strategic gift must be safeguarded at all costs; everything must be done to secure this unparalleled advantage that luck and providence had granted the American people.

It is within this broader chess-playing context that the president's actions over the Jay Treaty become explicable. For Washington and Hamilton, US foreign policy must be based, above all else, on practical interests rather than ideological passions of any sort. As Washington says in the address about the Jay Treaty, in a not so subtle dig at Jefferson's emotional Francophilia, "The nation which indulges towards another an habitual hatred, or an habitual fondness, is in some degree a slave."[7]

In the light of his view that neutrality remains the best strategy for America to safeguard its western frontier, suddenly Washington's entire foreign policy becomes eminently clear: he is not for neutrality for neutrality's sake; rather, given the highly favorable geopolitical position America found itself in during the 1790s, such a practical policy

[7]Ibid., p. 756.

is simply the best specific course of action for the young Republic. It is because of its geopolitical position, in other words, that, as Washington put it, "'Tis our true policy to steer clear of permanent alliances with any portion of the foreign world."[8]

Like any good chess player, not only could Washington see the grand strategic picture, but he also kept his eyes firmly on the geopolitical prize in day-to-day matters. America could successfully pursue a neutralist foreign policy specifically because it had two moats to protect it from foreign encroachments, the Atlantic and Pacific Oceans. The internal forces that might work against American continental hegemony—Canadians, Mexicans, and the various Plains Indian tribes—were obviously not going to be able to stop the American Republic over the long-term from dominating the whole of the North American continent.

Given this unique and highly advantageous geopolitical position, all the United States had to do was not mangle its foreign policy too badly, giving major European powers no diplomatic excuse to intervene in far-off America. As such, permanent and entangling alliances with one or another of the European powers was about the only foreign policy mistake that had to be avoided, as it was the only policy that could conceivably compel a major European power to intervene on the North American continent.

A foreign policy based on neutrality would safeguard against the only calamity that could possibly derail America's almost unbearably bright and inevitable future as a great power, master of the North American continent. It is in this chess-playing light that both Washington's highly successful foreign policy and his Farewell Address must be viewed. The Jay Treaty was the practical culmination of this chess-playing

[8] Ibid.

strategy, affirming America's neutrality vis-à-vis both Great Britain and France by correcting the pro-French tilt that had characterized US foreign policy in the earliest days of the Republic.

Washington's foreign policy strategy proved so successful that it was not until the founding of NATO in 1949 that America dispensed with the first president's advice, entering into a permanent military alliance with most of Western Europe. By then, Washington's impossible dream of America's halcyon future—made so explicit in the Farewell Address—had come to pass, largely as a result of his chess playing.

Julius Runs Rings around Borgia

Of course, not all (or even most) chess-playing successes are in the service of such a higher cause; in most cases the strategy simply furthers the ambitions of individual, clever men. But certainly, on average, it has historically been better to be ruled by successful chess players than by fools or by random actors. For often the wisdom of a good chess player secures other advantages for his people. This was certainly true in the case of Pope Julius II, the man to whom *The Prince* ought to have been dedicated by Machiavelli. In between pursuing his geostrategic ends, Julius found time to rebuild St. Peter's Basilica, commissioning Michelangelo to paint the unutterably lovely Sistine Chapel along the way.

It is intellectually striking, following on from the failure of Cesare Borgia and the undiluted success of Pope Julius, that Machiavelli—the supposedly grand theoretician—would damn him with such faint praise in *The Prince*, just as he stubbornly made rather wan allowances for his favorite, Borgia. Yet it was Julius, and not Cesare, who fulfilled Machiavelli's key strategic dictate: he reinvigorated a state (in this case the Papacy in terms of its temporal possessions), salvaging its stability for the future.

Basically, lacking any sort of systemic argument for explaining why Julius rose and Borgia fell, Machiavelli falls back on the excuse given by all poor geopolitical risk analysts: bad luck is the reason he was so wrong. He laments the fall of Borgia, sorrowfully noting that he was overturned "from the extraordinary and extreme malignancy of Fortune."[9] Alexander VI, Cesare's father and key patron, died in 1503 at exactly the moment Borgia himself was deathly ill and unable to effectively defend his realm.

Machiavelli slavishly accepts Borgia's own account of his fall from grace, going so far as to recount in *The Prince* a personal conversation the two had about Borgia's fate. "But he [Borgia] told me himself on the day on which Julius II was created [pope] that he had foreseen and provided for everything else that could happen on his father's death, but had never anticipated that when his father died he too should be at death's door."[10]

This terribly convenient excuse—wholly omitting Borgia's disastrously being taken in by the wily Julius during the just-concluded conclave—is buttressed by Machiavelli's assertion that we basically have to take his analytical word for things, still today a sure sign an analyst doesn't have much of a factual argument. Incredibly, despite Borgia's fall and Julius's rise, Machiavelli, supposedly the doyen of chess players, comes to the ridiculous conclusion that, "taken all these actions of the Duke [Borgia] together, I can still find no fault with him."[11]

---

[9] Nicolò Machiavelli, *The Prince* (Norwalk, CT: Easton Press, 1980), p. 60.
[10] Ibid, p. 68.
[11] Ibid.

As for Machiavelli's judgment of Julius, at best it consists of grudging praise, leavened with the reverse side of the pallid argument he just made for Borgia: if Cesare was supremely unlucky, Julius, in turn, was smiled on by the gods. While Machiavelli does admit that Julius, "more than any of his predecessors showed what a Pope could effect with money and arms," his halting praise ends there.[12] In *The Prince*, Machiavelli makes clear that he finds Julius impetuous and supremely lucky. He explains away Julius's chess-playing success, noting that "the shortness of his life did not allow him to experience reverses."[13] In fact, Julius reigned for nine years.

Machiavelli goes on, finding further fault with Julius's seemingly sterling record as a statesman. "But if times had overtaken him, rendering a cautious line of conduct necessary, his ruin must have ensued, since he never could have departed from those methods to which nature inclined him."[14] So Julius was lucky because his one-note bold nature suited his bold times; otherwise he would have met with disaster. Frankly, such sour grapes don't pass the laugh test as an argument.

Why was Machiavelli so down on Julius? The answer is deceptively simple. It was Julius who lent crucial support to Machiavelli's key Medici and Spanish enemies, leading to their triumph at the Battle of Prato in August 1512 and the personal ruination of Machiavelli himself with the downfall of the Florentine Republic. Machiavelli rightly saw Julius as the author of his own demise. His gripe with Julius is about as far away from chess playing as it is possible to be: a very personal and very emotional grudge got in the way

[12]Ibid., p. 91.
[13]Ibid., p. 177.
[14]Ibid.

of Machiavelli analyzing his world correctly. The personal will remain a difficult hurdle for geopolitical risk analysts to intellectually vault unto the end of time.

How does one get personal feelings out of analysis, dispassionately assessing things, even if one does not like the outcomes one reaches? To ask this question is to acknowledge that it is a great challenge to be a chess player, either analytically or as a decision-maker, given that we all have human emotions that can so easily cloud our judgment, despite our best intentions. The supreme irony is that it was Machiavelli—the man who did more than any other to stress the need for cold logic triumphing over more transient human feelings—who was analytically incapable of being the chess player he urged the world's princes to be.

The Prince with Julius as Hero

However, we have five centuries of distance from the swirling events of the Italian Renaissance, allowing us to take up the more dispassionate, chess-playing analytical view that Machiavelli urges on us. So let us here re-write the ending of *The Prince*, this time using Julius II as the proper analytical hero of the piece.

Julius was born Giuliano Della Rovere around 1443. Like Cesare Borgia, his path to power was speeded along by close familial contacts to the Papacy. Della Rovere was the much-loved nephew of Pope Sixtus IV, who took him under his wing as he rose through the Vatican ranks. Again eerily paralleling Borgia's career, Della Rovere's big break came when his uncle assumed the Papacy in 1471 and he was made a bishop. Quickly ascending to the rank of cardinal, Della Rovere became his uncle's de facto prime minister, accruing great political influence in the Vatican. As such, between 1480 and 1484, Della Rovere made the diplomatic rounds, serving in the crucial position of papal legate to France.

Following the death of his uncle, Della Rovere assumed that he would succeed him. However, he was beaten out by Cardinal Rodrigo Borgia, Cesare's father, who assumed the title of Alexander VI. Della Rovere, incredulous at his humiliating defeat, never forgave Alexander, accusing him of winning the Papacy through the corrupt practice of si-mony—selling church offices in order to get elected by the College of Cardinals.

Della Rovere was certainly not a very good loser; following Alexander's ascension, he fled to the safety of great power France—where he was well-regarded—to plot his next moves. Della Rovere urged King Charles VIII to march on Rome, overthrowing the newly elected Alexander. Charles invaded Italy, but Della Rovere's machinations were defeated when Charles was bought off by the equally conniving Alexander. However, with the death of his rival in 1503, Della Rovere sensed that his moment had at last come.

Rightly alarmed at the prospect of Della Rovere assuming the Papacy, Cesare Borgia managed to temporarily block his family's great rival, with the election of Pope Pius III. How-ever, Pius lasted only twenty-six days, one of the shortest reigns in papal history. It was at this critical juncture that Della Rovere—in true chess player fashion—deceived the supposedly worldly Cesare and ran rings around him dip-lomatically, securing the papal throne by means of bribery, both in terms of money and future promises. With Cesare's crucial support, the conclave was one of the shortest in his-tory, with Della Rovere winning on only the second ballot, taking all but two of the cardinals' votes. He ascended to the papal throne as Julius II at the end of 1503.

Having secured power through first-rate intrigues, Julius now set about fulfilling the second chess-playing maxim: retaining his power by strengthening his position, with political stability following on from this. Julius went about this in true chess player fashion—methodically and over a long period of time. However, Julius never for a minute lost sight of his ultimate strategic goal: ridding himself of the temporal powers in Italy that shackled his political authority, threatening to overwhelm him.

First, now that Cesare Borgia had outlasted his usefulness, Julius withdrew his political support from him in true Machiavellian fashion, seeing to it that the Borgias would find it impossible to retain their political control over the papal states of central Italy. Julius rightly reasoned that to fail to eradicate the Borgia principality would have left the Vatican surrounded by Borgia possessions and at Cesare's limited mercy.

Julius initiated a highly successful public relations campaign against the Borgias; let's face it, he had a lot to work with. Julius thundered on about his dead rival Alexander, damning him with the searing judgment that he had desecrated the Holy Church as none before him had done. Under pain of excommunication, Julius forbade anyone to speak of or even think about Alexander again, though how he planned to actually enforce such a ban is open to question.[15]

What is for certain is that Julius did not just defeat the Borgias—he eradicated them as any possible political threat to him. It is a telling sign of the Borgias' political extinction that the Vatican apartments in which Alexander lived were not re-opened, owing to Julius's fearful curse, until the nineteenth century.

Second, having stabilized the papal states surrounding the Holy See, Julius now brought peace to Rome itself.

---

[15]See Nigel Cowthorne, *Sex Lives of the Popes* (London: Prion, 1996), p. 219.

He managed to unify the often-fractious city, reconciling the powerful and constantly bickering Orsini and Colonna families. With this diplomatic coup, coupled with the undoing of the Borgias, Julius's domestic political position was now secure.

But Julius wanted to do more than merely safeguard what had been bequeathed to him with his election to the papacy; he was not nicknamed "The Warrior Pope" for nothing. Looking northwards, Julius saw the Republic of Venice as his next immediate target, gauging that its overthrow as the dominant local political actor in northern Italy was possible.

Over the next few years, the chess-playing pope doggedly set about that strategic task, always keeping his military campaigns highly localized, avoiding the fatal tendency to overreach. Using all his diplomatic guile in allying himself with outside great powers France and the Holy Roman Empire, Julius ousted Venice from the control of Faenza and Rimini before fighting the Republic in 1506 over Perugia and Bologna. With the decisive Battle of Agnadello on May 14, 1509, Venice lost most of its other Italian possessions, paving the way for Julius to fill the political void.

However, in succeeding in his immediate aim of ousting Venice as the dominant northern Italian power, Julius had encouraged powerful outside forces such as his erstwhile ally France to become entangled in Italian domestic politics. As such, and quite logically if treacherously, Julius switched sides, joining a chastened Venice in now taking on the overmighty French.

Julius's final, logical, calculating chess move was his effort to expel the French from Italy, a strategy that would have left him the dominant political force in both the northern and central portions of the peninsula. Allying with Venice, the Holy Roman Empire, and Spain, Julius was successful in driving the French across the Alps. However, before he could profit from this last brilliant masterstroke, Julius died of fever in 1513. He left the Vatican immeasurably stronger, but without having succeeded in expelling all foreign forces from domestic Italian politics.

That, Niccolò, is what a real chess player looks like.

The Analytical Riches That Come from Spotting Chess Players

Julius fits the chess player profile in a final way, one that makes the job of a geopolitical risk analyst infinitely harder. As has so often been the case throughout history, chess players manage to cloak their dogged, disciplined strategies, hiding them in plain sight from a world that does not generally follow such fixed principles and cannot really conceive of how others might be able to hold to a clear strategic line.

Beyond this intellectual incomprehension, chess players are hard to detect, as the din of the everyday world, the political noise we all have to contend with, so often obscures their longer-term machinations. For Julius, this was particularly true. He could so easily hide his chess-playing stratagems, cloaking them in the considerable tumult and chaos that characterized Renaissance Italy. In our own time, the constant choice our world gives us of reading literally hundreds of foreign policy articles on any given day, coupled with a media whose editorial attention span resembles a fruit fly's, creates a short-term news cycle whose endless churn provides a perfect hiding place for those rare political actors with more fixed policy strategies.

But despite the difficulty in spotting them, it is well worth the time trying to game out chess players, perhaps the rarest creatures in global politics. For once they are analytically brought to ground, the fixed, rational patterns that chess players live by means a true analytical understanding of them is possible, as well as a far better understanding of the world in which they live.

CHAPTER FIVE

1776: Everything to Play For

JOHN ADAMS AND GAME-CHANGERS

Adams Sees the Future, Jefferson Buys Gloves

Today when you enter the Independence Hall Assembly Room in Philadelphia you feel like an intruder. It is masterfully displayed as if the Continental delegates are really there, only having taken a break in their momentous deliberations and about to re-enter the room. Eerily, I kept looking around, expecting Adams, Franklin, and Jefferson—deep in conversation together—to come in at any moment. The walls are painted the same dark gray, while at the front of the room still sits the ornate chair of John Hancock, president of the Second Continental Congress.

In contrast, the colony's delegations all uniformly have the same straight-backed, austere chairs, clustered around a medium-sized table, covered by a green cloth. Books and quill pens are strewn willy-nilly on the tables, as if the delegates remain hard at work, which in a very real ideological sense they do.

Having spent a good deal of my life visiting historical sites, I was unprepared to find myself so moved by the perfection of the presentation of the room where it all began. I found myself thinking like the geopolitical risk analyst that I am. *The miracle of it all was that they did this not knowing they would succeed, fighting the greatest army, the greatest navy, and perhaps the greatest empire the world has ever seen.* I marveled at their courage, for signing the Declaration of Independence, as they were to do in July 1776, was as good as signing their death warrants, were the Continental cause to falter. But I also found incredible one man's foresight. For almost alone, John Adams managed to clearly see, beyond the immediate peril of what his contemporaries were attempting, the game-changing nature of the American revolutionary experiment.

The ability to know when game-changing events are actually happening in real time, as both Adams and later Winston Churchill managed to do, is to see history moving. It is an invaluable element in the mastering of geopolitical risk analysis, perched in the Pythia's fundamental admonition to "know thyself." To do so, the analyst must adopt an almost Olympian view, seeing beyond the immediate to make sense of what is going on now by placing it in the broader tapestry of world history itself. There is an almost mystical quality to the ability to spot game-changing moments, for in a very real sense to do so is to touch the face of God.

The rewards for this rare but necessary ability are legion, for it allows the analyst or policy-maker to make real sense of the present, assessing the true context of what is going on now and what is likely to happen in the future. It is jarring to compare the lackluster abilities of today's Western statesmen—so far behind the curve in seeing the game-changing rise of Asia and the rest of the world and the decline of the West, as we enter a new multipolar age—to the phenomenal analytical abilities of true statesmen of vision, such as the querulous, challenging, maddening, but overwhelmingly talented lawyer from Braintree.

For of the two great Founders of the American Republic, only one saw the happenings of early July 1776 as the game-changing, ground-breaking, epoch-shaking events that they were. Adams, the eloquent floor leader of the fight for independence, talked of people setting off fireworks in celebrations centuries hence owing to what was going on.

Adams wrote to his beloved wife and confidant, Abigail, on July 3, the day after Congress voted for independence (but the day before the Declaration itself was ratified), saying,

> You will think me transported with Enthusiasm but I am not—I am well aware of the Toil and Blood and Treasure, that it will cost Us to maintain this Declaration, and support and defend these States—Yet through all the gloom I can see Rays of ravishing Light and Glory. I can see that the End is more than worth all the Means. And that Posterity will triumph in the Days Transaction.[1]

While Adams was clear-eyed about the many struggles ahead that needed to be overcome to attain the dream of the American Revolution, he was also aware of the ground-shaking nature of the prize. In that same letter, Adams wrote to Abigail:

> The Second Day of July 1776, will be the most memorable Epocha, in the History of America. I am apt to believe that it will be celebrated, by succeeding Generations, as the great anniversary festival. It ought to be commemorated, as the Day of Deliverance by solemn acts of Devotion to God Almighty. It ought to be solemnized with Pomp and Parade, with Shews [sic], Games, Sports, Guns, Bells, Bonfires, and Illuminations from one End of this Continent to the other from this Time forward forever more.[2]

Looking back over the centuries, it is hard to think of a better piece of geopolitical risk analysis.

Thomas Jefferson, on the other hand, only mentioned in his diary that he had bought a thermometer from John Sparhawk (for three pounds fifteen) on the glorious Fourth, and

---

[1] John Adams, "Letter to Abigail Adams, July 3, 1776," Massachusetts Historical Society, www.masshist.org/digitaladams/archive/doc?id=L17760703jasecond.
[2] Ibid.

his wife some gloves. Nowhere is there the slightest mention of the enormous gravity of what was taking place. It is not that Jefferson was not fully aware that he was putting his life on the line; to sign the Declaration was to cross the Rubicon, engaging in what could only look like treason to the British crown. But Jefferson, unlike the prescient Adams, did not grasp what that moment in early July truly meant.

Losing the war to the most formidable army the world had yet seen seemed a likely conclusion. Indeed, as the political struggle for independence reached its climax in early July 1776, a combined British army and naval task force was about to inflict the worst defeat on the Continental Army of the entire Revolutionary War, at the Battle of Long Island. It was here that Washington himself escaped personal capture by only a whisker. Jefferson was well aware of the peril of what he and his colleagues were doing. However, there is no written record of him explaining the huge potential upside of what was transpiring, or revealing his awareness that this was a truly game-changing moment for all of human history.

But Jefferson is far from alone. Likewise, modern geopolitical risk analysts far too often cleave to the intellectual shore in a desperate search for analytical safety, when events have already shaken up the comfortable world they have grown used to describing. Knowing when a game-changing event has occurred (for instance, the recent, decades-long economic rise of China) and how it changes the old rules is a must for any world-class geopolitical risk analyst.

The Political Miracle of the Fourth of July

While Adams instinctively understood the game-changing import of what was taking place, he did fail miserably in picking the date that would be met by future generations with illuminations. But this is hardly surprising, as the struggle to enact American independence was far more of a process than a specific moment.

By the dawn of July 1776, Britain and America had already been at war for more than a year, as the Battles of Lexington and Concord had opened the conflict in April 1775. The actual state of hostilities, more than any other action, was the midwife to independence. As London haughtily dismissed petition after petition from a Continental Congress still desperately hoping for a rapprochement, political opinion in America inevitably hardened. For if the British were acting as if irreparable hostilities had broken out between the mother country and the colonies, why should not the Continental Congress follow in such logic? Jefferson's view was that the Continental Congress only needed to declare a fact that already existed.[3]

There were other factors pushing the cause of independence forward. Public support had been steadily climbing after the publication of Thomas Paine's explosive pamphlet, *Common Sense*, in January 1776. In it, Paine openly advocates the necessity of independence and the desirability of forming an American Republic, topics heretofore only whispered about. *Common Sense* proved enormously popular and discernibly moved Continental public opinion toward the political outcome that took place in July 1776.

But while support grew, something like 20 percent of the colonists—particularly in the Middle Colonies of New York, New Jersey, Maryland, Pennsylvania, and Delaware—retained an increasingly anguished loyalty to king and country. Advocates of independence such as Adams and Jefferson knew that to lose any of the colonies along the path to independence

---

[3] Merrill Jensen, *The Founding of a Nation: A History of the American Revolution* (Oxford: Oxford University Press, 1968), p. 689.

would be to doom their very fragile cause to defeat, as waging civil war—in addition to fighting the British crown—was a struggle beyond them. In many ways, independence had to proceed at the pace of the most hesitant of the colonies if the project was to prosper.

Here we must spend a minute looking at the incredible duo of Adams and Jefferson, the Lennon and McCartney of the Revolution. Just as was true for the two brilliant, feuding singers, Adams and Jefferson were truly frenemies—two parts creative and political soulmates to one part (and sometimes beneath the surface) ferociously competitive, talented, and proud men, with very different views of what America should become following the war.

It is hard to imagine two people with more different characters. Adams was eloquent, brilliant, fantastically well-educated, endlessly verbal, intense, vain, but possessed of the saving grace of a clear view of his own glaring foibles. Sent by Massachusetts to the first two Continental Congresses, Adams served there with singular distinction between 1774 and 1777. From the autumn of 1775 onwards, no single man in Congress worked more passionately to bring about independence.

In June 1775, with the political end in mind of promoting greater union amongst the colonies, Adams nominated the Virginian George Washington to be commander-in-chief of the Continental Army, meaning a Southern general would be commanding predominantly New England troops. Jefferson himself, years removed from the scene, described Adams as "the pillar of [the Declaration's] support on the floor of Congress, [its] ablest advocate and defender against the multifarious assaults it encountered."[4]

---

[4]Ciaran McEvoy, "John Adams Put Life and Career on Line for America," *Investor's Business Daily*, June 3, 2015.

Legendarily tireless, Adams sat on an astonishing ninety committees in Congress during the Revolution, chairing twenty-five; no other delegate came near to this work ethic. Crucially, from 1777, Adams served as the head of the Board of War and Ordnance, the committee that in essence oversaw the Continental Army's administration and ran the war effort. Nicknamed the "One man War Department," Adams regularly worked eighteen-hour days, mastering on the fly the detail involved in raising, equipping, and fielding an army from scratch.[5] This was Adams at his zenith, acknowledged by all as the most important man in the Congress.

Jefferson, by contrast, was a man of the pen, self-contained, quiet (but no less intense than Adams in his own peculiar way), extreme, bookish, and apt to settle scores behind the scenes. Jefferson served as a delegate from Virginia to the Continental Congress, starting in 1775, at the time of the outbreak of the Revolutionary War. There is little doubt that the early American Republic was blessed by the fact that both men were certified geniuses, but that made it more than a little difficult for them to work together. Over time the obvious contradictions in this enforced alliance were to drive them politically and personally apart. However, in July 1776, these two vital men worked amicably and in tandem over the single most important thing they would ever do in their lives.

Large, prosperous, and centrally located Pennsylvania became the key political battleground over the independence question. As late as May 1, 1776, a special state-wide election for the Pennsylvania Assembly, called over the question of independence, had left opponents of such a course in political control, with John Dickinson their leader.

---

[5] Joseph Ellis, *Passionate Sage: The Character and Legacy of John Adams* (New York: W. W. Norton and Co., 1993), p. 42.

Dickinson was by far Adams's and Jefferson's most effective political foe. Like Adams, Dickinson served in the first two Continental Congresses, from 1774 to 1776. Delaware's wealthiest farmer, Dickinson had significant political interests both there and in neighboring Pennsylvania. Later in the war, he served as chief executive of both states at the same time.

As verbally eloquent as Adams and as facile with a pen as Jefferson, Dickinson was a supporter of the necessity of taking up arms against Britain following on from Lexington, but lived in hope that a reconciliation was still possible, as he simply didn't believe—a supremely understandable view—that the ragged Continental Army could ever defeat the mighty British Empire.[6] Dickinson wrote the Olive Tree Petitions, which amounted to the Second Continental Congress's last attempt at formal reconciliation with Britain. Unbeknownst to Dickinson and his allies, George III in London didn't even bother to read them.

But even without assured victory, the proponents of independence felt the die was cast. On June 6, 1776, Richard Henry Lee of Virginia—by far the most populous and most important of the colonies—rose to his feet in the Second Continental Congress in Philadelphia proposing American independence. Adams immediately seconded a motion that he had helped the Virginian to draft beforehand.

Dickinson and his allies immediately countered, saying that while they admitted that reconciliation with Britain was unlikely, a call for independence was premature, and that seeking aid from a foreign power such as France should be the immediate priority. Adams in contrast argued that the only way to obtain such aid was to prove to the world that America was decisively politically separate from Britain, as

---

[6] His popular *Letters from a Pennsylvania Farmer*, written in 1767–68, had argued against unfair British taxation and made Dickinson famous throughout the colonies.

foreign countries were not going to waste their time if all this amounted to was an internal British matter.[7]

With the Congress deadlocked, on June 10, 1776, it voted to postpone further discussion of Lee's resolution for three weeks, as delegates from Pennsylvania, Delaware, New Jersey, Maryland, and New York still had not received instructions from their state legislators on how to vote over this central issue. During this lull, it was decided that Congress would prepare a Declaration, explaining before the world the reasons for American independence, in the event that Lee's resolution was to pass.

On June 11, the task of drafting the Declaration was given to the Committee of Five, comprising Adams, Jefferson, and their close ally the diplomatist Benjamin Franklin of Pennsylvania, along with Roger Sherman of Connecticut and Robert Livingstone of New York. Tragically for posterity, no official notes were taken of the proceedings, so we do not know exactly how the Committee set about working. It appears the Committee discussed as a group the general outline the document should take. We are aware that initially the Committee, including Jefferson, thought that Adams, as the acknowledged leader of the campaign for independence, should be the primary author of the draft.

Here Adams showed his greatness. He demurred, persuading the others that the relatively unknown Jefferson should be the primary writer. His arguments for this were many and telling. First, Jefferson was a Virginian, and unity would be better served if a representative of the most important colony was the principal drafter of such an important document. Second, Adams—always a deeply polarizing figure, as many great orators are—was unpopular with many mem-

[7] See Pauline Maier, *American Scripture: Making the Declaration of Independence* (New York: Alfred A. Knopf, 1997), p. 42.

bers of Congress, whereas the quieter Jefferson was liked by almost everyone. Third, Adams reasoned, Jefferson wrote ten times better than he did. While the last point may well have been a bit of Adams's famous false modesty, the rest of his reasoning hit home. Very reluctantly, Jefferson agreed to draft the Declaration.

It is likely that Jefferson wrote the draft quickly, consulting the other members of the Committee (particularly Adams, who had promised to work with Jefferson personally over the language and thrust of the text), then making a second draft, incorporating their suggested alterations. The Committee presented the Declaration to the Congress as a whole on June 28, 1776.

Then, to Jefferson's barely suppressed horror, the full Congress took a hacksaw to the document, amending it over the next two days, shortening the text by one-quarter. Crucially, Congress decided to remove Jefferson's sketchy charge that Britain had forced slavery on the colonies, in an effort to placate influential supporters in London who backed the American cause. For the rest of his life, Jefferson felt that Congress had "mangled" his soaring draft.[8]

Meanwhile, political events favored Adams and Jefferson. In Pennsylvania, controversies over what to instruct its delegates in Congress to do regarding independence led to the dissolution of the pro-Dickinson Colonial Assembly, and on June 18 the Pennsylvania state government switched course, authorizing its delegation to declare in favor of independence. With the critical vote looming on the horizon, only New York was unable to provide its delegates with revised instructions—its Provincial Congress had been forced to flee as British forces ominously approached the city.

---

[8] John E. Ferling, *Setting the World Ablaze: Washington, Adams, Jefferson, and the American Revolution* (Oxford: Oxford University Press, 2000), pp. 131–37.

Playing for time, on July 1, Dickinson tried to delay the decision, again arguing that Congress shouldn't declare independence without first securing a major foreign alliance and finalizing the Articles of Confederation, which served as America's first constitution. Adams replied (lamentably no copy of his pivotal speech exists), noting that Dickinson had it back to front. The colonial cause could only succeed if they declared independence and then found a foreign backer. There would be no such help without a declaration.

But the long-awaited vote did not result in a resounding triumph for the forces of separation. Each colony had only one vote, and the size of the delegations of each colony varied from two to seven. The delegates within a colony would argue amongst themselves as to what to do, with the majority determining the colony's vote. The July 1 vote found nine colonies in favor of independence, two against, and two abstaining. Dickinson's Pennsylvania and South Carolina voted against Lee's measure, with Delaware's two-person delegation split down the middle and New York unable to proceed owing to lack of instructions.

So, on July 1, Congress passed Lee's resolution as a committee of the whole, while the coming July 2 deliberation was over the formal vote for independence. It is easy to see why fixing a culminating date for this whole process was in retrospect beyond the Founders, but one thing was for sure: they were nearer the dream of independence than they had ever been.

This was the crucial political moment. For although the measure had been passed by the whole Congress out of committee, to do so by such an uninspiring margin could well spell doom for the Continental cause. Three major changes occurred with the dawning of July 2. South Carolina dramatically reversed position. Edward Rutledge, the state's young leading light, remained against the motion but—horrified at sundering his state's ties to the rest of the colonies—changed his vote. In Pennsylvania, for similar reasons, Dickinson and his ally Robert Morris abstained, allowing a 3–2 vote in favor of independence to be secured within the delegation. With the tie in Delaware broken by the just-in-time arrival of a third pro-independence delegate, Caesar Rodney, the political miracle had come to pass: twelve colonies in favor, none against, with New York abstaining.

On July 4th, the last day in this complex, riveting political process, Congress finally approved Jefferson's Declaration and sent it to the printer. As it was decided that no one should be allowed to sit in Congress without agreeing to sign the Declaration, John Dickinson illustrated his political commitment to the cause. Convinced the war would be lost, and despite his pacifist Quaker beliefs, Dickinson voluntarily left and instead enlisted in the Pennsylvania militia, with the rank of brigadier general. He would continue to serve his country faithfully for the rest of his life.

Given this complex story, it is easy to see why Adams, in writing to Abigail, thought that July 2 was the culminating moment in the drama. The independence voted for on that day had been a true game-changer, a decisive break with all that politically had come before, heralding a very different trajectory for both America and the entire world ahead. But history would have it be otherwise. The document justifying the act of independence would come to overshadow the act itself.

Churchill Rejoices over Pearl Harbor

In the hustle and bustle of the everyday world, recognizing game-changing events can prove exceedingly difficult, for both geopolitical risk analysts and policy-makers. Being surrounded by monumental goings-on makes separating the very important from the essential almost impossible. So it was in December 1941, undoubtedly the turning point of the Second World War. During that momentous time, Russia turned back the Nazi invasion at the very gates of Moscow, marking the first time Hitler's vaunted war machine had met with a real setback. But for all that the Battle of Moscow mattered enormously, it did nothing to change the overall balance of forces fighting the war, which had led to the outcome sitting on a knife's edge.

But half a world away, something else did. At 7:48 AM in Hawaii, on December 7, 1941, the Imperial Navy of the Empire of Japan, attacking without warning as it had done in the Russo-Japanese War in the early days of the century, unleashed itself against the American Pacific Fleet, serenely docked at Pearl Harbor that Sunday morning. 353 Japanese fighters, bombers, and torpedo planes swooped down in two devastating waves over a ninety-minute period, launched from six Japanese aircraft carriers.

The damage was immense. All eight American battleships docked at Pearl were struck, and four of them sunk. The Japanese attack destroyed 188 US aircraft (the vast majority of them on the ground, having never even made it into combat), while 2,400 were killed and 1,200 wounded. Japanese losses were negligible. At the same time Hawaii was under attack, there were coordinated Japanese strikes on the US-controlled Philippines, Guam, and Wake Island and on the British in Malaya, Singapore, and Hong Kong.

This thunderbolt from the blue enraged Americans, as the Japanese struck without formally declaring war. But the motivations for the strikes were borne out of strategic weakness. The attack amounted to a preventative action to neutralize the US Pacific Fleet, keeping it from interfering with Japan's coming military penetration into Malaya and the Dutch East

Indies, where it sought desperately needed oil and rubber to sustain its military might.

Given its resource-poor home islands, the Japanese military was living on borrowed time, as it was dependent on raw materials from abroad to sustain itself. It was faced with the prospect of either withdrawing from China (where it had been fighting since the early 1930s) and losing face or seizing and exploiting new sources of commodities in Europe's resource-rich Asian colonies. The true intent of the Pearl Harbor attack was to get Japan's only possible obstacle—the US Pacific Fleet—out of the way so that it could conquer Southeast Asia without interference.

With the American fleet literally in flames, the Japanese hope was that the devastation at Pearl Harbor would so crush morale in America that it would not move on Tokyo. To put it mildly, as was true for Hitler's strategic calculations made at the same time, this strategic rationale shows no cultural understanding of the United States at all. The following day, December 8, 1941, America declared war on Japan.

The Japanese attack on the central American naval base at Pearl Harbor changed the course of the war fundamentally, drawing in America as the decisive force which altered the correlation of power around the world. Stalin, with his back still to the wall in the snows of Russia, did not immediately grasp the game-changing significance of what had just happened any more than Franklin Roosevelt did, now grimly intent on surveying the wreckage of America's Pacific Fleet and marshaling the American public for global war. These were pressing times, and it is entirely human and understandable why both Stalin and FDR had other more immediate concerns to worry about during those early December days. But Winston Churchill, the last of the Big Three, immediately latched onto the game-changing significance of what had just occurred.

At the time of the attack, Churchill found himself dining at Chequers, the traditional country retreat of British prime ministers. Fortunately, his guests included US ambassador Gil Winant and Averell Harriman, FDR's special envoy to Europe and a member of Roosevelt's inner circle on foreign affairs. It was during the meal that a butler brought in a portable radio to the startled guests, so they could listen to the reports coming from the BBC Home Service.

At the precise moment the attack was announced, Churchill impulsively and magnanimously (if extra-constitutionally) leapt to his feet, offering to declare war on Japan at once.[9] Instead, the prime minister immediately got on the phone with Roosevelt, who coolly uttered that America and Britain were all in the same boat now. Churchill, never held back by the bounds of decorum, only partially managed to hide his glee at the catastrophe. For Churchill understood, even in the chaos of that moment, that the misguided Japanese attack had just won Britain and its allies the war and amounted to the game-changer a hard-pressed Britain had been praying for.

In his history of the Second World War, Churchill wrote of that seminal evening, "Being saturated and satiated with emotion and sensation, I went to bed and slept the sleep of the saved and thankful."[10] The great British prime minister slept well that night because he understood the fluidity of geopolitics, how a single event can change the overall balance of global power overnight, if one can but see.

For in a larger sense, Pearl Harbor brought to successful fruition years of Churchill wooing America to save the world from Nazism. With the defeat of France and the overrunning

[9] For setting the scene, see Peter Grier, "Pearl Harbor Attack: How Did Winston Churchill React?" *Christian Science Monitor*, December 7, 2015.
[10] Ibid.

of all of western Europe, Churchill was focused on the only possible geopolitical counter-stroke to this stunning revolution in global affairs—the entry of the United States into the war against Germany. Such an intervention—given America's armed forces, but even more its limitless manufacturing capacity—was the only possible geopolitical change that might yet save the day, overturning the outcome of the disastrous Battle of France in June 1940.

Britain's main immediate strategic task was simply to hold out, hoping for events to eventually push America to its side. This Churchill's country heroically managed, against long odds, during the Battle of Britain in the summer and autumn of 1940. But in geopolitical terms, all this victory secured was Britain's position as a small island redoubt of opposition to Hitler, forced to wait for something positive to turn up.

Then something did. Hitler's terribly rash decision to invade the Soviet Union in June 1941 made a two-front war—the everlasting dread of all German military planners throughout the twentieth century—a reality. While both Stalin and Churchill were pressed to their limits merely to survive, the very fact of the other front meant Germany had to divide its troops and resources, rather than single-mindedly finishing off one of its enemies before devoting itself to the eradication of the other. There is little doubt this was a crucial error. For with a little more strategic patience, Hitler could have concentrated his forces and destroyed both Stalin and Churchill, if he had taken them on in turn. The diffusion of effort that a two-front war made necessary saved both London and Moscow.

But while this good fortune—due to Hitler's strategic mistakes—kept Churchill in the game, he well knew this was not enough to ultimately win the war. Only America, with its endless resources, industrial might, and manpower, could do that. So Churchill went a-courting. He wrote FDR two to three times a week, almost stalking the American president. Roosevelt was sympathetic. Until December 1941, in the face of strong isolationist opposition, the United States had become Britain's lifeline. Under the terms of the Lend-Lease Act, America supplied Churchill with enormous quantities of food, fuel, manufactured goods, ships, arms, equipment, and loans. This assistance literally kept Britain going, but stopped well short of amounting to a formal military alliance, as America's domestic politics placed real limits on what Roosevelt could do.

While isolationism's heyday had been in the mid-1930s, before December 1941 it remained a potent force in American life. Polls taken in July 1940, just five months before Pearl Harbor, showed that a minuscule 8 percent of Americans supported war against Germany. While this number rose as 1941 came to its climactic end, in the weeks just prior to the attack another poll showed almost 75 percent of Americans remaining opposed to another war with Berlin.[11]

As threats from Germany and Japan had risen in the 1930s, it seemed to many Americans that it was more important to attempt to seal the United States off—long a possibility due to the Atlantic and Pacific Oceans serving as two formidable strategic moats—from an increasingly dangerous world, and especially from the looming threat of yet another global war. Pearl Harbor shattered this way of thinking, as it definitively made clear that American territory was indeed vulnerable to the reach of foreign aggressors. If this was the case, the United States had no choice from here on out but to engage in an internationalist foreign policy. At the time, such a policy meant above all else coming to the rescue of

[11]Stephen Frater, "December 11, 1941: Hitler and Arguably the Most Insane and Pivotal Decision in History," *The History Reader*, December 11, 2011.

Churchill's Britain. As Senator Arthur Vandenberg, a key Republican on the Senate Foreign Relations Committee and a former isolationist, put it, "The day [Pearl Harbor] ended isolationism for any realist."[12]

Pearl Harbor broke the logjam, discrediting isolationism in one fell swoop; it turned out that the problems of the wider world did directly impact America, as the blazing hulks of the Pacific Fleet's battleships attested to. Stung by the surprise attack, the direct domestic political consequences of Pearl Harbor gave Roosevelt a unified America heading into battle, and himself almost limitless room for maneuver. After the years of being shackled by a country intent on avoiding the troubles of Europe and Asia, it was a liberating moment indeed.

Hitler's Fatal Error

But for Churchill, the best was yet to come. For the unnerving fact remained that while declaring war on Japan was an obvious thing for America to do, Hitler—in both Roosevelt's and Churchill's eyes the supreme source of global danger—had not lifted a finger against Washington. It would have been very hard for Roosevelt to convince Congress to declare war on a country that had not directly done anything to America.

But then deliverance appeared in the unlikely guise of Hitler himself. On December 11, 1941, compounding Tokyo's incredible blunder, Germany suicidally declared war on America, getting Roosevelt out of a very tight political spot. Hitler had not even been directly informed by his

---

[12]Quoted in Manfred Jonas, "Isolationism," *Encyclopedia of American Foreign Policy*, www.encyclopedia.com/topic/Isolationism.aspx.

Imperial Japanese allies about the coming attack, so he was under no real compunction to commit the folly that he did. The terms of the Tripartite Pact between the Axis powers specifically promised German military help to Japan if it was attacked, but said nothing about Tokyo being the aggressor. The only vague commitment Hitler had made to Tokyo at all was his oral agreement given to the Japanese foreign minister that Germany would join Japan in a war at some point against the United States if it came to that; pretty thin gruel indeed.

The out-of-his-depth German foreign minister, Joachim von Ribbentrop, did meekly worry aloud of his fears of Berlin having another global enemy in the United States that in time could overwhelm the German war effort. But Hitler waved these concerns away, wrongly speculating that it was inevitable that the United States was about to declare war on Germany; better to beat them to the punch and show loyalty to his Japanese ally. Indeed, Hitler had a point in that the US navy was already engaged in an undeclared war with German U-boats in the Atlantic, safeguarding vital American matériel being brought to Britain. But in so cavalierly fanning the flames, Hitler sealed his own doom.

In the end, it came down to the Greeks. In his hubris, his belief in his own invincibility, Hitler grandly stated: what could the United States do that Britain, France, and the Soviet Union had not? Personally aware of the strategic perils of fighting a two-front war, Hitler went on to say that the United States would also have great trouble managing such a war, as had he. Japan, which had physically attacked America at Pearl Harbor, was likely to be the focus of Washington's efforts. And even if this proved wrong, the Germans knew that it would take the United States at least until late 1943 or early 1944 to enter the war in a big way. The simple truth is that Hitler, vastly underestimating the endless productive capacity of the United States, didn't think declaring war on America mattered all that much.

Almost all of this thinking proved to be catastrophically wrong for the Nazis, as America's entry into the war sealed their destruction. Politically unbound, Roosevelt and Churchill quickly agreed that defeating Germany rather than Japan would be their common strategic priority. Roosevelt directed an overwhelming 90 percent of America's military resources to defeat Germany, rather than Japan.[13] Japan may have attacked the United States, but it was undoubtedly Berlin that bore the immediate brunt of America's wrath.

But if Hitler and the militarists running Japan were entirely analytically wrong, and if Stalin and Roosevelt were respectively preoccupied with the momentous events in front of the gates of Moscow and in the Pacific, one man did see the big picture: the attack on Pearl Harbor had been a game-changing event in world history. Because of the strike, America would eventually save the world from the dark night of Nazi barbarism. In the course of less than a week (December 5–11, 1941), Stalin halted the German drive in Russia at the last possible moment; the Japanese attacked Pearl Harbor, ensuring decisive American participation in the war; and Hitler ensured Germany's defeat by disastrously declaring war on the United States.

Churchill, at that key moment, alone saw the game-changing consequences of what was going on. Later that pivotal month, on December 28, 1941, he addressed the US Congress for the first time. While this was a singular honor, for the prime minister the best news of his life had already arrived earlier that December. As he so perfectly put it, "The

[13] Frater, "December 11, 1941."

US, united as never before, have [*sic*] drawn the sword of freedom and cast away the scabbard."[14] December 1941 had saved the world.

The Declaration of Independence as Improbable Game-Changer

But sometimes, as in the case of the Declaration of Independence, it takes far longer for game-changing events to play out, particularly if they are based on ideas rather than events. For while the Declaration started out as a specific charge sheet against Britain, justifying American freedom, as the years wore on it became something very different—a universal ideological rallying cry for a newly formed political system based on the notion that the only legitimate government was government based on the consent of the governed.

By Jefferson's own admission, the Declaration contained no new ideas itself, but like many seminal writings it beautifully and soaringly (especially in the Preamble) synthesized the general beliefs held by the leading supporters of the American Revolution. Jefferson drew on a series of immediate sources, especially his own proposed draft of the Virginia Constitution and fellow Virginian George Mason's draft of the Virginia Declaration of Rights.

The Declaration laid out two specific themes at the time the Committee of Five drafted it, with Jefferson in the lead. First, it justified independence by a lengthy list of specific grievances it placed at the feet of George III. Curiously, and not very accurately, he was seen by the colonists as the villain of the piece, rather than the British prime minister and Parliament, who increasingly wielded the true power. Secondly,

[14]Grier, "Pearl Harbor Attack."

it asserted that the colonists had natural and legal rights—life, liberty, and the pursuit of happiness (property)—that had been violated by Britain and that included the right of revolution in response to this violation. In essence, the colonists were saying that what the crown viewed as an illegal rebellion was actually a legal revolution.

The reaction to the eloquent boldness and universality of the Declaration from America's enemies was immediate. British Tories denounced the signers of the Declaration (curiously much as today's presentist historians do) for not applying their universalist principles of "Life, Liberty, and the Pursuit of Happiness" to the Africans miserably shackled in Southern fields. While this is an entirely valid criticism, then and now, it assumes that the movement of man toward meeting the wildly idealistic political nirvana of the Declaration could be accomplished all at once, which is certainly a naive point of view for anyone who has bothered to study history.

In setting the bar so politically and morally high, the Founders had rightly opened themselves up to the entirely justifiable criticism of their falling far short of the Declaration's lofty heights. However, by writing, agreeing on, and signing it, they had changed the very political reference points for the world from that time forward, making such a criticism valid in the first place.

It is this second broader theme—rather than the laundry list of the king's crimes, which makes up the majority of the document—that has come to have real intellectual staying power. The Declaration's heady notions of self-evident truths of equality and inalienable rights, articulated in the second paragraph, have proven to be universally applicable.[15] The

---

[15] David Armitage, *The Declaration of Independence: A Global History* (Cambridge, MA: Harvard University Press, 2007), p. 93.

phrase "All men are created equal" may indeed be "the most potent and consequential words in American history."[16] For it means that humans have innate worth, rights, and value that not even the most powerful government in the world is legally or morally allowed to eradicate.

All the snide, present-day commentators who drone on about how conservative the American Revolution was—merely a group of slave-owning oligarchs trying to secure political power commensurate with their economic wealth—entirely miss this basic point. Fortunately for the country, neither Abraham Lincoln nor Martin Luther King Jr. did. But it was Adams, not Jefferson, who at the time of the Declaration's drafting seemed to sense that something even larger than American independence was at work here—that this was a game-changing moment for humanity itself.

As the Revolutionary War wore on, the Declaration was largely forgotten, lost in the drama surrounding the ultimate, miraculous victory of Washington's forces at the Battle of Yorktown in 1781. But with the Federalist/Jeffersonian split in the 1790s (a division that ended the Adams-Jefferson friendship for twenty years), interest in it revived. The Declaration was politically pitched by Jefferson's allies as a way to enshrine his place in the revolutionary pantheon, alongside the undisputed credentials of Washington, Adams, and Hamilton, his Federalist enemies. Over time the act of winning independence, to Adams's barely concealed annoyance, came to be synonymous with the document itself.

Marginalized groups, first in America and then around the world, turned to the beguiling promise and meaning of the Preamble of the Declaration—and not the more legalistic

---

[16] Joseph Ellis, *American Sphinx: The Character of Thomas Jefferson* (New York: Alfred A. Knopf, 1996), p. 50.

Constitution—for moral and political support. Over the next century, workers, abolitionists, farmers, and women would all base their calls for greater rights on the argument that what they wanted was merely the fulfillment of what the Founders had promised to them long before.

Perhaps no figure was as important in bringing about the ideological transformation of the document as Abraham Lincoln. He strongly believed all his life that Jefferson's language in the Declaration was deliberately universal in tone, setting the highest moral and political standard for the American Republic to aspire to. As Pauline Maier makes clear, Lincoln believed that "the Declaration became a living document with a set of goals to be realized over time."[17] Firmly convinced as to its universal meaning and import, Lincoln said, "I had thought the Declaration contemplated the progressive improvement in the condition of all men everywhere."[18]

This intellectual jujitsu has made the Declaration the ultimate work in progress, the yardstick that any American person or group cleaves to when asserting their own universal rights. A major part of the reason for Martin Luther King Jr.'s great success in the civil rights movement of the 1950s and 1960s was his eloquent ability to shame white moderates in America with their own founding document's stirring words, making it clear that African Americans merely wanted the very rights Thomas Jefferson had made clear were inalienably theirs.

From the tumult of the French Revolution of the 1790s onwards, the Declaration of Independence has become a global yardstick used by insurgents everywhere, justifying their acts of rebellion as being legal and necessary, owing

[17] Maier, *American Scripture*, p. 207.
[18] Ibid.

to the deprivation of the universal human rights Jefferson so ringingly set forth over 200 years ago. The Declaration amounts to a truly game-changing ideological and political moment for humanity. Far-seeing John Adams was right to think that generations hence, his countrymen would light illuminations because of what happened in that hot Philadelphia of July 1776.

The Limits to Even Adams's Sagacity

It is delightful to report that Adams's sagacity had its limits. The always difficult Adams-Jefferson friendship hit the skids in the 1790s as their very different political opinions drove them into the rival Federalist-Jeffersonian camps. But for Adams the final straw was his sense of personal betrayal when, as America's second president, he found out that his vice president, Jefferson, had been disloyal and sponsored harsh personal attacks against him. After Jefferson defeated his old friend for the presidency in 1800, the two did not speak again for more than a decade.

But Adams's fundamental magnanimity eventually triumphed. In 1812—prompted by their mutual friend, and fellow signer of the Declaration, Benjamin Rush—Adams wrote Jefferson a short New Year's greeting, to which the Virginian warmly responded. Over the next fourteen years, between 1812 and 1826, the two men began an extraordinary regular correspondence, exchanging 158 letters in which they discussed their political differences, debating the meaning of the revolution to which they had devoted "their lives, their fortunes, and their sacred honor."

Their mutual ends on the fiftieth anniversary of the ratifying of the document that had done so much to remake the world is a story line that simply could not have been made up, proof to pious Americans of the time that God really did favor America. As he lay dying on July 4, 1826, Adams clearly smiled and said, "Thomas Jefferson survives."[19] Given the communications of the time, it was impossible for Adams to know that his great friend and rival had expired earlier that same hallowed day. But if in the end Adams was only human, his analytical gift in recognizing the game-changing nature of what the stirring events of July 1776 were actually about stands out as an example of what great geopolitical risk analysis can lead to.

[19] David McCullough, *John Adams* (New York: Simon & Schuster, 2008), p. 646.

CHAPTER SIX

1797: Getting to Goldilocks

NAPOLEON AND THE VENETIAN REPUBLIC

The Dangers of Analytical Overreaction

A generation after the drama that played itself out in the sweltering Philadelphia of 1776, the Most Serene Republic of Venice, one of the most consequential states of the European Renaissance, ended the 1,100 years of its existence not with a bang but with a pathetic whimper. At its height, and for hundreds of years, the Venetian maritime empire dominated the Adriatic and eastern Mediterranean, as well as possessing a central land base in the Veneto on the northern Italian mainland. However, by the time the great Napoleon had fixed his sights on what he rightly called "the drawing room of Europe" and determined that the Venetian pearl would be his, the city-state was but a shadow of its former self, largely because of a simple failure of geopolitical risk analysis.

Alarmingly, the Venetians awaited their doom with little more than dignified haplessness. Why was this former great power so utterly defenseless before Napoleon's hordes? The simple, overriding answer to this question is that the Venetians had learned an important lesson down the centuries—war is often folly and always expensive—while entirely forgetting that they might need to keep other important—and countervailing—truisms about international relations in mind as well.

First amongst these is that having merely carrots (economic power) as an instrument on the global stage only works in a world populated entirely by rabbits; military power is sometimes required too. And whatever you might say of him, the young Napoleon was hardly a rabbit. Because of this fundamental misreading of human nature, the Venetian Republic responded with a feckless strategy of disarmament that erased its mighty position in the world. By the latter days of the eighteenth century, the city-state was so divorced from the reality of power politics that when threatened by the French, it had absolutely no choice but to surrender.

Likewise, in our own time, George W. Bush and Barack Obama, in espousing neo-conservative and realist views, respectively, both fatally over-corrected the flaws of what came before them. The Bush administration shot first in Iraq and asked strategic questions later. However, the overly cautious Obama White House over-corrected the Bush team's many errors by ceasing to see that force—while it must always be judiciously used—still plays an enduring role in global politics. Both of these mono-causal policies, like mono-causal analysis in general, were doomed to failure.

Geopolitical risk analysts tend to follow this understandable but dangerous intellectual pattern: making up for past failings, all the while not seeing that their lack of balance is dooming their assessments. Nestled in the Pythia's typology for geopolitical risk analysis under the overarching sub-heading of "nothing in excess" is a Holy Grail for any world-class geopolitical risk analyst: the element of "getting to Goldilocks"—making policy assessments that are neither too hard nor too soft, neither too hot nor too cold, by eschewing extremes and mono-causal answers and actually balancing the numerous important factors determining outcomes.

Much as was true of the fading Venetian elite, modern-day geopolitical risk analysts and decision-makers are all too often prisoners of Hegel: confronted with a flawed thesis, they respond with an overcorrected antithesis. They remind me of the Marxist bores of graduate school: having found one valid motive force for what moves history, they never seem to stop to think that there just might conceivably be others. It is this old and venerable element of intellectual balance that helps separate first-rate geopolitical risk analysts from the herd.

Venice's Slow Castration

In truth, the long, slow road of Venice's decline began as early as the sixteenth century. First, its pivotal role as the key trading hub between continents—a geographic advantage that had made the Republic impossibly rich—was challenged, and then superseded, as Portugal, Holland, France, and England all came to directly engage in the spice trade with Asia, without continuing to use Venice as their middle man. This change came about because the emerging great powers' ocean-going ships, which were technologically superior to the old Venetian galleys, allowed them to go to their Asian trade sources themselves.

Second, the next-door Ottoman Empire engaged in a concerted, enervating challenge to Venice's primacy in the eastern Mediterranean, slowly wresting away its empire, even as other city-states, such as Livorno and Genoa, rose to rival Venice in northern Italy itself.

Third, internal decay and decadence set in as the government of Venice became increasingly sclerotic and self-satisfied and the maritime empire's army, always relatively weak—by virtue of its geographical location—melted away into nothingness over the centuries.

The oligarchs who ran the Republic preferred to avoid the hard economic choices and belt-tightening that could have corrected this dangerous decline, nor did the leaders of the city-state attempt to overcome their chronic manpower shortage. But as Venice was still a very rich city, and as its elite's cosseted life of masked balls and opulence were hard to part with, it was far easier to do nothing about what seemed at the time to be merely a theoretical problem. It was only when Napoleon showed up at Venice's doorstep that theory became all too real.

As C. P. Snow has put it, by the time of the last half-century of the republic's existence, the Venetians well knew "that the current of history has begun to flow against them," and that any sort of renewal would require "breaking the pattern into which they had crystallized."[1] Yet, in their decadence, they found themselves "fond of the patterns and never found the will to break it."[2]

And to a point, of course, the Venetians were absolutely right. Often wars explode in the faces of those who engage in them, and almost always they are ruinously expensive. Peace is in general a better alternative for both the health of any state and the welfare of its people. In our present day, I recently asked a female friend of mine where all the decent young Ukrainian men were who should be courting her. Her sad answer was that all the good ones were off at war. No one is arguing that in general the Venetians were onto something with their peace-first strategy.

But having grasped one essential reality of the world, the Venetian Republic wholly ignored other, darker, but no less important lessons about the nature of human beings and international relations. By 1796, on the eve of Napoleon's brilliant Italian campaign, the Republic could no longer defend itself. Of its pathetic fleet of thirteen ships of the line, only a handful proved to be seaworthy. The army was in even worse shape, consisting of only a few brigades of Croatian mercenaries. The problem was that in policy terms the oligarchs who ran

---

[1] C. P. Snow, *The Two Cultures* (Cambridge: Canto, 1993), p. 40.
[2] Ibid.

Venice were not prepared to pay the steep price that would have been necessary to upgrade the Venetian fleet with the latest technology of eighteenth-century warfare. Venice had castrated itself long before.

Manin Goes Out with a Whimper

As Napoleon thundered down out of the Alps onto the northern Italian plain, miraculously defeating his Austrian foes in five separate campaigns, it was left to the 120th and last of the doges of Venice, Ludovico Giovanni Manin, to try to confront him. By all accounts, Manin was a perfect representative of Venice's oligarch class, being a very rich (he married an heiress), cultivated merchant. Born May 14, 1725, Manin had risen to the position of doge on March 9, 1789, just months before the cataclysm of the French Revolution upended Europe. At the time, Manin's elevation to the position was a popular choice, as he was selected on the first ballot by Venice's electoral assembly of forty-one oligarchs.

In a portrait of the time painted by Bernardino Castelli, Manin looks pale, sallow, and sensitive, possessing a long, thin nose and a worried manner. But then, Manin had a great deal to be worried about. Praised by his contemporaries for his generosity, honesty, and kindness, Manin, with his gentle humanism, was to prove no match for the grasping meritocrat Bonaparte. For if he was endowed with genuine personal virtues, Manin was also emblematic of his dying class, proving to be amongst the feeblest, weariest, and most defeatist of all the doges.

Crucially, in the city-state's waning days, Manin had done absolutely nothing to in any way upgrade Venice's defenses. Upon Napoleon's thrust against the Austrians in northern Italy, Venice immediately declared itself neutral in the conflict, as though this self-effacing gesture could somehow save it from Napoleon's clutches. But Bonaparte, heading the French Army of Italy at the precocious age of twenty-six, was in the process of becoming a living legend. During the Italian campaign, his troops would fight and win eighteen pitched battles, capturing 150,000 prisoners.[3]

On April 9, 1797, Napoleon himself thundered at Manin, threatening the peace-loving Republic with war. On April 25, he bellowed, "I shall be an Attila to the state of Venice," the correct real-world strategy for besting a state that wished to live in a fantasy land where force played no role in foreign policy.

The French at last turned to finish off the spiritless empire. Napoleon's subordinate, Marshall Junot, called for Venice's unconditional surrender. As Napoleon ominously moved on the city, the French instigated popular uprisings against Venetian rule in the Veneto, further weakening Manin's political grip. May 1, 1797, was the date when at last Manin and the other Venetian oligarchs had to acknowledge the reality they had spent their whole lives ignoring. Manin glumly told the Great Council that it was necessary to make peace with the French at any price, as the wholly defenseless city had no other choice.

The French fleet (apart from one ship sunk by a single lucky cannon strike from Venice's landward defenses) waltzed into the city, tying up at the famed Lido. The French had effortlessly claimed a city that had once been considered invincible but was now a dissolute shambles, wholly open to invasion. Manin abdicated on May 12 and left the un-imaginably beautiful doge's palace two days later. The Grand Council of Venice, bowing at last to reality, voted itself out of existence later in the month, ending 1,100 years of Vene-

[3] Frank McLynn, *Napoleon* (London: Pimlico, 1998), p. 135.

tian independence. Venice had proven itself to be so fragile that, "before the mere breath of his [Napoleon's] coming the Republic of Venice crumbled into dust."[4]

After haplessly watching the voracious Napoleon gobble up his city, Manin rather honorably disdained to be the conqueror's stooge, refusing an offer to be installed as interim head of a French-dominated Venice. Instead, he withdrew from society, so bitterly and personally did he feel his role in the Republic's demise. Determining on a life of Edgar Allan Poe–style seclusion, Manin withdrew to the Palazzo Dolfin Manin, his glorious residence on the Grand Canal, refusing to answer his door, even to his friends.

But this characteristic effort to keep life's painful realities at arm's length continued to bring Manin nothing but torment, even in his retirement. In his rare public appearances, Manin was sometimes overtly insulted by Venetians who cursed him for the city's fall from grace. They were especially angered by his decision in 1797 to avoid bloodshed, even though at that late date there was little else Manin could do. It was the utopian, pacifist, otherworldly philosophy of the city-state that doomed it, not Manin's supposed cowardice. His agonizing decision to surrender Venice without a fight was the culmination of its philosophical problem, not the cause of the problem itself. Manin died of dropsy and heart problems in his ghostly palace on October 24, 1802, his silent vigil to the lost world of Venice's past glories finally coming to an end.

Stripped of its independence, Venice became a plaything of the great powers of late-eighteenth-century Europe. In the aftermath of Bonaparte's wildly successful military campaign, he hoped to buy off his Austrian enemies, while gaining their diplomatic support for France's newfound dominance

[4] Thomas Okey, *Venice and Its Story* (London: J. M. Dent and Sons, 1910), p. 186.

on the continent. Austria's inducement would turn out to be prostrate Venice, along with Lombardy and the Veneto. So confident was Napoleon of conquering Venice that he signed the secret Peace of Leoben with Austria on April 18, 1797, even before his military campaign against the Republic reached its climax. The treaty offered up Venice to Austria as the price of peace with France.

Adding insult to Manin's injury, the later Treaty of Campoformio was signed at one of the ousted doge's own country houses—the Villa Manin—on October 18, 1797, confirming the terms of the earlier Peace of Leoben and making Venice and all her possessions Austrian. Campoformio definitively ended the European-wide wars during which France had fought what came to be known as the First Coalition, temporarily leaving Britain to stand alone against Paris.

The Austrians at the time were delighted with their diplomatic bribe, as Venice and the Veneto bordered Austria proper, offering them a vital outlet to the Adriatic. As such, the once-mighty Republic was now merely a small piece of the much larger strategic puzzle Napoleon was endeavoring to assemble. In turn, the Directorate then ruling France was entirely satisfied with the terms. Its legitimacy had been recognized by the Austrians, as had its conquests in Belgium, around the Rhine, and its forcible acquisition of the Ionian islands. With his victories and the subsequent peace treaties, Napoleon had managed to drive a political wedge between France's Austrian and Prussian foes, if only for the moment.

Having paid this great historical price for failing to see that a peace-only foreign policy would inevitably lead to its ruin, Venice never again regained its autonomy, or its glory. After being handed over to Austria in 1797, it was snatched back by the then-Emperor Napoleon in 1805, forming part of his new Kingdom of Italy. Following Napoleon's final defeat, Venice was once again handed over to Austria at the Congress of Vienna in 1815.

By ignoring the iron law of all of human history—that force has played a part in international relations since the dawn of mankind—Venice had lost its way in the world. Tragically seizing on the entirely correct notion that peace is usually better than war for both countries and individuals, the Republic had found one basic motive force of history and analysis, but had forgotten the vital point that there are indeed others. This was no mere intellectual error, as the young Napoleon was to make very clear. This lack of analytical balance made Venice's doom almost inevitable.

Napoleon's France as a Country on Military Steroids

In his bedazzled, gilded youth, Napoleon Bonaparte shone like the sun. Beyond Alexander the Great, it is difficult to think of any other leader in the history of the world to whom fame and glory came so early, and so overwhelmingly. Even later on, when some of the luster had worn off—after the retreat from Moscow and the decisive defeat of his army at the Battle of Leipzig in 1813—his nemesis the Duke of Wellington openly admitted that Bonaparte's mere charismatic, talismanic presence on a battlefield was worth 40,000 troops.

Supremely competent, decisive, preternaturally driven, eloquent, quick-witted, and far-seeing, Bonaparte was capable of inspiring almost religious devotion in both his marshals and his men. When Bonaparte slipped his exile in Elba and returned to France in 1815, Marshal Ney, the hero of the retreat from Moscow, promised his new overlord Louis XVIII that he would bring back Napoleon in a cage. Instead, upon spying Napoleon in the flesh ahead of him, Ney was so emotionally overwhelmed that he immediately switched sides and joined the march to retake Paris.[5]

The recent intellectual argument about whether Napoleon was a great man, sparked by Andrew Roberts's fine 2014 book *Napoleon: A Life*, seems to me to somewhat miss the point. In weighing whether the fabled French emperor ultimately did more good things than bad, the basic reality of the complicated, mixed historical record of any life—and certainly the life of a contradictory genius like Napoleon—gets thrown all too easily to the side of the road.

In 1797, Napoleon could uncannily see the inherent defenselessness of the Venetian Republic, a government that had chosen to simply ignore the basic imperative any state has to defend itself. However, Napoleon was to make a diametrically opposed analytical misjudgment himself.

The Venetians were undoubtedly lotus-eaters, basking in their tranquil apathy, as the forces of the real world slowly and ominously gathered around them. But in worshiping the god Mars, Napoleon was to make an equally disastrous geopolitical risk mistake. For behind all his highly impressive domestic reforms was an effort to increasingly militarize French society, to make it fit for purpose to take on the rest of Continental Europe for almost a generation. This overcorrection and imbalanced reliance on war was to doom the glorious Bonaparte. In always seeing the need for war, Bonaparte was as out of kilter as were the Venetians, who never saw the need for it.

This process of militarizing France characterized the whole of Napoleon's political dominance of the country.

---

[5] For this act of romantic folly, Ney would be executed by the once again restored Bourbons following the Napoleonic cause's final defeat at Waterloo.

Soon after seizing power from the Directorate on November 9, 1799, (he was only thirty years old at the time), Bonaparte set about his monumental efforts to remake French society itself.

His acceleration of the process of conscription, Revolutionary France's highly successful innovation to ward off its legion of foes, was one of the centerpieces of the Napoleonic strategy to transform France. During the 1790s, nearly 1.25 million ordinary Frenchmen were incorporated into the army, where they shared a common, highly militarized experience.[6]

Napoleon took this revolutionary innovation—which had the salutary twin benefits for him of meeting his ever-pressing need for manpower while at the same time remaking French society—and ran with it. During his rule, two million more Frenchmen joined the army, heightening the military socialization that had already occurred during the earlier revolutionary period. However, the overriding point of Napoleon's acceleration of conscription was obviously to keep the French war machine ticking over.

Bonaparte also transformed the French schools, founding what became an especially excellent system of centralized and standardized secondary education, which up until then had been highly uneven across the country. But the basic purpose of this highly useful reform was to provide an intellectually superior officer class for the next French military generation. It was not a coincidence that students were summoned to their lessons by drumroll.

A third great innovation was the desperately necessary reform of France's civil legal codes. In 1804, he established the Napoleonic Code, which finally did away with

---

[6] See Alan Forrest, *Conscripts and Deserters: The Army and French Society During the Revolution and Empire* (Oxford: Oxford University Press, 1989).

feudalism itself, undoing ancient laws that still dominated French jurisprudence, disorganized and contradictory as they were. The Code greatly extended the right to own property, opening France up to a far more meritocratic age than the fading feudal world had allowed for. The Code further enshrined equality before the law and religious toleration, at a stroke lessening what had been endemic French internal social tensions.

At the time of the Code's adoption, France was using forty-two separate legal codes; Napoleon standardized these into just one. This great, lasting, legal achievement has been adopted in various forms by around one-quarter of the world's legal systems. As Andrew Roberts, grandly but wholly rightly, claims, the Code amounts to "the greatest codification of laws since the fall of the Roman Empire."[7]

When Napoleon became first consul in late 1799, France was teetering on the abyss. The chaos of the Revolution had left it with massive inflation and the terrible after-effects of a bitter royalist civil war in the Vendée in eastern France; the whole country having also suffered through excruciating rounds of The Terror as the French Revolution—very unlike the American experience of Adams and Jefferson—came to eat its own children.

The reforms of the Consulate did nothing less than to dramatically transform France's fortunes. France rose, phoenix-like, from the ashes of being a near-failed state to become the greatest and most important power in Europe. Napoleon first saved the country from chaos; with his reforms, he then set about making it into a modern European nation.

Bonaparte also greatly encouraged science and the arts, beautified Paris, established the Bank of France (the first

[7]Kim Willsher, "Cruel Despot or Wise Reformer? Napoleon's Two Faces Go on View," *The Observer*, September 3, 2017.

central bank in French history), ushered in an era of sound finance, reformed the tax code, established the public accounts system, and imposed the uniform metric system on the country. All of these innovations have stood the test of time, enduring for these past 200 years.

But the overweening purpose of all of these highly admirable transformations was nothing more and nothing less than supporting and expanding the French war machine. As Simon Schama has put it, "Militarization spread like poison through French society."[8] The emperor's (he gave himself the imperial title on December 2, 1804) incessant centralizing urge, which animated all his reforms, was at base a policy strategy designed to make France more uniform, putting it on what was for the time a constant war footing. Thompson concurs, noting that Napoleon "reorganized France itself to supply the men and money needed for great wars."[9]

While analogies between Napoleon and Hitler are generally unfair to the Corsican, over one basic and decisive geopolitical risk point they are entirely congruent. As was true for Hitler, the French emperor transformed his society, making it fit for total war and thereby unleashing Napoleonic France's basic expansionistic dynamic. Both are classic examples of revolutionary powers, which have no desire to co-exist in the present power structure they find themselves in, but instead want to overturn it, making way for their newfound dominance. While it is possible for revolutionary powers to mellow into status quo powers over time, if they do not they either come to dominate the world or are destroyed. There is no middle way for them.

---

[8] Simon Schama, "Napoleon Bonaparte, French Emperor," *Financial Times*, June 19, 2015.

[9] J. M. Thompson, *Napoleon Bonaparte: His Rise and Fall* (Oxford: Oxford University Press, 1954), p. 285.

It was all or nothing for both the Austrian corporal and the French artillery lieutenant, as well as for the societies they remolded in their image. Both Napoleonic France and Nazi Germany were at their essence war machines, pursuing the endlessly expansionistic strategy of a revolutionary power. And it is this common dynamic that explains why their strategic overstretch and ultimate ruin were almost inevitable. For all his glittering domestic achievements, Napoleon's colossal efforts to dominate Europe cost the continent seventeen years of almost unremitting war, leaving six million Europeans dead.

The Continental System, another of the emperor's flagship reforms, was to directly lead to his ultimate demise. Imposed on a prostrate Europe in 1806, in theory it prohibited all French conquered territories and his terrified allies from trading with Britain, the last of his enemies standing and by far the most implacable of Bonaparte's many foes. This effort to militarize economics—there is a reason that in modern international relations embargoes are seen as highly aggressive acts—failed in two fundamental ways, as the Continental System was habitually violated.

First, as Britain possessed a maritime and global empire, the embargo—even if it had been successfully applied—would not have amounted to an economic knock-out blow, forcing London to accept Napoleon's dominance on the continent. Second, trade is a two-way street. With much of Europe dependent on its trade with Britain—even then the manufacturing powerhouse of the world—and with France unable to fill London's central trading role, the rest of the continent grew increasingly restive at this unintended threat to its own economic well-being. It is little wonder that the Continental System was highly unpopular and regularly breached, even at the height of French power. Napoleon's efforts to bend macroeconomics to military ends were to end in disaster.

Bonaparte's Predictable Fall
as a Leader of a Revolutionary Power

It was his vain attempt to try to enforce the Continental System that led Bonaparte to his two greatest military calamities: the Peninsular War in Iberia, and the epic assault on Moscow. But in reality, it was the militaristic, self-perpetuating expansionism of Napoleon's France that led to the setbacks in Spain and Russia. The Continental System was just Bonaparte's policy tool for implementing the strategy of a revolutionary power. Both the Spanish and Russian disasters arose out of Napoleon fighting wars of choice, conflicts that a status quo power would have entirely avoided.

Enraged at Portugal's brazen violations of the Continental System—Lisbon had long had well-established and lucrative trading ties with Britain—Napoleon ordered its invasion. Along with its Spanish allies, Portugal was quickly brought to heel in 1807. However, befitting its status as a revolutionary power, France simply could not bank its strategic winnings and leave well enough alone.

In 1808, the throne of Spain was unoccupied. Seeing his chance, Napoleon seized Madrid for his older brother, Joseph, whom he had crowned as the new king in the summer of that year. This high-handed blunder enraged Spain's deeply religious and conservative Catholic populace, particularly in rural areas. Thus commenced a six-year struggle that morphed into a vicious guerrilla war sapping French strength and would ultimately tie down 300,000 French troops in a never-ending struggle to pacify the Spanish countryside.

Britain immediately capitalized on France's strategic mistake, in 1808 sending troops under the Duke of Wellington to bolster the Spanish and the Portuguese, as well as vital supplies and economic backing. By 1814, with Wellington having masterfully made his name fighting in Spain, Napoleon was

forced by the crisis in Russia to withdraw French troops from
the Iberian Peninsula; the British, Portuguese, and Spanish
at last managing to dislodge the French, pushing them out
of Iberia. Napoleon's over-fixation on the military tool of
power—in his case, to the exclusion of basic economics—had
led directly to France's ruin in Spain.

But even worse was yet to come. A major strain on the
always tenuous Franco-Russian alliance between Napoleon
and Czar Alexander I was this self-same violation of the
Continental System by Moscow. Finally, unable to contain
himself any longer, and hearing reports of ongoing Russian
treachery with England, Napoleon fatefully invaded Russia
on June 24, 1812.

Due to the Russian army's scorched-earth tactics, Napo-
leon's troops found it increasingly difficult to forage for food
for themselves, and crucially for their horses, which began
dying in the thousands. Even when the Russians finally gave
Napoleon the fixed battle he so longed for, at Borodino on
September 7, 1812, his usual decisive victory eluded him.
As the emperor himself put it at the time at Borodino, "The
French showed themselves to be worthy of victory, but the
Russians showed themselves worthy of being invincible."[10]
Napoleon was, as so often, on the mark. For the tactical
success at Borodino did not yield the strategic success that
Napoleon desperately needed—the dispiriting of the czar
and his docile return to the negotiating table. Instead, the
war went on, as summer became autumn and the weather
grew colder.

Of course, the unendurable tragedy of the Russian winter
lay ahead for the Grand Armée. The proud French army had
begun the campaign with over 400,000 frontline troops. By
its calamitous end, fewer than 40,000—or one-tenth—made it

---

[10] Felix Markham, *Napoleon* (New York: Mentor Books, 1963), p. 194.

back from the desolate Russian steppes.[11] Though there were still brilliant moments ahead for him—from the genius of his desperate campaign within France itself in 1814 to the glory of the Hundred Days in 1815—Napoleon's empire never recovered from the Russian calamity. It was an entirely unforced strategic error, only explained by the excessive militarism of French society under the emperor, the imbalance in his geopolitical risk assessments, and the inherently expansionistic strategic outlook that flowed so seamlessly from that lack of balance.

The final, devastating proof of the over-militarization of French society under Napoleon—and the disastrous revolutionary power mindset that it enabled—is the French diplomatic record of the early nineteenth century. It makes for frustrating reading as Bonaparte spurned numerous chances to save his throne, all because if he could not have the whole world, he wanted none of it. It is hard to think of a better example of the revolutionary power mentality in all of international relations.

At Amiens, in March 1802, Prime Minister Henry Addington's government actually accepted in treaty form Napoleon's European conquests up to that point, in the hope that economic prosperity and trade would revive a recession-plagued London. However, this favorable deal for the emperor lasted only a year because Napoleon—ideologically incapable of consolidating his gains—always wanted something more.

In late 1813, even after the Russian campaign and the October 1813 Battle of Leipzig, where he had been soundly thrashed, as Napoleon fell back from central Europe and his many enemies circled around him, the emperor still rejected peace terms that would have allowed him to remain on the throne of a France bigger than it had been before the rev-

[11] McLynn, *Napoleon*, p. 541.

olution in 1789. Yet, extraordinarily, he refused this highly advantageous offer.

The Frankfurt Proposals of November 1813 stipulated that Napoleon could remain emperor of the French and be succeeded by his son, but that France would be reduced in size. However, it could still keep the gains it had made in Belgium, Savoy, and the west bank of the Rhine. In turn, it would be forced to cede back Spain, the Netherlands, and most of Italy and Germany. The only explanation for such highly favorable terms, given France's then-parlous military state, was that the myth of Napoleon was still alive and well. His enemies may have beaten him at Leipzig, but they still feared him.

Astoundingly, in the face of such terms, Napoleon dithered, and by December 1813 the allies had withdrawn their offer. Surely this amounts to a canary in the coal mine for any good geopolitical risk analyst, the telling sign that the over-militarization of French society had led the country to adopt a radical, utopian foreign policy that knew neither limits, balance, nor compromise.

Professor Charles Esdaile says of this diplomatic blunder that Napoleon "forgot statesmanship is the art of the possible."[12] But this is to miss the point of Napoleon, and to think like a conventional person. The whole point of a revolutionary power is to indeed ignore the art of the possible and use the dream of creating a different world as the basis to run a utopian foreign policy that ignores the half-measures that status quo powers—which make up the vast majority of countries—trade in. If Napoleon had done the sensible thing, if he had settled for less than everything, then the myth of French military *gloire*—which itself was based on

---

[12]Charles Esdaile, "Debate [between Professor Charles Esdaile and Professor Andrew Roberts]: Was Napoleon Great?" *British Journal of Military History,* vol. 1, issue 3, June 2015, p. 114.

the over-militarization of French society—would have been exposed as a fraud. That ultimately mattered more to the emperor than being just one of a series of dull, time-serving European monarchs.

Of course, Napoleon paid the ultimate price for his utopian folly, much as the Venetian oligarchs had done. Forced to abdicate on April 6, 1814, and exiled to the island of Elba in the Mediterranean, the genius of his era once again could not simply fade away, as the allies so hoped he would. Instead, Napoleon stormed back to the French mainland, briefly regained power, and then lost the decisive Battle of Waterloo in June 1815 to Wellington. This time the emperor was not to escape. Napoleon was exiled by his British rivals to St. Helena in the middle of the Atlantic, 1,162 miles from the west coast of Africa. On May 5, 1821, the great man died there, far from the trappings of his once-supreme power, an unwitting victim of having legendarily used the military lever of politics without ever learning that there are other motive forces of history as well.

The Benefits of Balance

Two major powers, the Venetian Republic and its vanquisher, the great Napoleon, were laid waste to when they could not overcome a fundamental geopolitical risk analytical error. Commercial Venice forgot along the way that a state's paramount need is to always defend itself, that there will always be creatures in the foreign policy jungle to be fought off. Evil and aggression in the world cannot be wished away just because it is far more pleasant to attend glittering seaside parties and to produce breathtaking works of art.

Some sort of balance is called for. Over the centuries, Venice's abdication of responsibility for seeing the world as it is left it entirely at the mercy of the young, covetous Napoleon when he made his way over the Alps. But given the Venetians' fundamental misreading of the world, it hardly mattered that it was Napoleon who brought the Venetian Republic down. Someone would have.

But Napoleon, in his own diametrically opposed way, made the same fundamental error as the Italian oligarchs he so effortlessly conquered. The sword had made Napoleon the most famous man in the world and had given him, a minor Corsican aristocrat, first a throne and then the dominant position in Europe.

It is human and understandable that even a man of Bonaparte's first-rate intellect, having personally experienced how far the military component of power could take both a genius and a country, failed to see that his reliance on the military instrument of power was highly skewed, to the exclusion of a more balanced strategy, such as that pursued by Pitt's England throughout the period. It is understandable, but Napoleon's sad end makes it clear that his failure of analysis was also absolutely toxic.

Modern geopolitical risk analysts would do well to take note of both of the historical examples of Venice and Napoleon. There are many motive forces of history and analysis, and the major ones must always be taken into account altogether if geopolitical risk analysis is to get anywhere. To forget the absolute need for "getting to Goldilocks"—the essential geopolitical risk commandment of finding an analytical balance—is to get every big thing wrong, no matter how right analysts might be about the detail. For both analysis and policy require more than merely one basic insight into how our complicated world works.

CHAPTER SEVEN

1863: The Losing Gambler Syndrome

ROBERT E. LEE AT GETTYSBURG

Why Casino Magnates Get Rich:
Gettysburg and Vietnam

The losing gambler syndrome is a fact of the human condition that casino magnates have come to well understand. When someone loses big at the tables, almost always they have an overwhelming urge to invest ever more resources to make good on their catastrophic losses, rarely bothering to think about the reasons for these losses in the first place. Dad cannot go back to Mom telling her he has lost the kids' college fund at the roulette table, so he keeps playing . . . and keeps losing. The reason for his demise—the terrible odds—is never analytically addressed.

Sadly, this dismal pattern of thinking has been repeated throughout all of history. The losing gambler syndrome is an overall element necessary for mastering geopolitical risk, clustered under the Pythia's admonition to "make a pledge and mischief is nigh." Analysts as well as policy-makers must be perpetually on guard against the Greek notion of *hubris*, assessing and re-assessing the effectiveness of their analysis. Sadly, the losing gambler syndrome—where analysts in all-too-human fashion park their brains at the door—occurs with tragic frequency and must be constantly guarded against.

I saw this doleful process up close and personal in Washington as the Iraq War slid toward the abyss; very often those policy-makers urging ever-greater efforts in Iraq from the American people were forced to admit that they did so largely to make good on their already monumental strategic losses. Geopolitical risk analysts are not immune to this folly, often doubling down on a bad assessment emotionally in order to wipe the slate clean of their intellectual mistakes.

Anyone who has ever walked the mile and a half in that beautiful, tragic open field between Seminary and Cemetery Ridges at Gettysburg knows that the Confederate assault on the third day of the battle should never have been made. The simple reason for Pickett's disastrous charge is that Robert E. Lee had emotionally invested too much at Gettysburg to easily turn back. The famed Confederate general was both desperate and overconfident, a fatal combination. Lee was held intellectual hostage by his relative failure on the second day of the battle, an unwitting prisoner of the losing gambler syndrome.

Likewise, as the years rolled by without the United States ever finding a political ally in South Vietnam with local political legitimacy, it never seems to have occurred to Lyndon Johnson that the lack of such a partner was a sure sign to get out, not to redouble his efforts. Avoiding the disastrous siren song of the gambler's curse, and instead limiting and mitigating past analytical mistakes, is a vital component of geopolitical risk analysis.

Joshua Lawrence Chamberlain Saves the Union

On July 2, 1863, Colonel Joshua Lawrence Chamberlain of the Twentieth Maine Regiment saved the United States and, because of what was to come in the next century, quite possibly the world as we know it.

In a desperate ad hoc maneuver (for incredibly, the Union Army had somehow neglected to fortify it), Chamberlain and his men found themselves on the extreme left flank of the US line on Cemetery Ridge, a defensive position shaped like a fish-hook, with a small hill named Little Round Top at the end. It was the absolute key to the entire Union position.

If the Twentieth Maine were to be dislodged from Little Round Top's rocky crags, allowing the crack Army of Northern Virginia to capture the hill and then bring artillery to bear there, it could decimate the entire Union Army, compelling either its destruction or its ignominious retreat.

The battle—and quite possibly the war—would be lost, and General Robert E. Lee's second invasion of the North would prove successful, with the Confederacy gaining its independence through the dash and brilliance of its generals.

It is a sign of its eternal good fortune that the United States always seems to find the right man for the job when the stakes are the highest—with the Republic itself in peril. As had proven true of the unflappable leadership talents of George Washington at the critical Battle of Trenton—when the Continental cause hung by a thread in the American War for Independence—so now in Chamberlain the man and the moment eerily suited one other.

Chamberlain, thirty-four at the time of the battle, preferred to be called Lawrence to his given name of Joshua. Before the war, he had been a professor of rhetoric at prestigious Bowdoin College in Maine. In the summer of 1862, when the college had refused to let him enlist in the army, Chamberlain had requested an academic sabbatical. Once granted, he used it to join up anyway.

Tall, handsome, boyish-looking, Colonel Chamberlain spoke nine languages other than English. His love for the Union and its cause bordered on the mystical, especially after President Lincoln's issuing of the Emancipation Proclamation in January 1863. Deeply idealistic, Chamberlain told his men that the war was now about more than even Union—it was a cause consecrated in the noble ideal that all men should be set free, that slavery must come to an end. For all his impressive credentials, Chamberlain had been in command of his regiment for only one week, since late June 1863, before the battle commenced.

The first day's preliminary fighting had gone well for the South as they drove the Northern forces back through the little, well-cared-for town of Gettysburg and up to the heights of Cemetery Ridge. But fatally, the Southern corps commanders, in particular General Richard Ewell, failed to finish off the North. Darkness was falling, and night assaults were very rare in this pre-modern war.

Ewell—a new corps commander having been promoted upon the death of the irreplaceable Stonewall Jackson after the Battle of Chancellorsville in May 1863—hesitated, leaving the North to dig in on the heights of the ridge, a fine natural defensive position.[1] The Union Army was able to catch its breath that evening, and as the second day dawned, rather than fleeing the field, it had established a strong perimeter from which to repel the Confederate troops.

Lee, slightly nonplussed, remained obviously encouraged by the first day's fighting. Given the mythical reputation for invincibility that both Lee and his army had acquired throughout the world, this was not an unreasonable response. For in many ways, Lee was the next world-historical military genius, following the demise of Napoleon in 1815. Since taking over field command from the severely wounded General Joseph E. Johnston at the Seven Days Battles in the summer of 1862, Lee had defeated Union generals George B. McClellan at Seven Days in June and July 1862, John Pope

---

[1] While counter-factuals are rightly called the fool's gold of historical analysis, it is almost impossible not to engage in them over the Battle at Gettysburg, as Stonewall Jackson's ghost hovers over the field. It is almost inconceivable that the hard-charging Jackson would not have pressed the Southern advantage at the end of the first day of fighting. The world might have been a very different place if he had lived, and done so.

at Second Manassas in August 1862, Ambrose Burnside at Fredericksburg in December 1862, and Joseph Hooker at Chancellorsville in May 1863. During that magical Southern year between the summer of 1862 and the summer of 1863, Lee's army could do almost no wrong.

Even Lee's sole failure, the bloody Battle of Antietam in September 1862, which had ended his first invasion of the North in Maryland, was something out of Homer. Despite the fact that the reinstated McClellan had unearthed a copy of Lee's precise orders to his generals, the Army of Northern Virginia had somehow fought the Union Army to a tactical draw. If the North couldn't win a battle outright when they knew exactly what the South was going to do, it didn't seem likely that the Army of the Potomac stood much chance when the Confederacy had more reasonable odds.

Throughout this mystical year, despite the longest odds, Lee had been supremely calculating, rational, and hard-headed. All these necessary analytical qualities were to desert him at Gettysburg at the worst possible moment for the Southern cause, as the losing gambler syndrome eclipsed Lee's greatness.

On the second day at Gettysburg, Lee ordered his best remaining corps commander, General James Longstreet, commander of the I Corps, to attack the Union left. As his ace in the hole, Longstreet had General John Bell Hood's division of Texans and Alabamians at the extreme end of his line. Hood, decisive and impetuously, even recklessly, brave, was commonly thought the best division commander in the Southern army.[2] These crack troops would be the men that Chamberlain would have to somehow overcome.

As they started out, the Confederates were unaware of the possible fatal Union strategic blunder in leaving Little Round Top undefended. Instead, asinine political appointee General

---

[2] Hood would be badly wounded during the attack, losing his arm.

Dan Sickles, commander of the Union III Corps, had—for reasons that still pass human understanding—moved his forces off Cemetery Ridge into a peach orchard in the far less defensible valley below. This monumental blunder left Little Round Top entirely exposed.

But here the North caught a break. Given that Lee and Longstreet did not want the Union to see the attack on its left that was coming, they were forced to reposition Southern troops for most of the day. Incredibly, the main attack didn't get under way until 4:00 PM on the second day. As such, the margin of error for Southern victory was very small, as the night sky threatened to fall again, halting any possible Confederate gains.

As Longstreet's attack swept the hapless Sickles back through the Peach Orchard, the Wheat Field, Devil's Den, and the Valley of Death, at last one Union commander recognized the danger. General Gouverneur K. Warren, the chief engineer of the Union Army, who had been sent by overall Union commander George Gordon Meade to scout out what was happening on his left, climbed Little Round Top and immediately recognized the peril.

Hastily grabbing any spare regiments he could find, Warren devised a makeshift defense on the crucial hill. Chamberlain was simply told, "Hold to the last." The regiment arrived at its position at the extreme end of the Union line only ten minutes ahead of the Confederate attackers. There could simply be no retreat for the Twentieth Maine, whatever the odds and whatever came. All told, there were only 385 men from the regiment on Little Round Top.

With no real time to think, Chamberlain acted on inspired instinct. At this moment of maximum peril, the colonel did have a few advantages working for him. The hill itself was steep and wooded, making coordinating an attack difficult. Likewise, and utterly unbeknownst to him, the Alabamian brigade of Hood's division that Chamberlain faced, commanded by Brigadier General Evander Law, had already marched twenty miles that day to be in position; they started the charge utterly exhausted. But for all that, as Chamberlain awaited what he knew to be the inevitable Southern attack, he had absolutely no cause for optimism.

For over ninety minutes, Hood's Texans and Alabamians came on, time after time, wave upon wave. Finally, in a lull between charges, Chamberlain's subordinates all came to him with the same cataclysmic news: they were almost entirely out of ammunition. At just that moment, men called out that the Southerners were advancing again. It was in this second that the fate of the Republic was decided.

Although at this point he was slightly wounded in the foot and the thigh, Chamberlain's thinking was crystal clear. Knowing that without ammunition the Maine regiment could not stay where it was and knowing equally well he could not retreat, Chamberlain decided upon the boldest of plans, one that quite possibly saved the Union.[3]

Commanding his men to fix bayonets to their bulletless guns, the colonel ordered a frontal assault, with the regiment racing down Little Round Top like a swinging gate. His line, bent back by repeated Confederate charges into a "U" shape, would now unfurl down the hill. While Chamberlain certainly had surprise on his side, the regiment by this time had lost fully one-third of its men. There were only 230 Mainers left to make the all-or-nothing charge.

It worked. Chamberlain's desperate troops utterly surprised the Southerners, capturing 101 prisoners during the stunning advance, a good portion of the Fifteenth Alabama Regiment. The line held, the flank was saved, and was immediately

[3] Also suffering from malaria and dysentary at the time of the battle, Chamberlain could hardly be considered a well man when he performed his miracle.

reinforced by large numbers of Union troops, transforming the Achilles' heel of Little Round Top into a now-impregnable fortress. Though no one knew it at the time, the best chance the South would ever have to win the war had been lost, owing to the improvisational genius of a college professor from Maine.

Lee had come within a whisker of another overwhelming victory, one that might have won him the war. As a result, his blood was up; beyond any analysis or strategic logic, in the fatal pattern of the losing gambler syndrome, he took his near-victory as a sign to double down, to commit everything to immediate triumph, rather than seeing Little Round Top as the defeat it really was. This analytical error was to seal his cause's doom.

The United States Tragically Doubles Down in Vietnam

But Lee is far from alone in falling into the losing gambler in Vegas analytical trap; there are a legion of twentieth-century American examples showing this to be an enduring, universal phenomenon. By the autumn of 1967, there were fully 500,000 US troops in Vietnam, with Commanding General William Westmoreland requesting 100,000 more. A primary American commitment had been made to a country that ought to have been only a negligible interest to the United States.

What analytical madness had driven this process? And why was it to take so long for the United States to agonizingly extricate itself from the endless morass that was Vietnam? The losing gambler syndrome is the clear culprit that answers both of these questions.

After my rather similar Iraq experiences in Washington, I am highly skeptical of the supposed analytical prowess of the Washington establishment. Saying this, incredulous shock and anger can be the only acceptable human emotions when assessing the decision-making over Vietnam of the senior members of the Kennedy and Johnson administrations.

David Halberstam's bold and utterly supportable position in his peerless work *The Best and the Brightest* is clearly vindicated: the Washington establishment of the Vietnam era was highly intellectually overrated, as they time and again fell foul of the losing gambler syndrome, alongside making myriad other basic analytical mistakes. At its essence, the best these supposedly worldly men could come up with as a rationale for escalating the Vietnam War was the highly dangerous analytical view that "because we are losing we must up the ante," without stopping to consider the more important geopolitical risk question as to why they were losing in the first place.

Perhaps the key moment in the Vietnam tragedy came on January 27, 1965, when the two key intellectual players in the Johnson administration, National Security Adviser McGeorge Bundy and Secretary of Defense Robert McNamara, wrote a wavering LBJ a memo strongly urging an enhanced military commitment to the flagging mission.

For no particular reason—for he had written no original books or developed any original thoughts to justify his Olympian position—Bundy was the preeminent foreign and defense policy intellectual of the Kennedy-Johnson era. Elitist, sharp, hawkish, good at the close verbal combat that is the key determination of bureaucratic success in Washington, Bundy was, at best, a bright process guy, adept at keeping the flow of decision-making going from his perch in the White House as national security adviser.

However, for all his supposed brittle brilliance, he lacked the ability to coldly assess policy decisions and neglected to constantly check to see if they were working, which is the mark of a first-rate foreign policy practitioner. Instead, in his enraging elitist manner, as the clouds darkened over Vietnam, he instinctively moved to shut down all discussion, to stifle all the reasonable doubts that were emerging.

Of the two, Secretary of Defense Robert McNamara is the more interesting, and the more tragic. Johnson was right to rejoice in his ability. Calm, analytical, driven by empirical data (a rarity then and now in the capital) rather than politics, McNamara seemed to be the harbinger of a beguiling new age when rational men eschewing ideology would reach the correct policy decisions for the right reasons.

Instead, he came to stunningly epitomize the peril of such a belief: if the data going into a system are junk, the outputs are bound to be junk too. By focusing on the more intellectually manageable policy specifics of Vietnam (body counts), without ever looking at the broader, less quantifiable, but more important strategic factors determining the result (the relative political will of the two sides and the discrepancy in political legitimacy between the north and the south of the country), McNamara's analysis was constantly missing the forest for the trees.

The Bundy-McNamara memo baldly acknowledged that the then policy of steering a middle course between full-out military support and withdrawal had been a failure, and it conceded—without once questioning why the present policy wasn't working—that continuing the present American policy would lead only to "disastrous defeat."[4]

Bundy and McNamara starkly outlined for the president that the United States needed either to move to negotiations with North Vietnam or deploy more force to right the sinking ship, particularly increasing the bombing of the north. They both came down strongly in favor of the latter option. It was

---

[4]David Halberstam, *The Best and the Brightest* (New York: Ballantine Books, 1993), p. 518.

particularly McNamara's great influence over the president that swayed LBJ into making this cataclysmic error.

The problem with increasing the bombing was that it organically led to a much larger troop commitment, without a definitive strategic decision ever needing to take place. As Halberstam notes, "If you bombed you needed airfields, and if you had airfields you needed troops to protect the airfields, and the ARVN [South Vietnamese troops] weren't good enough."[5]

This is the moment at which the analytical alarm bells should have been ringing. If after all those years of intense American military, economic, and political support, the South Vietnamese government couldn't field a credible army, the United States was surely supporting a regime incapable of standing on its own.

It was time to pare American losses and recognize that the fundamental lack of South Vietnamese political legitimacy (in contrast to the innate popularity of nationalist Communist Ho Chi Minh) meant that the war could *never* be won, as the United States was fighting for a wholly artificial political construct. Instead, those around LBJ, following on in true losing gambler fashion, used the failure of their current policy to advocate doing even more in the service of an obviously lost cause.

And following this perilous analytical logic, the United States was to do much more; before too much longer it totally dominated the war effort of the supposed South Vietnamese cause. US troops guarding airfields for increased bombing missions morphed into American troops leading the fight in the jungle against the Communists. Inevitably, American casualties began to mount, further playing into the losing gambler syndrome. As Halberstam acutely observes,

[5] Ibid., pp. 538–39.

"Each dead American became one more rationale for more dead Americans."[6]

Of the senior figures in government, only Undersecretary of State for Economic Affairs George Ball had a real sense of the ruinous analytical errors being made over the prosecution of the war. To Ball, "the arguments of Mac Bundy and Taylor[7] that we must bomb to shore up the morale of the South Vietnamese because the government was so frail that it would otherwise collapse was foolishness of a high order. It was all the more reason *not* to commit the power and reputation of the US to something that weak."[8] Ball was analytically on the money, but bureaucratically almost alone in his dissent. While Johnson mournfully listened to his doubts, he sided with the vast majority of the Washington establishment, terribly wrong though it was.

As the war inevitably lapsed into an unwinnable quagmire, a charnel house for a generation of young American men, the losing gambler syndrome—as it so perniciously does—further tightened its grip over American decision-making regarding Vietnam, precisely because things were going so badly.

First, there was the emotional commitment the war's original architects brought with them to subsequent decisions. General Maxwell Taylor came to be highly psychologically involved in the commitment, just as Secretary McNamara felt increasing guilt for both the war itself and the peril it posed for the president he had so ruinously advised.[9] In both cases, when the doleful real-world facts of the war began trickling back to Washington, causing both men acute discomfort, it

[6] Ibid., p. 299.
[7] General Maxwell Taylor, former chairman of the Joint Chiefs of Staff and later the US ambassador to South Vietnam.
[8] Halberstam, *The Best and the Brightest*, p. 498.
[9] Ibid., p. 497.

was this very sense of emergency and crisis that caused them to further embroil both themselves and the country in the Vietnam morass.

As for Bundy, he became so intellectually tetchy that when pressed by subordinates as to what the worst-case scenario in Vietnam looked like, he madly responded, "We can't assume what we don't believe."[10] Because failure was on the doorstep, it must not be discussed, or even thought about, even as America mindlessly doubled down on its commitment to Vietnam. All of official Washington was in the deepest throes of the losing gambler syndrome.

The last, terrible phase of this analytical breakdown played out—as the political and military situation in Vietnam went from bad to worse—over spurious debates about prestige already committed. Yes, the argument went, perhaps the war was initially a mistake, but as we have already committed so much blood and treasure to the effort, to leave now would negate such sacrifices. Worse, American credibility around the world was bound to suffer a calamitous setback. Such a disastrously reasoned argument did nothing to change the outcome of the war, though it did tragically extend its length as the Vietnam conflict went on, seemingly forever.

Hauntingly setting the precedent for the later pattern in Iraq, the worse things got on the battlefield in Vietnam, the less dissent was tolerated in decision-making circles. After it was apparent to all that Vietnam was a catastrophe, official Washington—almost universally complicit in the disaster—circled its political wagons. As Halberstam relates, "At first the critics were told that they should not be critics because it was not really going to be a war and it would be brief anyway; then, when it became clear that it was a war,

[10] Ibid., p. 528.

they were told not to be critics because it hurt our boys and helped the other side."[11]

The losing gambler syndrome compelled those in its grip to ferociously oppose any impulse to say that it was in American interests to cut its losses in light of the political unsustainability of the South Vietnamese cause. Things had progressed too far, and gone too badly, to even contemplate turning back. It is hard to think of a more damaging geopolitical risk analytical mistake to make than this.

What occurred at the political level in Washington decision-making circles was repeated in terms of geopolitics. After Johnson's presidency was destroyed by the war, his successor, Richard Nixon, also found it devilishly hard to quit the Vietnam morass. For Nixon himself at least partially believed in the losing gambler syndrome. He rationalized that if America threw in the towel in Vietnam, it would suffer a massive blow to its credibility around the world from which its prestige would not recover.

Beyond greatly historically overestimating the blow to American credibility that withdrawal actually caused (less than two decades later the United States triumphed in the Cold War), by this logic a country is forced to stay forever in a quagmire, endlessly pursuing an inherently unwinnable policy to prosecute an inherently unwinnable war. It is the losing gambler syndrome—and not the highly useful analytical ability to recognize when it is time to cut policy losses—that does more to destroy a country's credibility than anything else.

But as was argued on depressingly similar grounds over the Iraq debacle, the analytical breakdown over Vietnam culminated in this wan justification. So much had already been invested and lost that America must simply keep going. Dad, having lost the kids' college money, must stay at the

---

[11] Ibid., p. 620.

table, all evidence to the contrary that this will retrieve the situation. And so, tragically, the losing gambler syndrome claimed America in Vietnam as another victim.

Lee Fatally Goes for Broke with Pickett's Charge

Similarly, late into the night of July 2, 1863, and the early morning of July 3, Lee was about to look for a triumph where there was none to be had. At the time of Gettysburg, the South's beloved general was fifty-six, stood five-foot-ten, was red-faced, with his visage covered by a stately snow-white beard. Every inch the gentleman, Lee (like his idol George Washington) spent his whole life successfully mastering a ferocious temper. He never gambled, drank, or chased women, and like many in the South's senior officer corps, he was deeply pious. Whatever happened to Lee and his famed Army of Northern Virginia, above all else the great man never complained.

On this fateful evening, Lee called into conference, as he had done so often, the general he affectionately called his "war horse," James Longstreet of Georgia. Longstreet, forty-two, was the ablest of Lee's surviving corps commanders. "Peter," as he was known, was a large, quiet man, full-bearded, stubborn, and slightly deaf; a slow talker, he was one of the rare high-ranking officers not from the pivotal state of Virginia. Three of his children had died in a single week from fever in the winter of 1862, which had taken a great deal of the joy out of Longstreet. Before this overwhelming tragedy, Longstreet had been fond of gambling, especially poker. After his children died, he was never to play cards again.

Extremely close to Lee, and always physically in camp near him at both men's request, Longstreet was respected by the commander for his loyalty and for always speaking his mind to his famous leader. However, like the classical Greek story of Cassandra, Longstreet's curse throughout these fateful days at Gettysburg was to have his highly precise analysis of the calamities to come ignored by his superior, Lee; Longstreet was analytically right, but powerless to stop the disaster just ahead of him.

Lee began the strategy session by stressing how close they had come to total victory at Little Round Top that day. They had almost done it, and with such a crushing victory the road to Washington would lie open, heralding the triumphant conclusion of the South's struggle for independence. While that was true, "near-wins" are merely a euphemism in life for defeats. The opportunity for the South had been lost owing to the genius of Chamberlain, but Lee remained analytically mesmerized by the glittering possibilities, not noticing that they had disappeared.

In true losing gambler style, Lee went on, certain that one more push would do it. The Union right had been tried on the first day, and the left on the second, and both flanks had needed reinforcing by the North to hold. As such, Lee felt certain that the center of the Northern line—which, unlike the two flanks, had no defensible hills giving the Union an advantage—must be its weakest position.

The general went on to propose a massed infantry charge straight into the center of the Northern line, which would split it evenly in two. Longstreet was to be given operational command. At the same time, Lee would send his dashing (if slightly errant) cavalry commander J. E. B. Stuart around the Union line to pick off the two disorganized remnants of the Army of the Potomac, once it had been breached. Lee's second invasion of the North would be crowned by total victory, and the war would be won.

Longstreet was horrified. He said slowly, "It is my opinion that no 15,000 men ever arrayed for battle can take that position."[12] Longstreet correctly argued that after three days the federal line was now well entrenched everywhere on Cemetery Ridge; the Confederates would be crossing a mile and a half of utterly open ground and would have to attack uphill, straight into the Union artillery. The North could see the attack coming from literally a mile away and would be able to reinforce the center easily and quickly. Southern forces would be under direct rifle fire with a mile still to go from the Emmitsburg Pike, the road that bisected the field between the two ridges.

I well remember first walking that open field as a young boy with my father, and it dawning on me that men had been forced to march and then run across it under tremendous concentrated fire. As a seven-year-old, I recall thinking to myself, *Oh, my God*—the exact thought that must have been coursing through Longstreet's astonished mind on that night so long ago.

But Lee was not to be dissuaded. As was true over the vital Vietnam memo, he knew the strategic status quo was insupportable; the South either had to attack again or retreat from Gettysburg, leaving the Union victorious. Given how very close he had come to total victory, to try just one more time was a strategic temptation Lee simply could not resist.

There are a lot of understandable reasons this supremely talented general fell squarely into the losing gambler analytical trap. His army had so routinely defied the odds over the past magical year that Lee had begun to forget that the odds existed for a reason. The North had always had a decisive edge in manpower, matériel, and industrial production. All things being equal, it was going to win the war.

---

[12] Jeffrey D. Wert, *General James Longstreet: The Confederacy's Most Controversial Soldier* (New York: Simon & Schuster, 1993), p. 283.

By the time of Gettysburg, Lee had become overconfident in the invincibility of his men. With the death of the irreplaceable Stonewall Jackson, his subordinates' heretofore sterling performance declined, and the Army of the Potomac was better led than it had ever been (as attested to by the record at the battle of both Chamberlain and Second Corps Commander Winfield Scott Hancock). The law of averages had finally caught up with the South.

The problem was that Lee had come to believe the understandable myth about his own beloved men: that they could do anything, that no hurdle was too high for them to jump. While the attack on the third day was surely a desperate endeavor, all would somehow come right because Lee's men were untouchable, beyond normal human calculation. This tragic hubris led both the fabled Army of Northern Virginia and its commander to their doom.

As such, the losing gambler syndrome is directly responsible for the most catastrophic (and politically pivotal) assault in history, Pickett's charge. The false analytical logic behind making the attack led Lee to disastrously stake everything on one desperate throw of the dice.

Ignoring Longstreet's specific objections, Lee told him he could see no alternative to the frontal assault. Making the charge would be 12,500 Southerners, with Major General George Pickett's fresh 5,000-man division at its heart. The youthful Pickett himself is something straight out of a good Southern novel. Thirty-eight at the time of the battle, he was gaudy, perfumed, lusty, and exuberant. A personal friend of Abraham Lincoln's before the war, Pickett was peacock proud of both his personal bravery and of the fact that he had finished dead last in his class at West Point. When Longstreet somberly told him that he would lead the desperate charge, Pickett whooped with joy, as he saw it as his chance to win undying glory.

Pickett's men were to aim for a small clump of trees located directly in the center of Cemetery Ridge, a mile and a half away. At 1:00 PM, the largest artillery bombardment of the war, with 150 to 170 Confederate guns firing in unison, began. It was to precede the charge, in an effort to sweep the Union cannon away. For all the noise, the Southern guns failed to make a significant impact on the federal position on Cemetery Ridge. Northern guns returned fire, but after a while fell silent, all in the hopes of luring the Southerners out into that open field while conserving their ammunition for the charge everyone knew was likely to follow.

At 2:00 PM, Pickett asked Longstreet for formal permission to move forward. Overcome with emotion, and convinced he was watching the death of the Confederacy, Longstreet could not bring himself to speak; he only nodded. At around 3:00 PM, Pickett led his men out from their wooded position on Seminary Ridge with the exhortation, "Don't forget, men, today that you are from Old Virginia." The 12,500-man Confederate infantry began to briskly make their way into the open.

Just as Longstreet had feared, the Union forces had plenty of time after the bombardment for able II Corps Commander Winfield Scott Hancock to steady his line and to reinforce his position. All the while, Pickett's troops tramped across that beautiful, open Pennsylvania field. After crossing the Emmitsburg Pike, and still a mile away from the Union position, Southern troops came within range of the Union rifles. They almost couldn't miss.

From here on, and under the most intense fire from both cannon and rifles, the Southern battle line became confused, and no general orders could be given. Still, incredibly, the Southern advance carried on. At a low stone wall called "The Angle," Southern Brigadier General Lewis Armistead, placing his hat on his sword, managed to breach the Union lines.

Once over the wall, Armistead urged on his comrades to turn the Union guns—which had done such horrific damage to the attackers—around to confound the Northern men. He managed to seize a Union battery, only to discover that it had run out of ammunition. Already shot in the leg, Armistead was wounded three more times in the desperate hand-to-hand fighting that followed (the two sides were firing at each other from not five feet apart), in the side and the chest, before being surrounded by Northern troops.[13] Every single Confederate who had breached the Union line at The Angle was either killed or captured. Pickett's charge had failed.

And what a calamity it had been. Pickett's division lost 70 percent of its strength. Of the thirteen colonels leading the division, seven were dead and six wounded, for a casualty rate of 100 percent. Nearly one-half of all those who made the charge did not make it back to the line at Seminary Ridge. Years later, a still embittered Pickett recalled of Lee, "That old man destroyed my division."

As his sorrowful men streamed back to the safety of the Southern lines, Lee rode out to meet them, in what was perhaps his greatest moment. Thanks to the losing gambler syndrome, Lee had made the biggest mistake by any general on either side in the war. However, Lee's moral majesty allowed him to immediately admit that he had made the analytical error of all errors. He said, comforting the men, "It is all my fault." Longstreet, who had watched the attack unfold while sitting on a rail fence, simply wept.

Along with the fall of Vicksburg in the western theater of battle on July 4, 1863, Gettysburg was the turning point of the American Civil War. Following the Southern defeat, any lingering hopes of winning European recognition for

---

[13]The valiant Armistead was to die in a Union field hopsital two days later, succumbing to his wounds and to fever.

the Southern cause (such as vitally helped the colonists in winning independence from England in the Revolution) were definitively abandoned. After the battle, the Army of Northern Virginia never again went over to the general offensive, instead fighting a skillful (if doomed) defensive campaign in 1864–1865 against General Ulysses S. Grant. Lee's one, cataclysmic analytical error was nothing less than the determining factor in the war that made modern America.

The Losing Gambler Syndrome as Beguiling Analytical Trap

In both the tragic cases of Lee at Gettysburg and the decision to escalate the Vietnam War, the reasons for the decision-makers falling into the losing gambler syndrome are readily apparent, and all too human. That is precisely what makes it such a beguiling analytical trap for geopolitical risk analysts to this day.

Once resources and intellectual credibility have been expended, it is all too tempting, whether met with crisis or entranced by near-success, to keep doing what has been failing up until that point. It is entirely understandable to do this, but as Gettysburg and Vietnam point out, practically disastrous. Geopolitical risk analysts must instead have the courage to look at failure straight in the eye and make adjustments to mitigate its effects, rather than doubling down and inviting more.

CHAPTER EIGHT

1895: Knowing Your Country's Place in the World

LORD SALISBURY SAVES THE BRITISH EMPIRE

The Analytical Imperative of Seeing the World as It Is

Throughout history, any geopolitical risk analyst worth their salt has been able to clearly see one thing above all: the basic power structure of the world and their country's place within it. Whether it is Roman historians looking at the unipolar Mediterranean of the Augustan Age or Castlereagh and Metternich gaming out complex European multipolarity following the defeat of Napoleon, this is the starting point for all effective geopolitical risk analysis.

Nestled under the core typological admonition of the Pythia to "know thyself," seeing the world as it is—and crucially, knowing one's country's structural place within it—is an absolutely essential element for mastering geopolitical risk. In essence, what bedevils the overall foreign policies of both major American political parties today is their failure to clear this first intellectual hurdle. The world is neither nearly as unipolar as the neo-conservatives dream about nor as strictly multipolar (relatively equal great powers on the global scene) as Democratic Wilsonians assume.

In the late nineteenth century, following on from the American Civil War and with Great Britain still the undisputed greatest power in the world, one major British statesman, the brilliant, pious, gloomy Lord Salisbury, rightly sensed that while Britain's power was waning, it still had the ability to set the scene for the coming era. He based his new strategy on the correct and novel structural fact that while London remained first amongst equals, other great powers such as Germany, the United States, and Japan were relatively on the rise. Seeing the world dispassionately as it is in terms of power is the entry point for any successful geopolitical risk analysis, and there are few statesmen in history who displayed this talent as acutely as did Salisbury during the fraught days at the end of the Victorian era.

Salisbury's Intellectual Courage in Confronting His Changing World

He is not an easy man to love, Robert Arthur Talbot Gascoyne-Cecil, Third Marquess of Salisbury. A direct descendant of Lord Burghley, the able chief minister to Elizabeth I, Salisbury never let you forget for a minute that his family was used to running things. Aristocratic, brilliant, haughty, imperious, never giving an inch, he dominated late Victorian British politics after the colossal struggles of the earlier Disraeli-Gladstone era, serving as Conservative prime minister three times between June 1885 and July 1902.

A powerful speaker, a fine writer, and a first-rate intellect, Salisbury was faced with the gargantuan task of doing nothing less than preparing his countrymen to survive and thrive in a very different global order than the one they had been born into. Given the new structural state of play, he had to convince the British foreign policy elite, very used to having almost no limitations placed on their policies, to completely change their way of thinking, and in a remarkably short period of time.

This was a truly herculean endeavor. For to see the world as it is was as profoundly emotionally uncomfortable for the British foreign policy elite of the late Victorian era, as it is for today's American decision-makers. In both cases, London and Washington got used to an easy supremacy, where it was simple heresy to even suggest that their dominance might be passing away, as always occurs in history to every great power. Salisbury had to contend with rivals who thought him heretical, bordering on treasonous, to merely suggest the need to overhaul British foreign policy to make it fit for purpose in an age where London remained first amongst global equals, even while it was no longer wholly dominant.

The reward for Salisbury's intellectually heroic effort was that his cultivated allies, the United States and Japan, took up a significant portion of the global ordering slack from Britain, in the Western Hemisphere and Asia, respectively, without unduly harming major British national interests. Salisbury, with his brave, underrated far-sightedness, buttressed Britain's central role as the global ordering power, by paradoxically having it do less.

Salisbury is one of those curious transition figures in history, part a relic of a bygone age and part a very modern man. He was the last British prime minister to head an administration while sitting in the House of Lords, to which he had been elevated following the death of his father in 1868. A product of the old conservative British landed gentry to his fingertips (his family had vast land holdings in rural Dorset), Salisbury spent the better part of his adult life a reactionary in terms of domestic politics, skillfully if vainly trying to sweep the tide of universal male suffrage back to sea, even after his Conservative colleague, Prime Minister Benjamin Disraeli, had shrewdly come to accept it.

Perhaps it is because he was so obviously on the wrong side of history over this central point that Salisbury has become a relatively neglected figure in our own time, which is a great intellectual shame and far too easy a judgment to pass on him. For compared to the pygmies presently dominating both major American political parties, Salisbury ran a surprisingly modern, and very effective, foreign policy in his own day.

In contrast to his domestic failure to hold back the modern suffrage, Salisbury's foreign policy triumphs centered on his shrewd realist understanding of Britain's historic interests. This was combined with a keen appreciation that he and his country were living through a period of global structural change in foreign affairs: although the world of easy British dominance was finally giving way to a more competitive, more multipolar era, Britain remained the most important and powerful political force on the planet. His entire foreign policy was based on his unerring and correct reading of this global shift in power and Britain's changing place in the world.

Serving also as foreign secretary for the majority of his three premierships, Salisbury was the undisputed master of late Victorian foreign policy. It is even more to his credit that Salisbury was able to accurately assess that this global sea change in Britain's place in the world meant a diminution in overall British power. Salisbury's supreme intellectual ability to bravely look in the analytical mirror and see what was actually there did nothing less than save the British Empire, then the ordering power of the world, from catastrophe a generation later in 1918. With the fate of the modern world resting in the balance, long-cultivated allies, the United States and Japan, rode to Britain's rescue in that pivotal year.

Salisbury's entire foreign policy rested on the uncomfortable notion that Britain was in the very curious structural position of being in relative decline, but was still by a long way the greatest power in the world. However, he saw that the ascension of Japan in Asia, the United States in North America, and Germany in Europe to great power status could not be stopped. Instead, if Britain was to retain its pre-eminent place in the world, these emerging powers would have to be accommodated if possible, and opposed by a British-led alliance if necessary.

A few basic but vital truths underscored this shift in British strategy. Salisbury knew that most people would have little understanding of what he was attempting to do. As he said in criticizing British officials grappling with the Orissa famine in India, they were "walking in a dream . . . in superb unconsciousness, believing that what had been must be."[1] This is a key belief of Salisbury's: for all his conservatism, he knew it is poison in geopolitical risk terms to lazily assume that things will always be as they have been. His whole foreign policy was about avoiding this devilish analytical trap.

The second basic precept followed by Salisbury was to avoid wasting time, energy, and power worrying about what countries were doing in their internal affairs, as outside influences were highly unlikely to change things and would fritter away British power. While still a junior MP, Salisbury had argued in the House of Commons, "It is not a dignified position for a Great Power to occupy, to be pointed out as the busybody of Christendom."[2]

In sharp contrast to today's debilitating Western foreign policy views, so dominated (despite all facts to the contrary) by a moralistic Wilsonianism, Salisbury saw the world in starkly realist terms. His job was to secure Britain's place in the world, no more and no less. All foreign policy ventures would be judged only by this exacting if simple standard.

In line with this point, Salisbury firmly believed that Britain should not threaten other countries in general unless it was prepared to back up these statements with force. Otherwise,

---

[1] Andrew Roberts, *Salisbury: Victorian Titan* (London: Faber and Faber), p. 86.
[2] Ibid., pp. 40–42.

it would look increasingly weak and feckless in the world, the last thing he wanted at a time of such global structural change, as Britain grew relatively weaker.

While the British prime minister firmly believed that rising powers should be accommodated wherever possible, he also worked to make sure British security was bolstered, especially regarding Britain's vital Royal Navy. During Salisbury's second premiership (1886–1892), he crafted the Naval Defense Act of 1889, spending an extra 20 million pounds on the navy over four years, the largest-ever peacetime expansion of the fleet. The new money allowed the construction of ten new battleships and thirty-eight new cruisers.

Further, it led to the propounding of the new naval doctrine that the British Royal Navy must be maintained at the standard of the next two largest navies in the world combined, preserving the country's dominant military position even as other great powers were rising. For in the end the bolstering of the navy and the new, novel diplomatic approach Salisbury adopted were both there to serve the same overall purpose: securing Britain's dominant position in the world, even though it was in relative decline as other powers rose.

The Merits of Off-shore Balancing

Historians, in this as in so much else about the man, have generally been very confused as to what Salisbury was up to. The lazy, conventionally accepted view of him is to conflate his foreign policy with his predecessor Disraeli's and to wrong-headedly assert that they were both pursuing a policy based on what has been termed "splendid isolation." This term misleads, as it strongly implies that Britain adopted a passive approach to foreign policy at this critical juncture when in actuality the precise opposite is true at the strategic level.

At this highest level, Salisbury felt that the new world structure called for Britain to function as the global off-shore balancer. Staying aloof from the day-to-day quarrels and shifts in power in the various regions of the world, Britain would bring its power to bear only if these regional balances of power fell apart and any one rising power began to both dominate a region and threaten primary British interests.

Far from being a passive strategy, off-shore balancing calls for a constant assessment of what is going on within regional balances of power, as sudden shifts can result in dangers that must be quickly righted by the ordering power in question.

However, if a balance of power failed and one power began to dominate a region—as the Japanese did in Asia, the United States did in the Western Hemisphere, and the Germans did in Europe during Salisbury's premierships—Britain would be called upon to make a fateful strategic determination: was the rising power likely to be a status quo power helpful to Britain over the long run, or a revolutionary power deter-mined to upend the British-inspired global order? To answer this central question, it was vital to know in great detail the specific national interests of the rising powers in question before making a strategic determination as to whether they were best co-opted or opposed. Far from being a passive position, the "splendid isolation" of the Salisbury years re-quired an intricate, comprehensive, vigilant understanding of the world as it was.

Salisbury's overall foreign policy had several key planks. While alliances were acceptable, they must not be entangling, as Britain had to absolutely maintain its freedom of maneuver and its sovereignty to quickly and decisively right threats to regional balances of power throughout the world. Here the prime minister was supremely lucky in that the very character of his country—by virtue of its isolated location, dominant navy, and central position in the financial, trading, and industrial worlds—could with ease run such an independent foreign policy.

As such, safeguarding these unique national advantages became a cornerstone of Salisbury's thinking. Under his leadership, Britain was always protecting free trade around the globe, as no other nation benefited from it to such a degree. Likewise, as we have seen, preserving British naval dominance was a central plank of Salisbury's worldview.

Off-shore balancing freed Britain up to more narrowly focus on its primary national interest of the time: securing the colonies and dominions that comprised the British Empire, especially seeing to it that the vital sea routes between Britain and India, via the Suez Canal, were absolutely protected. At the core of Salisbury's overall foreign policy was a fervent desire for Britain—as the world's foremost status quo power and the global ordering power—to avoid war with rising powers if at all possible, thereby ensuring that these lines of communication throughout the Empire were unthreatened and British dominance could proceed in a non-dramatic and secure manner.

To live in this hoped-for peaceful world, Salisbury's last foreign policy plank amounted to what seemed at the time like an unnerving, almost humiliating climb-down for a proud country used to running the world as it saw fit. Britain as the primary status quo power would not stand in the way of the rising powers if it could possibly be helped.

Maintaining peace meant accommodating rather than opposing the United States, Japan, and Germany as far as possible, as this approach made it far more likely that they would emerge over time as status quo powers themselves—and as such, be prepared to help Britain defend the present global order—rather than as revolutionary powers determined to upend the world that Britain had largely created.

As Britain's power was due to continue relatively ebbing over decades, these new, emerging powers would determine the nature of the new era Salisbury was trying to birth: either they would come to safeguard the old order and peace would reign, or they would challenge it by force and inevitably tumultuous war would break out. Far from carrying out a placid, reactive foreign policy, as "splendid isolation" is often portrayed, Salisbury could not have been playing for higher stakes with his actual off-shore balancing efforts.

This radically different British policy of accommodating— rather than thwarting—rising powers required that Salisbury directly challenge the mindsets of the majority of British foreign policy practitioners of his own time, who were complacently used to living in a world where they could largely do as they pleased without having to worry over-much about accommodating anyone.

A similar problem bedevils American foreign policy at the present moment. Today's United States finds itself eerily in the same global structural position as Salisbury's Britain: it is still far and away the world's dominant power (and will be so for quite some time), even as it is relatively in decline as other great powers, such as China and India, rise from a low base.

As was true in the late Victorian era, the American foreign policy elite of today—as I witness every time I attend a Council on Foreign Relations meeting—still can't get its collective head around this complicated new era. As Anatol Lieven and I pointed out in *Ethical Realism,* Democratic foreign policy elites may think they can charm the world into doing as they want, and Republican elites may think the world can be bullied into doing as they wish, but the bottom line is that both the dominant Wilsonian and neo-conservative strains of thought still think they can pretty much tell the world what to do and it will happen.[3]

They are living in a time warp, still harkening back to the long period—during the Cold War and then the brief unipolar moment—when the United States had far more global power than it presently possesses and could easily afford to pursue a more aggressive and less subtle strategy. Salisbury ran into precisely the same sort of opposition, as he lived in a hauntingly similar structural world in terms of global power.

His nimble intellectual success contrasts sharply with the cloddish, dinosaur-like refusal of much of the present American foreign policy elite to simply recognize that the world has fundamentally changed, as has the country's place in it, and to act on this precious knowledge. Failure to do so, in geopolitical risk terms, poses the gravest threat for the United States today, as its elites fail to adjust to the basic power realities of the new era we presently find ourselves in. Salisbury's supreme triumph in accurately seeing Britain's true place in the changing world of the late Victorian era amounts to an argument against complacency and arrogance in geopolitical risk analysis, and in favor of the intellectual flexibility that is necessary to be strategically successful.

The Meiji Restoration Saves Japan

A generation earlier, in another part of the world, a very different great power was mastering the brave analytical art of looking in the mirror. The Meiji Restoration in Japan

[3] See Lieven and Hulsman, *Ethical Realism*.

(1868–1912) led to numerous advances in Japan's social and political structure, dramatically turning the country's fortunes around.

Whereas Japan had begun the period as a hopelessly out-of-touch declining power, ripe for Western domination, it ended the era as the greatest regional force in Asia. The key to this sea change was the exact same geopolitical risk calculation that Salisbury later undertook in London: to see the world as it was, warts and all, and Japan's specific place in it.

Japanese society, characteristically conservative and traditionalist, found itself surprisingly open to such a radical modernizing process. Critically, it had been made painfully clear to the Japanese elite that they were lagging behind the Western world in terms of power when American Commodore Matthew C. Perry finally opened Japanese ports to international trade, as he arrived in the closed society in large warships and with armaments that far outclassed the technology of the Empire.

When Perry's "Black Ships" arrived in Edo (soon to be renamed Tokyo) Harbor in July 1853, the country was an isolated, feudal state. His dramatic and forcible opening of Japan to the outside world ended the traditional Japanese foreign policy of *Sakoku*, whereby for 250 years foreigners had been put to death for entering the country, as were Japanese caught leaving it.

Perry's appearance also highly discredited the *Shogunate*, the hereditary warlords who had run Japan for centuries, as ordinary Japanese came to see how out of date and out of touch their rulers truly were. Knowing they couldn't possibly win a military conflict with the Americans, the *Shogun* was forced to sign a series of "Unequal Treaties" (as the Japanese rightly called them), giving up their power to levy tariffs on goods and also the right to try foreigners in their court system.

The origins of the coming Meiji Restoration can be found in the profound dissatisfaction amongst many nobles and *samurai* with the *Shogun*'s humiliating capitulation to the foreigners, a blot on the country's honor they grievously felt. Japan's fundamental geopolitical weakness had been made all too apparent.

Leaders of the Meiji reform movement (named after the sitting emperor) wanted to strengthen their country so that Japan would not become another plaything of the Western powers, a goal it shared with the Chinese government of the time but would be far more successful in achieving. The Meiji Restoration amounted to a very conservative revolution: traditional Japanese culture and values would be preserved, paradoxically, by adopting Western technology and modernization techniques. That this high-odds reform effort was crowned with success can largely be put down to its leaders' ability to bravely assess Japan's real, faltering structural position in the world, and then to decisively act to improve it.

The key figure who made the Meiji Restoration work is the rather mysterious Sakamoto Ryōma (1836–1867), whose diplomatic genius in 1866 brought together the powerful, traditionally warring heads of the Satsuma and Choshu provinces in western Japan. These reformist elements allied in their efforts to challenge the ruling and out-of-touch Tokugawa *Shogunate*.

While there are frustrating gaps in his life story, there can be no denying Ryōma's organizing genius or his centrality to the success of the Meiji movement. Ryōma was born into the lowest rank of the nobility (*samurai*); as a boy, he showed little scholarly inclination. However, Ryōma did achieve early notoriety as a master swordsman, which earned him official permission to travel more widely than was generally sanctioned at the time under the *Shogunate*'s highly restrictive laws.

Convinced that things could not go on for the country as they had, in 1864 he fled to Satsuma, an emerging center of anti-Tokugawa resistance. As he had left his home province without permission, a sister of his killed herself, believing that Ryōma had brought dishonor on his family in illegally leaving his Tosa clan. For Ryōma, there could be no turning back from his act of defiance.

Quickly rising through the ranks of the growing anti-Tokugawa forces, it was precisely because he belonged to neither province but was a sympathetic and neutral outsider that Ryōma was able to skillfully bring about the alliance between the Satsuma and Choshu regions, which had previously been intractable enemies.

Realizing that the rebellious provinces must almost instantly establish their armed forces to overthrow the *Shogunate*, Ryōma is also often considered the father of the Japanese Imperial Navy, as he established for Satsuma and Choshu a modern naval force that was to hold its own against the established navy of the Tokugawa *Shogunate*.

Critically in 1866, the forces of Choshu defeated the *Shogun*'s army. The omnipresent master diplomat Ryōma then played a key role in talks that led to the voluntary resignation of the last *Shogun* (Tokugawa Yashinobu) in November 1867, bringing about the Meiji Restoration, as oligarchs from the two rebellious provinces—the *Genrō*—dominated politics throughout the reformist period.

However, not long after this moment of triumph, the invaluable Ryōma was dead, struck down on December 10, 1867, by pro-Tokugawa assassins at an inn in Kyoto.[4] Oddly enough, Ryōma had been a transitional historical figure much as Salisbury was to prove to be in England. As a member of the feudal aristocracy who had risked his life countless times in

---

[4] The assassins were never caught.

the service of a cause that would lead to its abolition, Ryōma embodied these contradictions in the fact that he preferred to wear traditional *samurai* dress, but always coupled with modern Western footwear.

The *Genrō* Face the World

At first Ryomo's rebel movement—which arose primarily in response to the humiliations Perry had visited upon the *Shogun*—was strongly chauvinist in character. A radical political movement called *Sonnō Jōi*, which was part of the anti-Tokugawa forces, adopted the slogan "Revere the Emperor, expel the barbarians." However, after receiving critical military support from the British, upon coming to power the *Genrō* abandoned this utopian objective, not because they had come to love foreigners, but because they saw in the clearest-eyed way possible that strategically it was unachievable, as the West was simply too strong.

If they couldn't beat the foreigners, the Meiji reformers chose to join them. For the *Genrō* crucially understood Japan's perilous position in the world, and determined to improve it. Rather than expelling outside influences, the *Genrō* instead chose to learn from them how to modernize, paradoxically all in the effort of preserving Japanese society. Instead of outright chauvinism, the Meiji reformers adopted an overall policy of modernization, with an eye to improving Japan's position in the world, so as to renegotiate the "Unequal Treaties" with the Western states from a position of strength.

In just two generations—a blink of an eye in terms of Japanese history—the country was transformed from a feudal society into the foremost power in Asia, one with a modern market economy. For the first time, the central government in Tokyo exercised direct control throughout all its far-flung provinces. Feudalism itself was abolished, with the *samurai* class being gradually (and mostly peaceably) pensioned off.[5]

The country as a whole successfully underwent a crash course in industrialization. Out of nowhere, the Japanese constructed shipyards, iron smelters, factories, spinning mills, a national railway, and modern communications. With the abolition of feudalism, the Japanese people were allowed to move about their country far more freely, which led to a massive migration from the countryside to industrial cities, where they could earn more lucrative wages.

These basic and profound political and economic changes allowed other reforms to flourish. The army was radically modernized with the introduction of conscription in 1873. Profound land reform was introduced. The Meiji reformers established a dominant national language, *hyojungo*, as the norm, replacing the mishmash of local and regional dialects that had held sway under the *Shogunate*. Schooling was made compulsory, and all Confucian class distinctions were abolished. This all happened so quickly that it was almost as if Japan had gone to bed a feudal society and awoken a modern great power.

The *Genro*'s heroic efforts at reform were thoroughly validated by the two shock victories of Japan's armed forces in the Sino-Japanese War (1894–1895) and the Russo-Japanese War (1904–1905), which left the country as the undisputed rising regional power in Asia.

By having the rare intellectual bravery to look in the mirror following the country's humiliation at the hands of Commodore Perry—and the will to fundamentally reform, changing their very structural position in the world—the

---

[5]The *samurai*'s last stand, the Satsuma rebellion, was swiftly put down by the modernized Japanese Imperial Army.

Genrō had taken a country falling apart at the seams and in just over two generations left it a world power, in defiance of all the odds. Seeing where they were in the world allowed the *Genrō*, with such great success, to see where they needed to go.

Salisbury Finesses America over the Venezuelan Crisis

Much as proved true with the Meiji reformers, Salisbury's brave and correct analytical take on Britain's changed structural position in the world not only conditioned his overall foreign policy strategy but also provided the outlines for the tactics necessary to make such a game plan work.

Given Britain's relative decline, the three rising regional powers London had to try to accommodate—and if not, confront within a broader coalition—were the United States in the Western Hemisphere, Japan in Asia, and Germany in Europe. Matters with America were to come to a head first.

By 1895, an obscure border dispute between Britain and Venezuela had been simmering at a low boil for half a century; no one would have thought such a minor crisis would take London and Washington—Venezuela's champion—to the brink of war. The original dispute had arisen centuries before between the Spanish Empire and the Dutch Empire and was inherited by Venezuela (after its independence was declared from the former in 1830) and Britain (after it took over British Guiana from the Dutch in 1814).

The disputed territory had always contained the strategic mouth of the Orinoco River, and the crisis assumed more importance when lucrative gold mines were discovered in the region. More importantly, political feeling grew in the United States that Britain was throwing its weight around in the Western Hemisphere. From an American perspective, this was a clear violation of the Monroe Doctrine, then the primary pillar of American foreign policy, which had been formulated by Secretary of State John Quincy Adams in 1823.

The Doctrine stated that any further attempts by European powers to colonize land or interfere with countries in the Western Hemisphere would be viewed as unfriendly acts of aggression by the United States, requiring American intervention; in essence, Washington was declaring that the entirety of the Western Hemisphere was its specific sphere of influence.

While the Monroe Doctrine was unenforceable at the time, the United States had been lucky that, as it rose over the course of the nineteenth century as a great power, it had suited the ordering power in London to uphold the Doctrine based on the fact that it did not wish its own rivals to bolster their positions through the acquisition of colonies in the Americas. Now, however, the shoe was firmly on the other foot, as a rising United States saw Britain as the primary meddling outsider.

In February 1895, President Grover Cleveland signed into law the congressional injunction that Britain and Venezuela should settle the dispute by arbitration, meaning that Britain could not continue to blithely ignore Venezuelan claims to the territory.

Initially, the British behaved as they had throughout much of the nineteenth century: they haughtily dismissed American objections on the grounds of the Monroe Doctrine and went about their business as if they could do as they pleased anywhere in the world. But the emboldened Americans would not let the matter rest.

July 1895 saw Secretary of State Richard Olney send a diplomatic note to Britain, firmly insisting on the application of the Monroe Doctrine to the crisis and making it clear that Washington believed that "today the US is practically sovereign on this continent," and that British claims in the disputed region threatened primary American interests.[6] Still the British, so used to getting their way owing to their old structural position of dominance, did not budge.

So America simply upped the strategic ante. In December 1895, President Cleveland delivered an address to Congress, reaffirming the Monroe Doctrine and its relevance to the Venezuelan dispute. Couched in undeniably menacing tones, the address seemed to amount to a direct threat of war if London did not seek to take the matter to international arbitration, as Washington insisted on. Cleveland said that America would "resist by any means in its power" if Britain continued to ignore American and Venezuelan concerns and exercise jurisdiction over the disputed land.[7]

It was at this critical moment that Salisbury showed his true greatness. Surely no one in the haughty (to modern eyes) nineteenth century was so full of his own importance as was the British prime minister. However, at this pivotal moment he managed to master his own pride—as well as that of his country—in the service of his evolving foreign policy of accommodating the rising powers of the day.

In line with the later "Serenity Prayer" of that arch-realist, the American theologian Reinhold Niebuhr, Salisbury was guided by the pivotal notion, "God, grant me the serenity to accept the things I cannot change, courage to change the things I can, and the wisdom to know the difference."[8]

---

[6] R. A. Humphreys, "Anglo-American Relations and the Venezuelan Crisis of 1895," the presidential address to the Royal Historical Society, December 10, 1966, *Transactions of the Royal Historical Society*, vol. 17, pp. 131–64.

[7] Ibid., p. 150.

[8] See Lieven and Hulsman, *Ethical Realism*.

In January 1896, Salisbury's government decided to formally recognize the American right to intervene in the territorial dispute, accepting the American position that arbitration was necessary to resolve the controversy. Negotiations were conducted in a personally highly cordial manner, greatly and immediately improving US-UK relations. The tribunal met in Paris, where Britain largely persuaded the United States of its claims. In October 1899, the tribunal awarded Britain 90 percent of the disputed territory—and all of the gold mines.

However, and far more importantly, what had just happened was that the global ordering power, still by far the most important country in the world, had accepted that the United States—as the rising power in the Western Hemisphere—held regional primacy over what went on there. In recognizing America's right to intervene in the dispute as asserted by the Monroe Doctrine, Salisbury's Britain implicitly acknowledged American dominance of the Western Hemisphere itself.

Salisbury, in working through a seemingly obscure territorial dispute halfway around the world from London, had successfully broken the old mold of British foreign policy, making it fit for purpose in the new era that was just dawning. This was the very last time in the modern era that a possible war between the two great Anglo-Saxon powers would ever be contemplated. From here on out, the two great powers, as Salisbury had so presciently seen, worked together hand in glove as status quo forces, determined to defend the British-inspired global order.

Reaching an accommodation with rising Japan proved far easier—as well as far less dramatic—for the British. The Anglo-Japanese alliance, which came into force in 1902, implicitly did in Asia what the Venezuelan crisis had done in the Western Hemisphere: Britain as the ordering power tacitly ceded regional dominance to the primary rising regional power.

The treaty was renewed and expanded by the two powers in both 1905 and 1911. The aging *Genrō*, who still remembered with gratitude that Britain had supported their drive for modernization over the past two generations, had proved easier than the Americans to bring on board as a status quo power.

Tokyo's stunning victory in the Russo-Japan War of 1904–1905 confirmed Britain's analysis that it was Japan and not Russia that was the rising power to watch in Asia. Crucially, it was the alliance's provisions for mutual defense that prompted Japan to enter World War I on the British side, riding to the Empire's rescue in Asia, much as America was to do in Europe.

Salisbury Saves His Country, Long after His Death

Salisbury's tragedy was that while his creative foreign policy saved the British Empire, it did not do so without the shedding of blood in a world war. For while the United States and Japan proved malleable to his plans for rising power accommodation, the Kaiser's Germany did not.

The dramatic German efforts to threaten Britain's naval supremacy—a cornerstone of Salisbury's foreign policy strategy—from 1898 onwards led to the Anglo-German arms race, causing Britain (unlike in the cases of the United States and Japan) to perceive German efforts to achieve regional dominance in Europe as fundamentally hostile to its interests.

The off-shore balancer would now have to get far more involved with the intricacies of European politics, using its weight to directly offset growing German power. As such, the British entente with first France and then Russia—originally agreements limited to colonial affairs—gradually over time became a fully fledged alliance. The civilizational disaster of

World War I was not far away. And for all of Salisbury's imaginative foreign policy, it could not avert the catastrophe.

But if Salisbury's innovative foreign policy—predicated on the key geopolitical risk imperative to look at the structural position of the world (and yourself in it) as coldly and as clearly as possible—had not averted war, it largely managed to win it. For in 1918, it was Salisbury's cultivated rising powers, the United States in Europe and Japan in Asia, that contributed mightily to ultimate victory and the securing—for a little while longer yet—of Britain's preeminent place in the world.

Far before those pivotal years, on July 11, 1902, in failing health (largely due to his great weight) and distraught over the recent death of his beloved wife, the old man finally resigned the premiership in favor of his nephew, Arthur Balfour. Salisbury died quietly a year later in 1903. But this forgotten man, by mastering the key geopolitical risk tenet of seeing the power structure of the world as it actually was and Britain's place in it, saved his country from disaster a full fifteen years after his death.

CHAPTER NINE

1898–1912: The Promised Land Fallacy

VON TIRPITZ DISASTROUSLY BUILDS A NAVY

The Dangerous Mirage of the Promised Land Fallacy

Distantly related to the losing gambler's syndrome is the promised land fallacy, the naive view that one attribute of power or one strategy is sufficient to overcome the complexity of the world and—in silver bullet–like fashion—change the terms of the geopolitical game. In essence, it's a very human effort to falsely manufacture a game-changing strategy rather than recognize that a game-changing event generally happens organically. This element of geopolitical risk analysis, nestled under the Pythia's strident admonition "make a pledge and mischief is nigh," calls upon analysts and policy-makers alike to resist this beguiling intellectual trap. Geopolitical risk analysts throughout the ages, frustrated by the constraints of living in the world as they have found it, are often highly susceptible to dreaming up analysis designed to liberate them from the shackles of reality. Ruinously, reality always wins.

In the years following the innovative genius of Salisbury's foreign policy, Anglo-German relations nevertheless spiraled out of control. No one was more responsible for this than Alfred von Tirpitz, whose wrong-headed strategy to supersede the British navy instead led Germany directly over the cliff into the charnel house of the Great War.

For Wilhelmine Germany, the building of a fleet from scratch to challenge the mighty Royal Navy was meant to be the country's ticket to its place in the sun. The German political and military elite, frustrated that the world (especially haughty Great Britain) failed to recognize the ascension of Germany to great power status, set about rushing the forces of history, rather than merely waiting for their yearly relative gains in global power to become apparent over time. Already possessing the greatest army in the world, the kaiser became intent on building a threatening navy.

Instead of heralding an era of German dominance, the elite in Berlin unwittingly started a process that led to its doom. The naval race awoke an alarmed London to the coming German threat to its position as the greatest single power in the world (though one in relative decline, as we have seen), a fact that helped directly lead to war and ruinous German defeat.

Far from leading to the promised land, this approach puts geopolitical risk analysts forever at the mercy of the latest intellectual fad, often leading to simplistic analysis that doesn't stand up to the realities of a complicated world.

Von Tirpitz Recklessly Challenges British Naval Dominance

Grand Admiral Alfred von Tirpitz became the living embodiment of the kaiser's drive to build a world-class navy, almost from scratch. Born March 19, 1849, pictures of von Tirpitz show a man looking like nothing so much as an enraged walrus, with his long, flowing beard, fierce eyes, and stern countenance.

Yet von Tirpitz was much more than this caricature of a stiff-necked Prussian. For one thing, he knew the English personally and well, spoke the language fluently, and even sent his two daughters to the prestigious Cheltenham Ladies' College. For another, von Tirpitz rose through the German navy's ranks largely through his own merits, something unheard of at the time. In the 1870s and 1880s, he was at the forefront of military technology, championing the development of a new class of torpedoes and torpedo boats for the puny German navy. Tirpitz, for all the Prussian glowering, was essentially a creative, outward-looking, self-made man.

His big break came in 1887, when he escorted then Crown Prince Wilhelm across the English Channel to attend the Golden Jubilee celebrations of his grandmother, Queen Victoria. On the way over, von Tirpitz managed to persuade the excitable prince to focus in the future on building battleships as the linchpin of the fledgling German navy. The future kaiser fell in immediately with these ambitious plans, and von Tirpitz was transferred back to Berlin to begin work on setting out a strategy for creating a powerful German High Seas Fleet.

On December 1, 1892, von Tirpitz presented his recommendations to Wilhelm, who had unexpectedly succeeded his father as kaiser. As a sign of his continuing favor, Wilhelm made von Tirpitz chief of the naval staff in 1892, and a rear admiral in 1895. However, for all his laurels, von Tirpitz chafed at the fact that his ambitious recommendations had yet to be acted on. In the autumn of 1895, he asked to be replaced from his senior strategic planning position.

The kaiser, not wishing to part with his guru, instead asked him to prepare a new set of recommendations for all future German ship construction. It was at this point, in 1897, that von Tirpitz was made head of the powerful Imperial Navy Office, an unassailable bureaucratic perch that allowed him to relentlessly focus on making the German navy a force to be reckoned with.

On June 15, 1897, von Tirpitz presented his review on the composition and strategic purpose of a new German navy to the Kaiser, overtly identifying Great Britain as Germany's principal foe for the first time. The primary recommendation was that Germany must build as many battleships as possible, if it was to challenge British naval hegemony. Initially, von Tirpitz advocated the creation of two squadrons of eight battleships, plus a fleet flagship and two reserves.

For its time, the first von Tirpitz plan was revolutionary in that it made a clear, unambiguous strategic statement of Germany's naval goals and how to meet them, rather than following the then-accepted custom that military expenditures would be considered piecemeal, and year-to-year.

The initial impetus spurring on this ambitious German naval program had been the threat the British Foreign Office made to Berlin in March 1897 following the outbreak of the Boer War. London had made it abundantly clear that, owing to broad German sympathy for the Boer cause in South Africa, the Royal Navy would blockade the German coast, and thus cripple its emerging economy, if Berlin intervened on the Boers' side.[1]

This intolerable affront to the thin-skinned kaiser allowed von Tirpitz to skillfully use the crisis to win the kaiser over to his point of view that Germany would only be taken seriously as a great power if it built a navy that reflected its new status in the world.

Initially, conservatives in the Reichstag felt that any significant expenditure on the puny navy was wasted, as any extra money available should go to Germany's powerful army, which would doubtless be the deciding factor in any coming European war. While this was to be borne out by events of World War I, von Tirpitz managed to overcome his critics, correct as they might have been on the policy.

Heading the German Imperial Naval Office from 1897 to 1916, von Tirpitz was what today would be classed a "political general," having almost magical powers to secure

---

[1] Christopher Clark, *The Sleepwalkers: How Europe Went to War in 1914* (London: Allen Lane, 2012), pp. 148–49.

appropriations for the German navy from what had been up until then an extremely reluctant Reichstag. His great talent was not as a strategist, but rather his uncanny ability to arouse German public interest and support for the country's naval expansion, while successfully leveraging the Reichstag to do his bidding and fund his incessant naval requests. To the kaiser's delight, the First Naval Bill was passed on March 26, 1898, by a vote of 212–139.

This political victory ensured that von Tirpitz would be at the center of German strategic thinking for the next nineteen years. Von Tirpitz came to be nicknamed "The Eternal," for he remained firmly ensconced at the German Imperial Naval Office, while all those politically around him came and went, victims of the whims of the mercurial kaiser. This bureaucratic staying power added to von Tirpitz's luster, giving him enduring leverage within German defense policy-making circles.

For all that the First German Naval Bill looked ominous to London, it did not directly threaten British naval doctrine, as the fledgling German navy was still playing catch-up; it remained roughly the size of the French and Russian fleets, a full rung below the British in terms of naval power.

However, in January 1900, at the height of the Boer War, a British cruiser intercepted three German mail steamers, high-handedly searching them for supplies that might help the hard-pressed Boers. German public outrage was skillfully stoked by von Tirpitz, enabling him to pass a Second Naval Bill, which did threaten the strategic balance of power. It called for a doubling in the number of German battleships from nineteen to thirty-eight, making the German fleet the second largest in the world. The bill sailed through the Reichstag on June 20, 1900.

Between 1898 and 1912, von Tirpitz managed to get four naval acts through the German Parliament, greatly expanding the size of the country's High Seas Fleet. Over time, von

Tirpitz's clearly stated strategic goal became to construct a navy that was two-thirds of the size of the dominant British fleet. In the narrowest of terms, von Tirpitz was successful, in that he took the very meager German navy he found in the 1890s and transformed it into a world-class force. He was rewarded by being made a grand admiral by Wilhelm in 1911. However, the strategic cost of doing so far outweighed the tactical gains.

The irony was that, for both von Tirpitz and the kaiser, the German naval build-up was essentially defensive in nature. They did not wish to overwhelm Britain as a revolutionary power, but merely to be taken seriously by it as a valued guarantor of the status quo. The von Tirpitz strategic plan was to build the world's second-largest navy after Britain's, announcing Germany's arrival on the world stage as an undisputed great power.

In this vision, the naval build-up would get the Germans to the promised land, making the British see sense and accommodate Germany's rise to great power status. Yet, as so often has proven the case for those whose geopolitical risk analysis leads them to adopt the promised land strategy, unintended consequences overwhelmed these initial goals.

In direct reaction to von Tirpitz's naval program, Britain (between 1902 and 1910) embarked on its own massive naval build-up, with the express purpose of safeguarding its naval dominance and seeing off the perceived German strategic threat. Standard British defense policy, inaugurated under Salisbury's premiership, held that Britain must ensure that its navy remained at least the same size as the world's next two largest flotillas combined if London's dominance was to be maintained. As such, von Tirpitz's build-up, far from cowing Britain into supporting Germany's overall geopolitical rise, instead threatened basic British strategic doctrine.

Owing to the obvious superiority of the German army in Europe, Britain was forced to wholly rely on its preponderant naval position to secure its far-flung empire and its own great power status. As such, the German naval challenge was one that Britain simply could not afford to ignore, as it threatened Britain's core interests. Following the Reichstag's passing of the Second Naval Bill, the British responded in kind, ordering eight King Edward–class battleships as a direct response. The naval arms race was on, sparked by von Tirpitz's flawed promised land thinking.

The British also developed a revolutionary new class of ship, the "dreadnought," modeled on HMS *Dreadnought*, which was launched in 1906, quickly making all previous battleships obsolete. The dreadnoughts amounted to a strategic paradigm shift in that technologically they were the first capital ships to be powered by steam turbines, which enabled them to do a world-beating twenty-one knots, making them easily the swiftest battleships in the world at the time.

Dreadnoughts had very accurate twelve-inch guns capable of long-range fire, as well as a very short construction time: they could be built in just fourteen months. HMS *Dreadnought* was the first modern warship of the twentieth century. Immediately, von Tirpitz's navy rushed to match England's breakthrough. The naval arms race had reached its zenith.

The unintended result of the von Tirpitz plan was to leave Germany in the worst of all possible strategic worlds. Its efforts to catch up to the dominant British navy—seeing this as the ticket to the promised land of acceptance of Germany as a great power—narrowed, but did not eliminate, Britain's maritime advantage. By 1914, Germany did indeed possess the second-largest naval force in the world, though it still remained roughly 40 percent smaller than the Royal Navy. In an immediate, limited sense, the Germans won the naval arms race by whittling down British dominance. But the cost of this pyrrhic victory was exorbitant.

Salisbury's strategic doctrine—that the Royal Navy was to remain at least the size of its two largest competitors put together—was indeed upended by 1914, owing to the explosive growth of the German and American flotillas. This change in strategic circumstances was enough to alarm Britain into fundamentally changing its foreign and strategic policies, but did not alter the overriding fact that in 1914 it still possessed by a long way the most powerful naval force in the world.

At the start of World War I, Britain had forty-nine battleships to Germany's twenty-nine, meaning that Berlin had failed to meet von Tirpitz's ultimate goal for the German navy to be two-thirds of the size of its rival in London. Even worse, in 1914 London had twenty-nine of the cutting-edge dreadnoughts, and Berlin just seventeen.[2] However, it was the naval arms race that persuaded Britain to wholly adopt Salisbury's evolving policy and instead look for allies to deal with what was seen—as a result of the von Tirpitz plan—as an increasingly malevolent German threat.

As the German navy posed an increasing challenge to Britain in its home waters, London shifted the bulk of its navy back to the North Sea and the English Channel to protect its very existence. The logical corollary following on from this strategic shift was to make it necessary for London to make diplomatic arrangements with other global powers, such as it was already doing with Japan and the United States, to see that the international commons remained open, and the British Empire safeguarded.

Unwittingly, the promised land fallacy, epitomized by the von Tirpitz plan, led directly to the closer Anglo-French ties that were to form the basis of the resistance to Germany in

World War I. With Britain pressed to withdraw its Mediterranean fleet to its home waters to fend off the impending German naval threat, much closer ties with Paris became an absolute strategic imperative so as to safeguard the Suez Canal, the jugular of the British Empire.

Britain, turning its back decisively on its nineteenth-century post-Napoleonic foreign policy heritage, formally allied itself with European powers France, in 1904, and Russia, in 1907. Incredibly, the Germans—pursuing their promised land strategy to secure in von Tirpitz's words German "political independence" from England—had just forced the British into their eternal enemy France's waiting arms, the worst possible strategic thing Berlin could have done.

Khrushchev and the Limits of Brinkmanship

But von Tirpitz is far from alone in falling into the trap of the promised land fallacy. More recently, the Soviet Union—under Nikita Khrushchev—became ensnared in precisely the same morass. As was true for Wilhelmine Germany structurally, the Soviet Union under Khrushchev was seen as a rising power, struggling to be taken seriously as an equal by the dominant power of the day, in this case the United States.

Just as it was von Tirpitz's dream to establish a world-class navy to cow the British, Khrushchev used Communist ideology to reach for a silver bullet to right the strategic equation, using aggressive brinkmanship to help the developing world wage wars of national liberation against the dominant West. As was the case with the kaiser, for Khrushchev catching up was vital, but brinkmanship was also intended to keep his stronger American opponent off balance. This he certainly did, but as happened with Wilhelmine Germany, this led to predictably disastrous consequences. In Khrushchev's case, brinkmanship directly caused his ouster in 1964.

Soviet support for "wars of national liberation"—bolstering rising global anti-colonial movements from Algeria to Cuba to Vietnam—had its roots in the far-off writings of Lenin, specifically his work *Imperialism: The Highest Stage of Capitalism*.

As William Odom puts it, for the Soviets, nationalists in colonies "were objectively 'progressive' political forces. Furthermore, because capitalism had become a world imperialist system, revolutions in the colonies might well break the 'weakest link'" in imperialism's chain of control, enabling a war in the colonies to bring down the whole imperialist structure.[3] Strategically, Khrushchev dreamed of a world where a Communist East allied with the developing world would overturn the dominance of the West.

If Communist ideology as derived from Lenin's anti-colonialist writings provided Khrushchev with the intellectual material for his silver bullet strategy, standard Soviet military doctrine provided the tactical form that such a strategy would take. Soviet ideas about war were based on a "belief in the primacy of the offensive form of warfare."[4]

So if the developing world amounted to the soft underbelly of capitalism and its chief champion, the United States, it had to be attacked aggressively through strategic, diplomatic, and, if necessary, military means. As was true for von Tirpitz and Kaiser Wilhelm, Khrushchev would play a dangerous, high-stakes game of brinkmanship with the world's dominant power to secure the Soviet Union's place in the sun.

But if the Khrushchev era was to be characterized by his blustering on the world stage—thereby fooling many Amer-

---

[3] William E. Odom, *The Collapse of the Soviet Military* (New Haven, CT: Yale University Press, 1998), pp. 4–5.

[4] Ibid., p. 13.

ican strategists into thinking they were outright losing the Cold War to an inevitably rising Soviet power—the reality of the situation was far different. The Soviet leader was attempting to make the Soviet Union a viable global power, knowing that the country he had inherited from Joseph Stalin had been isolated, handicapped by a war machine it could ill afford.

As Aleksandr Fursenko and Timothy Naftali point out, when Khrushchev came to power, his "long experience as an agricultural and industrial manager made him more sensitive than Stalin or Molotov to the cost of military confrontation with the West and its effects on the standard of living within the Soviet Union and its Communist allies. His few foreign travels, all of which had been to socialist countries—to East Germany, Poland, and China in 1954— had reinforced his belief that economics was the Achilles' heel of the Soviet bloc."[5]

Khrushchev was acutely aware of the structural flaws marring Soviet power, even if his Western adversaries were not. He knew that enhancing Soviet economic growth was the absolute key to the country's future geopolitical success, and that its oversized conventional military was a drag on its prospects. At the same time, Khrushchev was determined to pursue his aggressive "wars of liberation" foreign policy strategy. The key intellectual tension throughout the period of Khrushchev's dominance was how to address the Soviet Union's acute economic needs while at the same time implementing its expansionistic foreign policy designs.

Unlike the kaiser, who could simply have waited a few years until Germany's growing economic dominance would have inevitably granted it a seat at the global top table with

[5] Aleksandr Fursenko and Timothy Naftali, *Khrushchev's Cold War* (New York: W. W. Norton and Co., 2006), p. 23.

Britain, Khrushchev was working from a structural position of relative weakness compared with the United States. The Soviet leader made this clear in a speech to his colleagues on January 8, 1962.

"He adopted the metaphor of a wineglass that was filled to the brim, forming a meniscus, to describe a world where political tensions everywhere were brought to the edge of military confrontation . . . so long as the Soviet Union was the weaker superpower, it had to practice brinkmanship to keep its adversary off-balance."[6] The unanswered metaphorical question in all this was, what was to be done if the meniscus was broken and the wineglass did overflow?

Khrushchev was certainly a true believer in the historically inevitable victory of communism on the world stage, and did all he could to enable the Soviet Union to overtake and supplant the United States over time as the world's dominant power. But when push came to shove in the crises he so often caused, the Soviet leader shied away from war, having seen a great deal of it as a political commissar at the pivotal Battle of Stalingrad in World War II.

So at the exact same time Khrushchev embarked on his ambitious promised land strategy of using "wars of national liberation" to best the United States, he was simultaneously pushing for deep cuts in Soviet conventional forces across the board, while also disdaining a build-up of tactical nuclear weapons, for fear they would lower the atomic threshold and increase the chances of nuclear war.

Khrushchev was relying instead on strategic nuclear weapons, only to be used as an absolute last resort. So beneath all the bombast and his dangerous silver bullet strategy hinging on "wars of national liberation," in reality Khrushchev simultaneously pursued a very conservative and cautious

[6] Ibid., pp. 5–6.

nuclear policy. Unhappily for him, this nuance was lost on both his allies and his enemies.

Yet, on the other hand, "Khrushchev was convinced he could play on the nerves of his adversaries by threatening nuclear strikes he had no intention of undertaking. He tried out that tactic during the Suez Crisis, and was convinced that it worked; he used it again during the Berlin crisis and tried to repeat it in Cuba. But instead of cowing his adversaries, his bluster and bluff alarmed them and mobilized them to undertake resistance that forced him to back down."[7]

As had been true for the kaiser, Khrushchev's menacing "wars of national liberation" policy was the worst of all strategic worlds. It did just enough to alarm the United States to check Soviet advances without amounting to enough to overturn the established order.

Over the eleven years he was in charge of the Soviet Union, Khrushchev aggressively pursued the strategic offensive in the Cold War, through threats to use nuclear weapons, but primarily through the Soviet Union's sponsorship of what were deemed "progressive" anti-colonial movements throughout the world. As Robert Donaldson and Joseph Nogee put it, Khrushchev viewed his "wars of national liberation" strategy as "an arena in which the Soviets could compete with the West with a high likelihood of success, but with less risk than would result from a direct challenge."[8]

Khrushchev practiced what he preached. In June 1955, during a state visit to India, a leading light of the anti-colonial world, he promised that the Soviet Union would finance and construct the giant Bhilai steel mill, as a form of economic

[7] William E. Taubman, foreword to Sergei Khrushchev, *Nikita Khrushchev and the Creation of a Superpower* (State College: Pennsylvania State University Press), pp. viii–ix.

[8] Robert H. Donaldson and Joseph L. Nogee, *The Foreign Policy of Russia: Changing Systems, Enduring Interests* (London: M. E. Sharpe, 2009), pp. 80–81.

assistance for its developing world ally. This cemented a special relationship between Delhi and Moscow that lasted until well after the Cold War.

There is little doubt that Khrushchev's foreign policy thrust the Soviet Union into truly global involvement. Besides India, he forged ties with radical anti-colonial movements in the developing world, such as the Castro regime in Cuba and Ho Chi Minh in Vietnam. For these nationalist Communists, the Soviet Union represented a welcome alternative to the United States as a source of economic and military support. In the wake of Stalin's narrow focus on Eastern Europe, Khrushchev expanded the parameters of Soviet foreign policy.

In pursuing the "wars of national liberation" strategy, the Soviet Union provided logistical, financial, and ideological support to Communist as well as anti-colonial groups. For example, in 1959, Khrushchev provided military assistance to Patrice Lumumba in Congo and supported his diplomatic initiatives at the United Nations. The Soviets also supported the Laotian Communists, but only within the parameters of the broader neutralist United Front, giving military aid to the allies of Souvanna Phouma.

The overall strategy called for picking away at imperialism in the developing world, as dismantling it over time would cause capitalism's ultimate collapse. The Soviet Union challenged the United States in every single region of the globe. And that was precisely the problem with Khrushchev's "wars of national liberation" policy. The United States was challenged across the world, but the Soviet Union, as very much the junior superpower, was in no position to compete with America everywhere. As such, geopolitical realities doomed the policy to failure, eventually merely highlighting the very glaring Soviet weaknesses that Khrushchev's bluster had been designed to hide.

Khrushchev's Ill-Fated
"Wars of National Liberation" Strategy

Nikita Khrushchev was born in 1894 in the village of Ka-linovka, close to the present-day border between Russia and Ukraine. The son of poor peasants, the future leader of the Soviet Union received only four years of formal schooling, working to help feed his family from a very young age. Eventually, Khrushchev found a trade, becoming a skilled metalworker.

Meanwhile, in the tumult of the 1920s Soviet Union, Khrushchev advanced quickly through the Communist ranks. Initially a protégé of Lazar Kaganovich, a major Party figure, Khrushchev was tasked by Stalin with helping to rule Ukraine, the Soviet Union's second-most-important republic. In 1934, in recognition of his rising status, Stalin brought Khrushchev to Moscow itself, where he was made Party leader and set about constructing the city's subway system. In late 1937, as he unhesitatingly supported Stalin in his murderous purges, he was sent back to Ukraine as head of the Communist Party. Khrushchev was made a full member of the Politburo in March 1939, on the eve of the Second World War.

During the war, Khrushchev served as a senior political commissar, a vital liaison between Stalin and his generals. He was present for the pivotal Battle of Stalingrad, a fact of which Khrushchev remained proud for the rest of his life. After the war, the icy Stalin—who was surprisingly affectionate toward his bumptious aide—installed Khrushchev as one of his senior advisers.

During the latter part of Stalin's reign, Khrushchev continued to alternate between assignments running Ukraine (which he governed for over a decade in total) and serving as Party chief in Moscow, at the center of Stalin's court. At one late-night drunken dinner with the Soviet dictator,

Stalin dangerously insisted that Khrushchev, then almost sixty, burst into a traditional Ukrainian folk dance, which Khrushchev—despite the intense humiliation—immediately did. When later asked about it, Khrushchev, displaying his native cunning for survival in Stalin's shark tank, said simply, "When Stalin says dance, a wise man dances."[9]

After Stalin's death in 1953, Khrushchev, with the firm support of the Soviet military, somewhat surprisingly emerged the victor in a complicated, many-sided power struggle with Georgy Malenkov, Lavrentiy Beria, and his former patron, Kaganovich. However, though from 1953 to 1964 Khrushchev was the preeminent Soviet leader, he enjoyed nothing like the absolute control Stalin had possessed.

On February 25, 1956, at the Soviet Twentieth Party Conference, Khrushchev finally laid Stalin's homicidal ghost to rest. In a secret speech, he shockingly (to senior Party ears) denounced Stalin's reign of terror, inaugurating a less repressive era in Soviet history. Khrushchev set about doing away with the special tribunals that had been operated by Beria's secret service, which had been the means to carry out the purges. In direct contrast to his bloodthirsty predecessor, no major political show trials were conducted during Khrushchev's leadership.

But if the Khrushchev era was a time of domestic relaxation, in terms of foreign affairs it signaled the tensest days of the Cold War. The Suez Crisis, the Soviet crushing of the Hungarian revolt of 1956, the U-2 spy plane crisis, ongoing tensions over Berlin, the Bay of Pigs, the Vienna summit debacle with JFK, and most importantly, the Cuban Missile Crisis—all were moving the world perilously close to the brink of all-out nuclear war.

---

[9] William Taubman, *Khrushchev: The Man and His Era* (New York: W. W. Norton and Co., 2003), pp. 211–15.

This was partly the result of the West perpetually underestimating the new Soviet leader. Short, stocky, and ac-
customed to wearing ill-fitting suits, Khrushchev at times
reveled in playing the role of the Russian peasant he had
long since ceased to be. Yet the act often took in supposedly
more worldly observers. Then British foreign secretary Harold
Macmillan, upon meeting the loud, ebullient Soviet leader,
wondered, "How can this fat, vulgar man with his pig eyes
and ceaseless flow of talk be the head—the aspirant Tsar—of
all those millions of people?"[10]

Yet this was the same man who worried incessantly that
the huge, bloated Soviet military would continue to eat up
his country's limited resources, making his longer-term goal
of improving the lot of average Soviet citizens impossible to
achieve. This was the impetus for the major cuts the Soviets
made in conventional forces, hoping instead to strategically
rely on nuclear weapons and improved missile technology
for national defense, as Eisenhower (unlike Kennedy) had
done in America in the 1950s.

In 1955, Khrushchev—unlike the kaiser—overturned Stalin's plans for constructing a large navy to challenge American
maritime dominance. Likewise, in January 1960, Khrushchev
took advantage of a momentary thaw with the Americans
to order a massive one-third cut in the overall size of the
Soviet armed forces.

Yet Khrushchev was ultimately trying to change the nature
of the strategic game, not to end the Soviet Union's rivalry with
America or to acquiesce in Western dominance. Convinced
that Moscow could not challenge American pre-eminence
through continuing the tired old Stalinist policy of maintaining the vast, bloated Red Army and focusing almost ob-

[10]William J. Thompson, *Khrushchev: A Political Life* (New York: St. Martin's
Press, 1995), p. 149.

sessively on Eastern Europe—which made the Soviet Union only a regional power at best—Khrushchev sought to globalize the Soviet Union's contest with America, contradictorily at the same moment as he was cutting back on conventional military capabilities.

These realities directly led to Khrushchev's reach almost always exceeding his grasp as he carried out his "wars of national liberation" policy. Ginned up by his brinkmanship, the Kremlin would have to brandish the threat of nuclear war. If the West failed to back down, that left Moscow with only the option of a humiliating climb-down. As such, the Soviet Union's search for a promised land strategy to overturn Western dominance, in the form of the "wars of national liberation" policy, led directly to the humiliating outcome of the Cuban Missile Crisis.

In October 1962, the Soviet Union, in an effort to further its "wars of national liberation" strategy by bolstering the Castro regime, sought to install medium-range nuclear weapons on the island of Cuba, having the effect of dangerously altering the global strategic balance of power, as Castro sat a mere ninety miles off the US coast.

Eventually found out by irrefutable American U-2 spy plane evidence, Khrushchev, true to form, almost immediately adopted a defensive posture, in line with geopolitical realities. Fearing an overwhelming American invasion of the island, Khrushchev crucially ordered the Soviet troops stationed there to resist by all means short of nuclear weapons.[11] There were obvious limits to how far this past master of bombast was prepared to go.

By October 25, 1962, in the face of the creative and forthright resistance of the Kennedy administration, Khrushchev decided that the offending missiles would have to be with-

---

[11] Fursenko and Naftali, *Khrushchev's Cold War*, pp. 469–77.

drawn from Cuba. Khrushchev's bluff had been called. By October 27, terms with the Americans had been hammered out.

The Soviets agreed to withdraw the missiles from Cuba and to allow UN inspections to determine that this had been accomplished. In turn, the Kennedy administration made assurances not to again attempt to invade Castro's Cuba. Further, in a secret protocol, Khrushchev managed to elicit a promise from the Kennedy administration to withdraw obsolete Jupiter missiles from Turkey, where they were perched all too close to the Soviet heartland.

On its surface, these terms were not unduly unfavorable for the Soviet Union. Although they had been humiliatingly found out in trying to alter the global strategic equation on the sly, on its merits the "wars of national liberation" strategy ought not to have come unstuck by the Cuban Missile Crisis. A major ally in that policy, Fidel Castro's Cuba, had just been guaranteed its continuing existence, right under America's nose. Further, the offending Jupiter missiles in Turkey would now be removed, in line with the strategic reciprocity of the deal, much as the missiles of October so obviously worried the Americans.

Yet less than two years later, Khrushchev was unceremoniously unseated, largely as a result of the outcome of the Cuban Missile Crisis. Fursenko and Naftali are right to point out how the basic contradictions in Khrushchev's overall "wars of national liberation" policy contributed to his demise. Prior to Cuba, "Khrushchev increased the number of Soviet commitments overseas, providing weapons at cost or below to Iraq, Egypt, Syria, Afghanistan, Indonesia, India, Laos, North Vietnam, Congo and Cuba. The effect was to make him [Khrushchev] increasingly reliant on the appearance rather than the reality of Soviet power."[12]

[12] Ibid., pp. 543–44.

Khrushchev's strategy rested precisely on his bluffs not being called, but whenever they were he backed down, both because he did not have a preponderance of military power behind him to secure his strategy, and because— despite all the bombast—he had no intention of starting World War III.

The Soviet Union's relative rise was nowhere near great enough strategically to accommodate this dramatic increase in ambition. This disconnect left the Soviet leader perpetually bluffing until, over the Cuban Missile Crisis, the Kennedy administration finally called his relatively weak hand. Like the kaiser, Khrushchev had bet everything on the promised land strategy, and lost. Following the Cuban Missile Crisis, like the Wizard of Oz, Khrushchev was shown to be blustering in a desperate attempt to hide weakness. After Cuba, Khrushchev's credibility had been fatally undermined.

Before the Cuban Missile Crisis, in June 1962, food prices had begun to rise in the Soviet Union. This was particularly true of the staples of meat and butter, which shot up in price by an astronomical 25 to 30 percent, inciting domestic discontent. This would be exacerbated by the drought that struck the Soviet Union in 1963. Along with the seeming humiliation of the Cuban Missile Crisis, the time was ripe for Khrushchev's downfall.

Khrushchev himself made things easy for Leonid Brezhnev and the other plotters, as he was absent from Moscow for a total of five months between January and September 1964.[13] At last, Brezhnev and his cronies struck in October 1964, as Khrushchev returned from holiday. He was met at Moscow's Vnukovo Airport by KGB chief Vladimir Semichastny, a supposed ally, who had come supported by guards from the

---

[13] Taubman, *Khrushchev*, p. 617.

intelligence agency. Bluntly informed of his ouster and told not to resist, Khrushchev bowed to this last insult, as he had earlier acquiesced in dancing for Stalin.

Pensioned off by the coup plotters, Khrushchev was allotted an apartment and even a small dacha in the countryside. Nevertheless, the man used to frightening the world fell into a deep depression upon his forced retirement, as he was largely ignored, becoming the latest Soviet "nonperson." When Khrushchev died of a heart attack on September 11, 1971, he was denied a state funeral by his enemies.

The Haldane Mission as the End of Tirpitz's Promised Land

Despite von Tirpitz's Germany being in a far superior geopolitical position to Khrushchev's Soviet Union, the wheels began to come off his promised land strategy as well. By 1912, German Chancellor Theobald von Bethmann-Hollweg sought to end the naval arms race that the kaiser's disastrous decision to build a navy had provoked, instead seeking a belated rapprochement with London.

The menacing growth of the Czarist Russian Army to the east was forcing the Reichstag to spend more money on the German army, and correspondingly less on von Tirpitz's navy. The naval race had succeeded in alarming Britain—and throwing it into the arms of Germany's enemies France and Russia—all without overtaking the Royal Navy as the preeminent maritime force on earth. In short, it was a strategic disaster.

Given these new military realities, Bethmann-Hollweg was desperate to reach an agreement with London that would allow Germany a free hand to deal with a vengeful France. The German chancellor needed to perform a diplomatic sleight of hand that even his famous predecessor Otto von Bismarck would have admired: offering London enough enticements to seduce it to leave the entente alliance it had formed with France and Russia. The germanophile secretary of state for war in the Asquith government in London, Viscount Haldane, was sent on a secret mission to Berlin, February 8–12, 1912, to see if this early form of arms control could be achieved.

In retrospect, it is hard to see any way in which the Haldane mission could have ended in success, as it would have required Britain to completely overturn its foreign policy of the past decade in order to reach a new and definitive understanding with Germany. But the diplomatic initiative was killed at birth, largely owing to the opposition of von Tirpitz, who narrow-mindedly was not about to allow his creation to be dismantled. Von Tirpitz opposed any change in Germany's ambitious naval policy. By this point, the promised land fallacy had completely clouded the judgment of Germany's sea lord.

Meeting alone with the kaiser and von Tirpitz, Haldane proposed that to end the naval arms race, both sides had to agree to voluntarily limit the number of ships—particularly dreadnoughts—they were allowed to build. Such an outcome would have secured British naval superiority into the medium-term, and tensions would have dissipated.

However, these ambitious diplomatic maneuverings were stillborn. The day before Haldane arrived in Berlin, the kaiser chose to present an ambitious new naval bill to the German Parliament, purposely sending precisely the wrong message to London about Germany's future intentions.

When they finally met, Wilhelm offered to Haldane that Germany would slow construction of its navy, but not halt it. Crucially, he linked this offer to an agreement by both sides not to join with any combination of powers directed against the other, both promising to remain neutral if the other was forced into a war.

In essence, the obviously not-up-to-scratch deal amounted to Germany agreeing to slow the naval arms race if Britain relinquished its vital alliance with France and Russia. While Asquith's government in London was prepared to make some limited concessions to Berlin to satisfy German colonial aspirations in Africa, it was completely against Germany's diplomatic linkage of the cessation of the naval arms race to its turning its back on its allies.

This otherworldly German offer to the British amounts to the Waterloo of von Tirpitz's entire naval policy. The whole strategic point of the German build-up had rested on the hope that the naval arms race would force Britain to agree to some sort of strategic "grand bargain," whereby London would allow Berlin to dominate Europe in exchange for a German promise not to interfere with Britain's colonies.

Such a reading of London showed absolutely no understanding of the most basic of strategic precepts that have guided British foreign policy since time immemorial: to remain strategically secure, Britain must never let any one continental power (be it Louis XIV, Napoleon, the kaiser, or later, Hitler) dominate the whole of Europe.

As such, Britain's historical strategy was always to ally with the smaller continental powers, balancing against any would-be hegemons. Britain was not about to throw away this guiding light of its strategic culture on the anemic German promise to slow down a naval arms race London had already won.

Far from cowing Britain into submission, as von Tirpitz and the kaiser had hoped, all the naval arms race had done was to alarm Britain into putting its usual European strategy into practice, allying in this case with the French and the Russians to prevent German continental domination. With the abject failure of the Haldane mission, von Tirpitz simply returned to his promised land strategy and began another counter-productive round of ship-building, further confirming British suspicions. Catastrophic war was not far away.

Von Tirpitz was to perform one last major strategic disservice to his country. As World War I ground into the bloodiest of stalemates, he advocated the use of unrestricted submarine warfare to bring England to its knees. This new promised land strategy merely succeeded in bringing the antagonized United States into the war, decisively shifting the correlation of forces in the entente's favor. Falling out with Wilhelm over the restrictions he had sensibly placed on the U-boat campaign, von Tirpitz was shocked when his resignation of March 15, 1916, was accepted.

In 1917, von Tirpitz helped found the Pan-Germanic, ultra-nationalist Fatherland Party, agitating for a military dictatorship to be formed around Paul von Hindenburg and Erich Ludendorff. Never learning his lesson, after the war von Tirpitz supported the far-right National People's Party, sitting for it as a member of the Reichstag between 1924 and 1928, though he never regained his pre-war eminence.

Von Tirpitz finally died in Munich on March 6, 1930, having unwittingly presided over the destruction of his country, due to his slavishly following the pernicious promised land strategy on more than one occasion. It is well that geopolitical risk analysts remember the doleful story of this talented man as a cautionary analytical tale; manufacturing game-changing strategies cannot be relied upon, often leading to outright calamity.

CHAPTER TEN

1970: Knowing the Nature of the World You Live In

OR THE TRIALS AND TRIBULATIONS OF GEORGE HARRISON

The Imperative of Understanding Time in the Analytical Equation

Even if a geopolitical risk analyst is able to correctly see the basic power structure of the world at any given moment, how does his analysis allow for slow, organic, but very real change in that global system? How can time be factored into the analytical equation? All too often analysis tends to be both static and reactionary, not allowing for the relative rise and fall of countries within the existing global order, let alone fundamental change in the power structure of the world itself. If this is the case, even analysts who are right at the time of their initial analysis over time will become increasingly wrong.

Understanding global power systems is absolutely crucial to being a world-class geopolitical risk analyst. Located under the core typological sub-heading of "know thyself," gaining an understanding of the nature of power within the world system—and vitally assessing whether it is stable or not—is a core element upon which mastering geopolitical risk is based.

The best (and most entertaining) way to look at the change of power dynamics in a successful order is to chronicle the startlingly quick unraveling of the greatest pop group in history, the Beatles, contrasting it with the entirely unexpected longevity of their closest rivals, the Rolling Stones. The Fab

Four went in lightning fashion from a period of artistic and commercial dominance in the mid-1960s (with *Rubber Soul, Revolver,* and *Sgt. Pepper's Lonely Hearts Club Band*) to their demise in 1970 (following *Let It Be* and *Abbey Road*) in a blink of a historical eye.

A basic reason for their collapse was the inability of John Lennon and Paul McCartney to make creative space for the burgeoning talents of their quiet and under-rated lead guitar player, George Harrison. By assuming, as geopolitical risk analysts so often do, that the present state of the dominant Lennon-McCartney duopoly would go on forever, the Beatles fell victim to a reactionary form of thinking that led directly to their downfall.

In this case, what is true for rock bands holds for the global order as well. A seminal geopolitical risk question of the present age revolves around whether a dominant but relatively declining West can cajole and entice the rising rest of the world to join a revamped global system, or whether— much like the Beatles' guitarist—the world's rising regional powers will simply go their own way.

The Beatles' System Falls Stunningly Apart

The brilliant system the Beatles created for working together failed to evolve as the relative creative powers of its members changed over the course of the 1960s. By failing to proactively reform a system that had so recently seemed etched in stone, the Beatles' abrupt end is a cautionary tale for today's Western world as a whole, and is an abject lesson for geopolitical risk analysts and policy-makers as to how to factor time into the systemic analysis which is so central to their work.

It is hard to think of a more successful system for working together than that conjured by the Beatles in the mid-1960s.

With the release of *Rubber Soul* (1965), *Revolver* (1966), and *Sgt. Pepper's Lonely Hearts Club Band* (1967), the Fab Four were at the apex of their creative and commercial power.

The rather rigid structure lying behind this creative and commercial success—on most albums their lovable drummer Ringo Starr was given at most one song, George Harrison had two or at best three, with the rest being Lennon-McCartney originals—became the group's unquestioned modus operandi. The system was working in that it reflected the creative power realities within the group.

This pattern—the accepted rules underlying a bipolar world dominated by Lennon-McCartney—was followed with metronomic efficiency. On *Rubber Soul*, there are eleven Lennon-McCartney tunes, two penned by Harrison, and one by Ringo (with the help of John and Paul). *Revolver* is graced by eleven Lennon-McCartney songs, while Harrison had three and Ringo none. *Sgt. Pepper's* in many ways amounts to the apogee of John and Paul's creative dominance; fully twelve of the thirteen songs on this masterpiece were written by Lennon-McCartney, with George managing only one and Ringo none.

But by now George Harrison had had enough. In any other group, he would have served as a first-rate front man, as both a performer and a writer; now he simply couldn't get much of his increasingly prodigious output on the records. The creative balance of power within the group was decidedly shifting, even as the Beatles' modus operandi stayed the same. Chafing at the creative bit, and frustrated that he simply wasn't allowed to crack the Lennon-McCartney duopoly, Harrison grew increasingly resentful that his efforts to grow as an artist were being given short shrift.

In a sense, such a rigid response to Harrison's rise is entirely understandable. John and Paul echoed back to him what great, established status quo powers have been saying since time immemorial: "Why should we change anything, given how well things are going for us?" While that certainly was true in this case—the Lennon-McCartney duo had taken the Beatles to undreamed-of creative heights—so was the fact that George Harrison, an immensely talented man in his own right, was not being given real opportunities to rise in the Beatles' system.

As was true for John and Paul, geopolitical risk analysts all too often get in the habit of looking at global power systems as if they will last forever, failing to note the small but definitive changes taking place over time that can dramatically alter the very essence of what is being analyzed.

The Rise of George Harrison

The lead guitarist of the most creatively and commercially successful pop group in history was born (like the others) in Liverpool on February 25, 1943, at the height of World War II. The youngest of four children, George came from a tight-knit, working-class family. He was particularly close to his mother, who throughout his tumultuous life provided him with unstinting support.

In 1956, George's father gave him his first acoustic guitar, and he was hooked for life. On the bus rides to school, George bonded with another music-mad boy named Paul McCartney, forming an indelible love-hate relationship that was to last for the rest of their lives.

In March 1958, Paul introduced the young George to John Lennon, then the undisputed leader of the pre-Beatles incarnation, the Quarrymen. For the next twelve years, these three creative giants were to uneasily co-exist, trying to accommodate increasingly disparate tastes in what was only a four-piece band. Because George was the youngest member of the group (he joined the Quarrymen when he was just fifteen) and by temperament the quietest—surely compared with the charming and gregarious McCartney and the witty and often outrageous Lennon—he initially was happy to take a backseat to the other two, who became the most successful song-writing duo in history.

But as the Beatles hit their creative apex in the mid-1960s, things slowly began to change. Up until then, George had been known to the public as "the quiet Beatle," unsung if generally respected for his guitar playing. Now his tastes and interests began to positively affect the overall direction of the band itself. The 1965 album *Rubber Soul* was heavily influenced by folk rock, mirroring George's friendships with Bob Dylan and the best-selling Los Angeles band, the Byrds. Later, George was to say that *Rubber Soul* remained his all-time favorite Beatles album.

Rubber Soul also provided the first artistic glimpse of what would become the great creative love of George's life, when he played the sitar, a traditional Indian instrument, on John's song "Norwegian Wood." For the rest of his life, George would serve as an ambassador for classical Indian music, popularizing it in the West. At the same time, his interest in Hinduism and Indian philosophy came to dominate his private life, giving Harrison a very different persona from that of his early Liverpool days.

But while George led the charge in popularizing Indian mysticism and introducing Indian instrumentation into Beatles music specifically and Western music more generally, increasingly he chafed at the creative bit as the Lennon-McCartney duopoly reached its climax with *Sgt. Pepper's Lonely Hearts Club Band* in 1967. George later said of it, "There's about half the songs I like and the other half I can't stand."[1] As a

---

[1] Alan Clayson, *George Harrison* (London: Sanctuary, 2003), pp. 214–15.

perfect illustration of his creative frustrations, Harrison did not manage to get even one of his songs promoted as a single until "The Inner Light" was made a lowly B-side in 1968.

While on a visit to his friend Dylan in Woodstock, New York, in late 1968, he found himself drawn to the Band's (Bob's highly creative backing group) vision of making music communally as equals. This way of working contrasted mightily with the Beatles' rigid Lennon-McCartney bipolar creative domination and spurred Harrison's increasing yearnings to assert his abilities, either within the band or on his own if need be.

The Rolling Stones Regroup

In 1967, no sane person would have bet the Rolling Stones would outlast the Beatles. While, at least on the surface, the Beatles seemed to epitomize hippy togetherness, the Stones were characterized by endless fist-fights, girlfriend swapping, drug arrests, and chaos. The Beatles were part of a stable creative bipolar system of Lennon-McCartney dominance, while the Stones were a volatile multipolar system, uneasily ruled by Mick Jagger, Keith Richards, and Brian Jones, all of whom at various points seemed to openly loathe one another.

Yet at Glastonbury in far-away 2013, the creaky, aged—but still very good—Stones headlined the most important music festival in Europe, forty-three years after the seemingly indestructible Beatles had acrimoniously split up. Why did the Stones' apparently unstable system last forever, and why did the Beatles' placid facade crumble so easily? What is going on here, and what can geopolitical risk analysts learn from it?

Ironically, the key to the Stones' long-term success was the demise of the group's founder, the talented, troubled Brian Jones. With his passing from their creative scene, the Stones were to be led by the surprisingly stable Jagger-Richards bipolar duopoly, one that would survive arrests, addictions, and just plain dislike, for the rest of time.

The Fall of Brian Jones

Lewis Brian Hopkin Jones, the founder and original leader of the Rolling Stones, was born February 28, 1942, in Cheltenham, England. His middle-class parents were always interested in music: his mother taught piano, while his father led the local church choir. From early on in his life, Brian was a jazz enthusiast, being given his first acoustic guitar at the age of seventeen.

Already promising, Jones did well at Cheltenham Grammar School for Boys, but loathed the school's rules and regimentation. Further marring his childhood, Jones was sickly, having severe attacks of asthma that would recur throughout his life.

Late in the summer of 1959, at seventeen, Jones's life was thrown into turmoil when his girlfriend became pregnant. He was forced to abandon school and his promising future and leave home in disgrace. His chaotic personal life was to continue over the next few years as he had five children in all, by five different mothers.

Wandering, Jones drifted with the wind, traveling in Scandinavia, surviving by busking as he went, before returning to London, where he became a fixture at the local blues and jazz clubs. Always ambitious, Brian placed an ad in *Jazz News* on May 2, 1962, inviting local musicians to audition to be part of his new rhythm and blues band; it was the birth of the Rolling Stones.

Along with Jagger and Richards, Jones set about nurturing the fledgling band. He made up its name on the spot—taking it from an old Muddy Waters tune—in order to secure desperately needed gigs. For a year, between September 1962 and September 1963, Jones, Jagger, and Richards all shared an incredibly dingy flat, 102 Edith Grove, Chelsea. Here Jones and Richards, then comfortably sharing the lead guitar duties, spent most days endlessly playing guitar together and listening to blues records.

Uniquely, and as a definitive sign of their initial real but fleeting personal harmony, Jones's and Richards's guitars were interchangeably playing lead and rhythm guitar, without the usual clear boundaries between the two, more like traditional jazz musicians. By January 1963, bassist Bill Wyman had joined the band, along with world-class drummer Charlie Watts.

At this point in time, Jones was the undisputed leader of the Stones, which functioned as a unipolar system centered on him. As Bill Wyman later put it, "He [Jones] formed the band. He chose the members. He named the band. He chose the music we played. He got us gigs . . . he was very influential, very important."[2]

But Brian was always his own worst enemy. While acting as the band's business manager, he secretly saw to it that he received five pounds more than the others. When this became known, it created deep resentment within the band, especially with Jagger and Richards.

As Keith later disclosed in his wonderfully revealing memoir *Life*: "The first demonstration of Brian's aspirations was the discovery on our first tour that he was getting five pounds more a week than the rest of us because . . . he was our 'leader.' The whole deal with the band was we split everything like pirates. You put the booty on the table and split it, pieces of eight. 'Jesus Christ, who do you think you are?

[2] Rob Lowman, "Roll of a Lifetime: Founding Bassist Bill Wyman Looks Back at the Stones," *(Los Angeles) Daily News*, October 27, 2002.

I'm writing the songs round here, and you're getting five pounds extra a week? Get outta here!' It started with little things like that, which exacerbated the friction between us."[3]

Not helping matters, when the first lengthy tours were arranged in 1963, Jones chose to travel separately from the rest of the band, staying in different hotels and continuing to demand extra pay. While all agreed that Brian could be charming, friendly, and thoughtful, he was just as likely to be cruel and unbearably difficult. As Wyman observed, "He [Brian] pushed every friendship to the limit and way beyond."[4]

As ever, Brian lacked staying power, tiring of playing the guitar. Instead, he evolved into a multi-instrumentalist, playing everything from guitar, marimba, Appalachian dulcimer, and organ to the sitar, recorder, autoharp, and saxophone on the Stones' mid-1960s records, *Aftermath* (1966), *Between the Buttons* (1967), and *Their Satanic Majesties Request* (1967). However, by now the creative power shift in the band was apparent to all, with Jones increasingly being seen by the others as an erratic, annoying distraction.

Many factors led to Jones's fall from grace as the Stones gradually morphed from a unipolar power system dominated by Jones to the unstable, multipolar power triumvirate of Jones-Jagger-Richards, to the enduring bipolar world of Mick and Keith.

First, the hiring of Andrew Loog Oldham as their permanent manager abruptly ended Jones's unique position as leader. Oldham, seeing that Jagger had the potential to be the best front man in rock, made Mick's flamboyance and swagger the focus of the band's live performances, further enhancing his role in the Stones.

[3] Keith Richards, with James Fox, *Life*, large-print edition (New York: Little, Brown and Co., 2010), p. 289.

[4] Bill Wyman, with Ray Coleman, *Stone Alone: The Story of a Rock 'n' Roll Band* (New York: Da Capo Press, 1997), p. 76.

Second, and perhaps most crucially, following the overwhelming success of their friendly rivals Lennon-McCartney, Oldham clearly perceived the financial advantages to the group of writing their own songs rather than merely performing the blues covers that Jones adored. As the song-writing duo of Jagger-Richards came to rival Lennon-McCartney, Brian—who was incapable of sustained song-writing—became increasingly overshadowed by his two bandmates. As Mick and Keith creatively grew, Jones stagnated.

By the time *Aftermath* was released in the spring of 1966, all the songs on the album were Jagger-Richards originals. Their song-writing dominance was to eventually form the core of the enduring creative bipolar duopoly that was to characterize the band for the many years to come following Brian's eclipse. While with the rise of Harrison the Beatles' bipolar power structure was in relative decline, with the advent of the Jagger-Richards song-writing partnership, the Stones' formerly unipolar power structure had obviously ceased to exist, as the group's creative realities were so at variance with this.

Instead, the Stones temporarily transitioned into an uneasy multipolar division of power. Keith unerringly sensed the shift: "What probably stuck in Brian's craw was when Mick and I started writing the songs. He lost his status and then lost interest."[5]

If Jones couldn't write, he increasingly couldn't play either, owing to his growing problems with drugs. Keith puts it bluntly: "And he became a pain in the neck, a kind of rotting attachment. When you're schlepping 350 days a year on the road and you've got to drag a dead weight, it becomes pretty vicious."[6] Time and time again, Richards was forced to cover

---

[5] Richards with Fox, *Life*, p. 293.
[6] Ibid., p. 291.

for a debilitated Jones at concerts. He bitterly remembers: "And I never got a thank-you from him, ever, for covering his arse. That's when I had it in for Brian."[7]

Brian's creative demise coincided with a general moment of systemic crisis for the Stones as a whole. December 1967's *Their Satanic Majesties Request* was conceived under very difficult circumstances, as Jagger, Richards, and Jones were all dealing with legal issues relating to various drug arrests. Late 1968's *Beggar's Banquet* saw Jones increasingly absent and only able to haphazardly contribute to the band.

During this period, Andrew Oldham, the Stones' manager, walked out on the Stones, feeling the end was near. Keith's recollection of the period is equally apocalyptic: "We'd run out of gas. I don't think I realized it at the time, but that was a period where we could have foundered—a natural end to a hit-making band."[8] The unstable multipolar system the Stones had evolved into was simply not working. The band would have to either adapt or die.

The final straw that broke the camel's back concerned Richards going off with Jones's girlfriend of two years, the sexy, dangerous actress Anita Pallenberg. Mired in an increasingly abusive relationship, matters came to a head in March 1967 when Jagger, Richards, Jones, and their entourage retreated to Morocco for a much-needed holiday. Following one particularly violent domestic incident with Jones, Pallenberg left the country with Richards, leaving Brian stranded at their Moroccan hotel. Richards later recounts: "It's said I stole her. But my take on it is that I rescued her."[9] Richards and Pallenberg were to remain together for twelve years. Jones's humiliation was complete.

[7] Ibid., p. 292.
[8] Ibid., p. 361.
[9] Ibid., p. 339.

Following this, Jones and Richards's relationship was irretrievably shattered. As Keith puts it: "All of my plans for rebuilding my relationship with Brian were obviously going straight down the drain. In the condition he was in, there was no point in building anything with Brian."[10]

The Stones wanted to tour the United States in 1969, but Jones was in no fit condition to join them and was further constrained from doing so as a second drug arrest made getting an American work visa highly unlikely. Given the doldrums the band was then in, the Stones could little afford to cancel the tour if the band was to survive.

But the supposedly radical and rebellious Stones were at heart Burkean conservatives—desperately searching for stability—as they unsentimentally morphed once again into a different creative structure, this time an enduring bipolar duopoly that actually suited the real creative realities within the group. As Richards puts it, "You can't work with a broken band. If there's something wrong in the engine, an attempt has to be made to fix it."[11] Bill Wyman has been equally incisive about Jones's fall from grace, saying that he "just kind of wasted it and blew it all away."[12]

On June 8, 1969, Jagger, Richards, and Watts traveled down to Jones's new house, Cotchford Farm, the former residence of author A. A. Milne, the creator of Winnie-the-Pooh. Their purpose was anything but childlike. Jones admitted to the three that he was in no fit state to go on the road again. Unceremoniously, they told Jones he was out of the band. It was left to him to decide how to break the news to the public. Then his former bandmates left as abruptly as they had arrived, going on to a record of lon-

[10] Ibid., p. 337.
[11] Ibid., pp. 296–97.
[12] Lowman, "Roll of a Lifetime."

gevity that is unmatched by any other major band in the annals of rock music.

But for Jones there were to be no more tomorrows. Less than a month later, on July 3, 1969, Brian Jones was found dead in his swimming pool under mysterious circumstances. While there were certainly signs of foul play and one deathbed confession by a local builder years later that he had killed Jones, the autopsy of the time noted that his liver and heart were greatly enlarged, owing to massive drug and alcohol abuse. Keith's philosophical view of what happened is perhaps best: Brian, he says, "was at that point of his life when there wasn't any."[13] Of his former bandmates, only Watts and Wyman attended Brian's funeral.

While Jones's demise and ultimate death were undoubtedly tragic, inadvertently these events gave the band he founded a second lease on life. For with Jones's passing from the scene, the Stones completed their lengthy metamorphosis from a unipolar creative structure dominated by Brian, through the uneasy Jones-Jagger-Richards triumvirate, to the far more stable bipolar creative construct that has characterized the band for decades. As Keith forthrightly puts it of his famously volatile relationship with Mick, "It was like two alphas fighting. Still is, quite honestly."[14]

But the bipolar partnership at the heart of the Rolling Stones was to endure, surviving Mick's fling with Pallenberg (and Keith's with Mick's long-time girlfriend Marianne Faithfull), Keith's recovery from drug addiction and further arrests, and these two gifted musicians growing personally apart through the decades.

The stable systemic nature of the relationship, something every first-class geopolitical risk analyst must grasp, is the

[13] Richards with Fox, *Life*, p. 420.
[14] Ibid., p. 395.

obvious explanation for the longevity of this highly unlikely partnership. With the necessary removal of Brian Jones, the band was able to adopt a power relationship that still mirrors its basic creative forces. The Stones, after all the chaos, managed to adopt a stable system allowing for their remarkable—and seemingly endless—run.

The Beatles as a Frightening Metaphor for Today's World

But while the Stones were improbably coalescing around an enduring system reflecting the creative realties within the group, at the very same time the seemingly impregnable Beatles were falling apart. Worse still, and carrying the systems analogy one step further, the Beatles' demise sets a very bad precedent for the world we happen to find ourselves in just now, as the terminal demise of the Western-ordered system that characterizes our own era appears well advanced.

So let's jump through the looking glass, taking our Beatles analogy a geopolitical step further. View John Lennon in the mid to late 1960s as a stand-in for the Europe of today: increasingly preoccupied with Yoko Ono, self-involved with the many demons of his past and present, more worried about his own problems and situation than about the Beatles as a whole, and eager to shed his responsibilities in the band.

See Paul McCartney as the United States, unhappily aware he is the last man standing, the force (after the death of their unsung manager Brian Epstein from a prescription drug overdose in August 1967) holding the group together. As John commented on Epstein's death, "We collapsed. I knew that we were in trouble then. I didn't have any misconceptions about our ability to do anything other than play music. I thought, 'We've had it now.'"[15]

It fell to Paul, both by virtue of his ambitious personality and John's lack of interest, to take over the running of the band. The others resented his increasing dominance, even as he resented the fact that they all benefited from his drive to keep the show on the road, the system ticking over. Paul is a harassed ordering power.

Imagine George Harrison as today's rising powers (China and the other major emerging market powers), resentful and distrustful of the old system of Western dominance (epitomized by Lennon-McCartney) and eager to strike off on his own, to take charge of his own destiny either within the established group or in a new band.

And finally, conjure Ringo up as the world's smaller powers, desperate to work with everyone, to keep a stable system working, even as he is glumly aware that whatever happens will affect him far more than he can impact any outcome. Strikingly, the Beatles of the late 1960s and the global political world of today are eerily in line with one another.

The Beatles were either oblivious to, or did not want to accommodate, the rising creative force that was their quiet and underrated lead guitar player. Their temporary solution in 1968 while making *The Beatles* (universally known as "The White Album," for its arresting minimalist cover) was anarchy, to let everyone put everything they wanted on the album.

Sadly, it shows. "The White Album" is a good double album that should have been a classic single album. Instead, it is a pudding that lacks a theme, the Beatles' formerly disciplined structure having broken down in favor of a free-for-all. As John later acknowledged, "Every track [on "The White Album"] is

[15] The Beatles, *The Beatles Anthology* (San Francisco: Chronicle Books, 2000), p. 268.

an individual track; there isn't any Beatle music on it. [It's] John and the band, Paul and the band, George and the band."[16]

"The White Album" acknowledges that the Beatles' old creative power structure no longer works, that the old system is in peril, but it is unable to put anything in its place. The exception to this is that all the singles issued at the time remained the province of Lennon-McCartney, again denying Harrison his creative due. "The White Album," good as it certainly is, amounts to a missed opportunity to reform the Beatles' creative structure to allow for rapidly changing circumstances. Later, both John and Paul openly admitted that it was during the making of "The White Album" that things grew openly fractious for the first time and the breakup started, with Ringo even quitting for two weeks.

By the time of *Let It Be* (1970), it is all over. For anyone who has watched the excruciating May 1970 film of the making of the album, the lowlight has to be when an exasperated Paul runs into a beyond-caring George, who mockingly tells him he will play whatever Paul wants, however Paul wants, all the while meaning the exact opposite. George later called the making of the album "the low of all-time."[17]

Frustrated by the poor working conditions in the frigid Twickenham film studio, and rightly perceiving that John was disengaging himself creatively from the group just as Paul was annoyingly becoming increasingly domineering in an effort to keep the Beatles together, George quit the band for twelve days in January 1969, only to be temporarily lured back.[18] It was still a year before the final breakup, but

[16] Jonathan Gould, *Can't Buy Me Love: The Beatles, Britain, and America* (New York: Three Rivers Press, 2007), p. 509.

[17] Mark Lewisohn, *The Complete Beatles Guide: The Definitive Day-by-Day Guide to the Beatles' Entire Career* (Chicago: Chicago Review Press, 2010), p. 310.

[18] Peter Doggett, *You Never Give Me Your Money: The Beatles After the Breakup* (New York: HarperCollins, 2009), pp. 60–63.

Harrison not only correctly analyzed that the Beatles' finely honed system was collapsing but also understood all too well the reasons for it in the changing status within the band of himself, Lennon, and McCartney.

Harrison has had enough because the world around him hasn't changed, even as his song-writing abilities have. A Lennon-McCartney duopoly no longer makes sense to two of the three key protagonists. George Harrison no longer wants to wait for the other two to take notice of his creative flowering. John Lennon no longer wants to carry the significant burden of keeping the group together, given his other preoccupations and weariness at being the co-leader of a system he increasingly cares less and less about.

Neither of these systemic shifts happened out of the blue, and both had been commented on for several years. But nothing systemically changed to keep up with these altered creative realities. As such, a system—the Beatles—that had flourished so magnificently for so long, came to an abrupt end with *Abbey Road* (ironically when George wrote the masterpieces "Here Comes the Sun" and "Something").

Things were so bad at the start of *Abbey Road* that John proposed that the Beatles put all of his songs on one side and all of Paul's on the other. (Tellingly, George was still left out of John's suggestion.) Ironically, it was only at this late stage that Harrison truly emerged, becoming the surprise creative force on the Beatles' last album. The majestic "Something" from *Abbey Road* became Harrison's first A-side single ever, and the second-most-covered of all the Beatles' songs. At the time John admitted it was the best track on this very strong swan song for the group.

The great irony was that just as the Beatles were disintegrating, Harrison finally achieved the hard-won creative equality that he had yearned for over the past years. During the making of the album, Harrison asserted far more creative control than he had up until then, aggressively rejecting suggestions for changes to his contributions, especially from McCartney. The Beatles were at last evolving into a multipolar order that suited the new creative power realities in the band. But for the group it was too little, too late.

The world had changed. The creative power constellation within the Beatles had changed. But the power dynamic within the group had not. This is the classic definition of a failed system. Everyone knew exactly what he was referring to when Harrison named his fine first post-Beatles record *All Things Must Pass.*

How the West Can Avoid the Beatles' Fate

The West must adopt a three-pronged strategy if it is to avoid the systemic fate of the Fab Four. First, it must re-engage George Harrison—the emerging market powers—on new terms that actually reflect today's changed multipolar global geopolitical and macroeconomic realities. It must forge a new global democratic alliance with rising regional powers, connecting itself more substantially to South Africa, Australia, Canada, Israel, Japan, Indonesia, Brazil, Mexico, and India.

The single greatest strategic challenge for the next generation is determining whether the emerging regional democratic powers can be successfully integrated into today's global order. To save the world we live in will be a tall order, but not an impossible one. However, the only chance of success is to first take a long look at the Beatles story, at how systems fall apart— realizing how perilously close to the edge of the cliff we truly are.

Second, the West itself must be bound together anew; Lennon-McCartney must recommit to the band, in this case the project of serving as the ordering powers in an increasingly factious world. The common grand strategic project of enticing the emerging democratic powers into becoming stakeholders of the present international order can serve as a large portion of the glue that relinks Britain, Europe, and America.

Finally, the revitalized global order must repel any and all revolutionary challenges from revisionist powers; the Beatles must see off Led Zeppelin. Over time China must be economically lured into defending the present order, even as it is strategically hedged against in the South China and East China Seas.

Russia, merely a fading, if dangerous, regional power at best, must be firmly contained within its very limited sphere of influence while endemic economic pressures increasingly cripple the Putin regime.

Bloodthirsty ISIS, which can be given nothing in terms of concessions as it wants everything, must simply be eradicated over time, as is presently happening. Each revisionist challenge, then, is very different, but all must be seen to if the present global order is to endure.

But the Beatles analogy holds, as does what it fundamentally teaches geopolitical risk analysts everywhere. Seemingly stable systems can be fragile things, requiring constant analytical reassessment and the advocacy of proactive policies to nurture them, flowing from this analysis. A geopolitical risk analyst's work is never done.

The Analytical Imperative
to Closely Track Changes in Systems

Ironically for Harrison, the freedom he had craved for so long when he found himself confined within the Beatles never fully yielded the creative renaissance he had dreamed of. Following the great success of *All Things Must Pass* (which was number one in both the United States and the United Kingdom), Harrison's post-Beatles career, as with the rest of the Fab Four, was commercially and creatively uneven. No member of the band was ever able to fully replicate the magic the Beatles had conjured up together.

Along with his close friend, the sitar virtuoso Ravi Shankar, Harrison was so moved by the plight of the refugees from the conflict in South Asia in the early 1970s that he organized the 1971 Concert for Bangladesh, the precursor to the many later benefit rock events that have become an enduring part of the cultural landscape.

In the late 1980s, Harrison founded the short-lived but platinum-selling super-group the Traveling Wilburys, along with rock legends Bob Dylan, Roy Orbison, and Tom Petty. On December 30, 1999, in a frightening reminder of the earlier murder of John Lennon in New York in 1980, Harrison and his wife Olivia were attacked by an unhinged fan wielding a kitchen knife in their England home. Before Olivia managed to subdue him with a lamp, the assailant stabbed Harrison more than forty times, puncturing a lung and causing him head injuries.

Sadly, George's reprieve from death was to be short-lived. Just under two years later, on November 29, 2001, Harrison, a long-time smoker, died in Los Angeles at the untimely age of fifty-eight from throat cancer. Per his wishes, George's ashes were scattered in the Ganges and Yamuna Rivers in India, his spiritual home.

After the Beatles' breakup, George drifted away from John Lennon, largely because of his strong and enduring dislike of John's controversial second wife, Yoko Ono. However, as time went by, George and Paul McCartney made a sort of peace with one another, even working together on the successful *Beatles Anthology* documentary. However, to the end of George's days, both these boyhood friends admitted that, with prolonged contact, they still tended to get on one another's nerves, echoing the dark days of *Let It Be*.

Paul's honest response to George's death mirrored the ambiguous relationship the two had long had. One part love and another part slightly patronizing, McCartney responded to George's untimely death by referring to him as his "baby brother."[19] Both the closeness and the sense of systemic hierarchy remained, even after all the years.

For geopolitical risk analysts, assessing global power systems and closely tracking their changes over time is a major part of the job. A failure to do so, to keep up with evolving trends, can lead directly to analytical and policy disasters, as happened in the case of the Beatles. However, to paraphrase the etched in stone Jagger-Richards partnership, if analysts try sometimes—ever re-checking their systemic analysis for signs of change—they might just get what they need in terms of understanding the world.

[19] Oliver Poole and Hugh Davies, "I'll Always Love Him, He's My Baby Brother Says a Tearful McCartney," *(London) Daily Telegraph*, December 1, 2001.

CHAPTER ELEVEN

1978: The Butterfly Effect in Political Risk

OR DENG XIAOPING AND THE PERILS OF A DRUNKEN SEA CAPTAIN

Mastering Real-World Bolts from the Blue

Geopolitical risk analysis is only as good as the unplanned-for real-world events that it rubs up against. However elegant the assessment, however spot-on the analysis, it must survive contact with the random. Or, as when John Kennedy asked British Prime Minister Harold Macmillan what worried him, the sage old premier supposedly responded, "Events, dear boy, events."

While by definition such random events are beyond human control, that does not mean they cannot be analytically managed. It is the job of the geopolitical risk analyst to identify weak spots in today's political constellations, links that could be broken when an unforeseen event blows up, where a single spark can ignite a prairie fire, such as occurred following the assassination of Archduke Franz Ferdinand in Sarajevo in 1914, precipitating the calamity of the Great War. Dealing with the "butterfly effect" in foreign relations—wherein small random events have outsized consequences—is a major element necessary for mastering geopolitical risk analysis, coming under the Pythia's typological sub-heading "Make a pledge and mischief is nigh." Analysts must check, and check again, for a system's weak links, waiting for the day when they must be instantly shored up in order to head off potential disaster.

Chinese paramount leader Deng Xiaoping is the most important great man of the twentieth century whom the average Westerner has no real idea about. Following the lunacy of Mao's Cultural Revolution, Deng almost single-handedly changed the course of Chinese and world history by rationally and methodically opening up the Chinese system, thereby laying the groundwork for Beijing's astonishing rise.

Further, Deng propagated a foreign policy expertly and rationally calibrated to limit Chinese geopolitical risk at the very time when the country was precariously beginning to economically take wing. Yet for all his work, China's future stability and prosperity hangs by a thread. For this thoughtful, subtle, intelligent foreign policy legacy is increasingly in peril, both at the hands of more bellicose successors, like current paramount leader Xi Jinping, and owing to Macmillan's "events."

For Beijing, the unforeseen event is the problem its undoubted rise has caused for both its nervous, immediate neighbors and the United States, the greatest power in both the world as well as in East Asia. The countervailing strategic pressures that have naturally been brought to bear to contest China's ascension to great power status make the region as a whole susceptible to the butterfly effect, whereby a single drunken sea captain could usher in a time of war and chaos in East Asia, presently the economic powerhouse for future growth in the world.

Preparing for the unplanned is a last and vital elemental weapon in a first-rate geopolitical risk analyst's armory. No analytical structure, no understanding of grand geopolitical systems, no incisive political or economic assessment, is worth the paper it is printed on if it cannot survive contact with the unforeseen circumstances that make up so much of real life. Supplely adapting to the unknowable—along with possessing the humility to know that the unforeseen is sure to happen along the way, jarring the best of analysis—is an absolutely essential quality for a world-class analyst to make their own.

Deng Xiaoping Crafts China's Successful Mercantilist Foreign Policy

China has been blessed in that its stratospheric rise to global economic and political prominence was guided by Deng Xiaoping, one of the most important and underrated statesmen of the twentieth century. In contrast to his colleague (and often rival) Mao Zedong, Deng understood that foreign and domestic policy are about limits, and that China's foreign policy strategy must be indelibly tied to its specific domestic circumstances.

For Deng, this meant that just as China was economically taking off—albeit from a very low base—Beijing's foreign policy had to be characterized by caution, almost quietism; nothing could be allowed to get in the way of economic growth, which Deng knew would bring China at last back to the top table of great powers within a generation. As he put it in the 1990s, "Keep a cool head and maintain a low profile. Never take the lead—but aim to do something big."[1]

It is not that Deng did not ultimately share the seemingly more aggressive foreign policy goals of today's Chinese leadership. Rather, he knew that achieving them would take time and was entirely predicated on Beijing continuing to grow at an astronomical rate, without external forces threatening that growth.

In fact, the genius of Deng—following the calamity of the Cultural Revolution—was to re-harness the Communist

---

[1] Malcolm Moore, "China: The New Rulers of the World," *(London) Daily Telegraph*, April 19, 2008.

Party's legitimacy (its "Mandate of Heaven") to two forces that were both organically and indelibly a long-standing part of China's political culture: capitalism and nationalism.

With Hong Kong and Macau reverting to China as a result of his initiatives, and with the Party retaining a firm grip on both Tibet and Xinjiang provinces, Deng's generation fulfilled its nationalist goal: providing China—with the glaring exception of the Tiananmen Square tragedy—with the magic elixir of stability. In turn, Deng's market opening made China the unquestioned great economic success story of the latter part of the twentieth century. This is why, despite the recent (and economically inevitable) slowdown, China's ruling elite is in no immediate danger.

It is perhaps unsurprising that since China's rise in the late 1970s, it has broadly followed the foreign policy contours of another ascending power that burst upon the international stage two centuries before—the United States of America. Under the dominating genius of Alexander Hamilton, America perfected a mercantilist international stance, desperately trying to avoid political fights with the great powers of the day, France and England. Trading with everyone, the United States kept the lowest of political profiles, all in an effort to secure its tremendous economic potential.

Since the days of the equally impressive Deng, Beijing has followed a similar strategy throughout the world. Even now, as Paramount Leader Xi Jinping finally alters the terms of Deng's engagement with China's nearby Asian neighbors, opting for a more aggressive and interventionist approach, Beijing continues to hew to its old mercantilist foreign policy the further from China one gets. That the policy has remained largely unaltered for almost forty years is evidence of its tremendous success.

In late 1978, as Deng rose to ultimate power, China found itself a poor, isolated country, just getting back onto its feet following the ravages of the Cultural Revolution of the 1960s and 1970s. While the internal Chinese market was even then a source of great hope for China's future, economic success—after all of the Maoist failures—seemed an implausibly distant dream. This was the domestic context in which Deng's foreign policy was born.

China's stupendous economic growth has been significantly bolstered by its low-key foreign policy, which has placed the avoidance of disputes and war—never beneficial for a country enjoying rapid catchup growth—at its core. China's mercantilist strategy was further reinforced as securing long-term supplies of raw materials to feed its ravenous manufacturing industries became a centerpiece of both Chinese economic and foreign policy thinking.

However, if the mercantilist strategy is simple enough, the tactics to achieve its end goals are daunting. Looking at China's regional policy in the Middle East provides a fine illustration of how Deng's foreign policy works in practice today.

First, China talks to absolutely everyone in the region—with the exception of ISIS—playing no favorites whatsoever with the five great regional powers: Turkey, Iran, Saudi Arabia, Egypt, and Israel. It is one of the only countries in the world to truly get on with all of them. Above all else, and ruefully noting the catastrophic American example, Beijing wants to avoid becoming militarily entangled in the cesspool of Middle Eastern regional politics.

The second rule of China's mercantilist strategy is that its foreign policy is like water: it flows along the path of least resistance—in this case, away from its established and still stronger American rival. This is the reason China has made such a big push for raw materials into Africa and other emerging market countries: precisely because the Americans have fewer interests there. In this conflict-free zone, Beijing can quietly secure its economic goals away from the limelight.

Third, China's policy in the Middle East is heavy on economics but very light on politics. For example, during the nuclear crisis with Tehran, Beijing largely accommodated but also restrained the United States and Europe over confronting Iran, just as it has largely accommodated but also restrained Russia over its support for the murderous Assad regime in Syria. In both cases, China has managed to successfully walk a very fine tactical line, remaining a valued part of outside great power coalitions, all the while being seen inside the Middle East as a necessary force for moderation.

Deng's masterful foreign policy has fulfilled its overall strategic purpose. Two generations of tranquility have allowed China's astounding rates of growth to continue, without the outside world imperiling its takeoff, and propelled the country to great power status. But even so rational, so calibrated, and so well crafted an analysis as Deng's is at the very real mercy of outside events that simply cannot be controlled.

China is haunted by the specter of calamity in the seas surrounding it, finding itself subject to a mythical figure who could at a stroke undo all of Deng's genius: the drunken Chinese sea captain. So finely balanced and on edge are the South China and East China Seas—hauntingly like Europe in 1914—that a very plausible and utterly uncontrollable series of events could in an instant destroy decades of Chinese subtlety, plunging the whole world into calamity.

Deng Survives Mao and Transforms China

Deng Xiaoping, the paramount leader of the People's Republic of China, was born in Sichuan province on August 22, 1904. Encouraged by his relatively prosperous landowning father to live abroad, Deng spent much of his youth in the 1920s studying and working in France, where he met fellow expatriate Zhou Enlai, who became a lifelong political ally. Deng joined the Chinese Communist Party in 1923.

During the 1930s Chinese civil war between the Communists and the nationalists under Chiang Kai-Shek, Deng served as a political commissar in the rural hinterlands of the country. A veteran of the fabled "Long March" of 1934–1935—the iconic strategic retreat that saved the Red Army from total defeat at the hands of the nationalist Kuomintang (KMT) forces—Deng endured the epic 5,600-mile trek in just 370 days as the Communist armies in the south of China managed to re-locate to the country's vast northern and western provinces. Deng became part of the Party's great survival myth; his later power partly emanated from having participated in this seminal event.

It was on the Long March that Mao became the preeminent leader of the movement, at the time having Deng's unstinting support. In fact, from the mid-1930s onwards, despite the many dramatic political twists and turns in store for the Chinese Communist Party (CCP), Mao and Zhou Enlai (who was also in a key command position during the Long March) would de facto retain the top two positions in the Party until their deaths in 1976.

Following World War II, the final defeat of the KMT, and the founding of the People's Republic of China (PRC) in 1949, Deng served in Tibet and other southwestern provinces, consolidating fledgling Communist control over this vast region.

From 1958 to 1962, Mao put in place his disastrous Great Leap Forward, the economic and social campaign designed to vault China almost overnight to the first rank of powers. Almost instantaneously, the impatient revolutionary attempted to transform China from its traditional agrarian base into a modern socialist society, through breakneck industrialization and collectivization.

Such horribly misplaced revolutionary fervor was directly responsible for the Great Chinese Famine that ensued, the deadliest such catastrophe in the history of the world: an unfathomable 23 million to 46 million people were killed. For a time following this unmitigated disaster, Mao's power waned.

In 1960, with the cataclysmic failure of Mao's Great Leap Forward, more moderate forces such as Deng, now in charge of the Party's secretariat, along with Premier Zhou and President (and head of state) Liu Shaoqi, set about reconstructing the Chinese economy from the ashes.

Deng's pragmatic economic policies were for the first time in direct opposition to Mao's far more doctrinaire political ideology. As he put it famously in July 1962, "It doesn't matter whether a cat is black or white, as long as it catches mice."[2] From this point onwards, Deng and Mao were in almost constant opposition to one another in terms of both policy and ideology.

But the master revolutionary was just biding his time. Mao's startling comeback came with the unleashing of the Cultural Revolution in 1966—a populist, radical leftist reassertion of the CCP's revolutionary roots—which was to last the better part of a decade and throw China into chaos again, even as it elevated Mao to semi-divine status in his country.

Insinuating to the fanatical students who comprised his personal Red Guards militia and to the army that hidden rightist, bourgeois elements in the CCP itself had perverted his revolutionary vision, Mao called on his allies to set things back onto their proper revolutionary path.

[2] Hung Li, *China's Political Situation and the Power Struggle in Peking* (Hong Kong: Lung Men Press, 1977), p. 107.

In theory, the Cultural Revolution set out to purge China once and for all of any lingering capitalist and traditionalist elements, replacing them with Mao's ideological disciples. In practice, it marked the return of Mao to a supreme position in the CCP, allowing him to settle scores with the moderates who had sidelined him following the calamity of the Great Leap Forward.

In October 1966, both Liu and Deng were branded as leaders of these hidden bourgeois, reactionary forces. Both were purged, with an ailing Liu first being placed under house arrest, then being denied medical treatment; he died in 1969. Deng was forced by the Red Guards to confess to his capitalist ways of thinking. He was then sent away from Beijing to be "re-educated": in his mid-sixties he worked for four years at the Jiangxi tractor factory.[3]

Tragically for his family, Deng's first son, Deng Pufang, in 1968 jumped out a window at Peking University while being interrogated and tortured by the Red Guards. His back broken, he was rushed to a hospital but was denied admission. By the time he reached a clinic that would accept him weeks later, he was paralyzed.

But the chaos of the Cultural Revolution could not continue forever. By 1974, with the economy once again in dire straits and Zhou (the last moderate standing) falling ill to the cancer that would eventually kill him, Deng was rehabilitated at Zhou's urging to manage the country. Deng was simply too able to be squandered by a hard-pressed China.

After Zhou completely withdrew from politics in January 1975, Deng was placed in charge by a wary Mao of the government, party, and military, serving as the chief of staff of the People's Liberation Army (PLA). True to form, Deng

---

[3] Fortunately, Deng was sent to work at the tractor factory as a fitter, a job he had performed in his youth in Paris.

immediately initiated far more pragmatic economic policies, much as he had done after the Great Leap Forward.

But the dysfunctional cycle of Deng's personal relations with Mao continued. In late 1975, Mao came to fear and resent Deng again, calling him China's foremost "rightist" and directing Deng to write a self-criticism of his own views in November. Deng was formally purged again on April 7, 1976, and stripped of all his positions.

But while Deng was awaiting his uncertain fate, Mao finally died, on September 9, 1976. Shortly thereafter, the Gang of Four—Mao's most radical supporters, including his ferocious wife Jiang Qing—were arrested, and the fevered horror of the Cultural Revolution at last passed from the Chinese scene. By July 1977, Deng was back again as vice premier, in essence becoming China's second-most-powerful figure.

Hua Guofeng, Mao's lackluster chosen heir, wanted to reverse the social damage caused by the Cultural Revolution, but also ruinously intended to keep the Chinese economic system firmly wedded to Soviet-style central planning. Unlike Hua, Deng felt that no policy should be rejected outright merely because it was not associated with the thoughts of Mao. He would usher in a new and necessary age of pragmatism that dramatically bettered China's fortunes.

Deng spent the next few years outmaneuvering the hapless Hua. On December 18, 1978, at the pivotal Third Plenum of the Eleventh Central Committee, Deng called for "a liberation of thoughts" and urged the CCP to abandon rigid ideological dogma and "seek truth from facts."[4] Hua was sidelined (he was allowed to quietly resign in September 1980), and the definitive break with Maoism was made. The economic reform era of Deng Xiaoping had begun.

[4]Ironically, an old Maoist adage.

While named the core leader of the second generation of the CCP, Deng set about governing in a very different style from his long-time rival. Adopting a far more collegial approach than the dictatorial Mao, Deng never held office as president, premier, or general-secretary of the Party and instead shared power with a group of his senior Party cadres called the Eight Elders, appointing allies to the key formal governmental positions.

Deng's only senior position was to serve as chairman of the Central Military Commission, seeing to it that both internal and external security matters were under his direct control. In this hidden-hand form of collegial government, important decisions of the Eight Elders were often informally made in Deng's private residence.

For all this, Deng was the undoubted paramount leader of China from December 1978 until 1992. With the Eight Elders, Deng was able on three occasions to displace Party leaders he felt were imperiling his reforms: Hua in 1980–1981, Hu Yaobang in 1987, and Zhao Ziyang over the Tiananmen crisis in 1989. Without a significant rival blocking his path, Deng initiated the most successful and far-reaching market economy reforms of the latter half of the twentieth century, catapulting China in a historical instant back to great power status.

Abandoning Mao's ruinous policies, Deng initiated an economic plan that called for "Socialism with Chinese Characteristics," a form of state-directed market economics light-years away from Mao's desire for complete control of the forces of production in that it allowed for significant economic liberalization, all the while retaining complete political control. Encouraging private competition, Deng opened China to foreign investment and the global marketplace.

The new regime's priorities were blessedly clear after all the years of chaos caused by the Cultural Revolution. Deng's "Four Modernizations" focused on the economy, agriculture, science and technological development, and national defense. His pragmatic reforms dramatically shifted China's overall development to a strong emphasis on export-led growth.

Most importantly, Deng provided a new ideological template and political support, allowing bottom-up economic reform to take place. He was recognized officially and correctly as "the chief architect of China's economic reforms and China's socialist modernization." Boldly, Deng provided ideological cover for the first generation of Chinese businessmen, saying, "There are no fundamental contradictions between a socialist system and a market system."[5]

Typically, and in complete contrast to the top-down policies of Mao, Deng would allow local, bottom-up reforms to proceed, then adopting the successful efforts at a regional or national level. For example, in a practice a universe away from the Great Leap Forward's forced collectivization, Deng's regime allowed peasants to earn extra income by having private plots of land. Deng also established Special Economic Zones, where foreign investment and market liberalization were actively encouraged and GDP boomed.

But for all his many successes, the widespread dissatisfaction with corruption, the Party's stranglehold on political power, and the increased inequality that China's economic success brought in its wake led to the Tiananmen Square crisis (April 15–June 4, 1989), the most serious threat to the Party during Deng's administration.

Sparked by mourning at the death of reformist Hu Yaobang, a Deng associate who had been sidelined by the

---

[5]"Socialism and Market Economics Aren't Incompatible," *Time*, November 4, 1985.

Eight Elders earlier in the decade, the daily protests in the center of Beijing led to an ominous split within the Party itself: General Secretary Zhao Ziyang, Deng's pro-market ally, actively sided with the student and worker protesters against hard-liners in the Party, who were clustered around Premier Li Peng.

After hesitating, the Eight Elders, at last convinced that the survival of the Party was at stake, and having just seen revolutions threaten socialism in much of Eastern Europe, declared martial law, sending more than 200,000 troops into Beijing to quell the protests, by force if necessary. On the night of June 3–4, 1989, hundreds, if not thousands, of protesters were killed. Zhao was placed under house arrest for the rest of his life. It was the darkest event of Deng's life, one which temporarily led to a real diminution in his power.

With hard-liners in the ascendant in the immediate aftermath of the Tiananmen crisis, Deng saw the impetus for his economic reforms falter as an increasingly powerful faction in the Party opposed them. In his last contribution to the life of his country, Deng jump-started the reform process, following the publicity of his 1992 southern tour.

Deng had officially retired in 1989, stepping down as head of the Central Military Commission. However, even without holding office of any sort, he was still widely viewed as remaining the paramount leader of China, wielding power behind the scenes. In the spring of 1992, using his latent grip over the CCP to reinvigorate the economic reform process, Deng set out on his southern tour of the country.

Visiting Guangzhou, Shenzhen, Zhuhai, and Shanghai, Deng made a number of speeches generating local support for his economic agenda and criticizing those in the Party who were against further opening of the country. Strongly backing the rise of Chinese entrepreneurs, Deng bluntly said that leftist elements in the country were more dangerous than rightist ones. He insisted that Maoism must not be allowed to undo the economic reform program that was remaking China.

At first, the national media, which was under the sway of his political enemies, ignored Deng's tour. However, Jiang Zemin, since 1989 the general-secretary of the Party, eventually sided with Deng, and the national media belatedly but lavishly reported on the importance of Deng's tour, now several months after it had taken place. With Jiang's support, Deng's southern tour enshrined his economic reforms as a permanent feature in Chinese life, safe-guarding the country's astounding economic rise.

Having personally lived through every major event in the Party's history throughout the tumultuous twentieth century, Deng died on February 19, 1997, at the advanced age of ninety-two. Since his death, the CCP has broadly maintained his policy of strict political control coupled with economic openness.

Deng's remarkable life left China with one other enduring legacy: a quietist, mercantilist foreign policy. Such a calibration makes entire sense, as China needed peace and stability in order for Deng's audacious economic reforms to take root and grow.

But for all Deng's undoubted genius in bequeathing China a rational, joined-up, and coherent foreign and domestic policy, like all man-made constructions, the continued success of such a strategy rests on the slender reeds of random events not being allowed to undo Deng's work of a lifetime. His inspired analysis, like the best work of geopolitical risk analysts, must survive the chaos of unforeseen events that can—from out of nowhere and at a stroke—destroy the most inspired insights.

Macmillan Salvages Britain's Place in the World

All through his passage through time he had been haunted by unwanted ghosts, both of his own life and also that of his country. Now, in December 1962, Harold Macmillan found himself in the Bahamas, attempting to save what could be saved—to salvage the reputation of Great Britain as one of the world's great powers.

The broader context of the Nassau Conference was that of Britain's place in a post-Suez world. The Suez Crisis—initiated by President Gamal Abdel Nasser when he nationalized the Suez Canal in Egypt on July 26, 1956, a butterfly effect event that had come seemingly out of nowhere—had been the acknowledged swan song both of European imperialism and of Britain and France as superpowers.

Macmillan had not personally covered himself in glory during the debacle. Serving at the time as chancellor of the exchequer, the number two in the British government, he told Prime Minister Anthony Eden (whom he disliked) that he would resign if force was not used against Nasser. This threat bolstered Eden's bellicosity, and Britain—along with France and Israel—subsequently invaded the canal zone, as European imperial countries habitually had done for centuries to put a little local difficulty right.

But times had changed. Most damaging, both Macmillan and the Eden government had entirely misread the anti-colonial position of President Dwight D. Eisenhower. Serving as a protégé of Winston Churchill during World War II, Macmillan had achieved cabinet rank and real power as Britain's minister resident for the Mediterranean. From 1942 to 1945, Macmillan had worked hand in glove with Ike, and a mutual admiration followed. Eisenhower said of Macmillan later that he was "a straight, fine man, and so far as he [Eisenhower] is concerned, the outstanding one of the British he served with during the war."[6] Macmillan and the Eden cabinet blithely thought that wartime camaraderie would sway American opinion.

Instead, Suez proved to be the bolt from the blue that signaled the definitive end of the British Empire. Macmillan met with his old friend Eisenhower privately on September 25, 1956, coming away again misjudging the US response to Nasser. In November 1956, Britain invaded Egypt, in collusion with France and Israel, only to be shocked by America's vehement anti-colonial response.

The run on sterling—a financial crisis caused directly by American pressure on London in the wake of the invasion—caused Macmillan, serving as Britain's chief financial officer, to dramatically change his mind about the incursion. As was bitterly noted by Eden's dwindling band of supporters, Macmillan was the first one in and the first one out of the crisis.

With his political position utterly untenable, Eden resigned as prime minister on January 9, 1957, and Macmillan took over the next day. Following the Suez shambles, the new prime minister told the queen that he could not guarantee his government would last six weeks. In the end, it endured for six years.

But Suez was not the first bolt from the blue to dramatically alter Macmillan's life. As was true for so many of his generation, the Great War of 1914–1918 changed everything. The scion of the famous publishing house, Macmillan was at Balliol College, Oxford, from 1912 to 1914, the halcyon days of his life. With the dramatic advent of European-wide war in August 1914, he did not hesitate to immediately volunteer for service. Little did Macmillan—or the millions of others who followed his brave example—realize it, but the world and the life he had known were coming to an end.

[6] D. R. Thorpe, *Supermac* (London: Chatto and Windus, 2010), pp. 352–53.

Serving with distinction in the Grenadier Guards, Captain Macmillan was wounded three times in the war, most severely in September 1916, during the Battle of the Somme. Badly shot through the hip, Macmillan lay in a trench for ten hours, sometimes feigning death as German troops passed over him, sometimes reading the Greek playwright Aeschylus for comfort, in the original Greek.[7]

Macmillan spent the final two years of the war in various hospitals, undergoing a seemingly endless series of operations; his hip would take four years to finally heal, and the pain from the wound would never entirely leave him.

But if Macmillan's physical pain from the war was considerable, the psychological cost was even greater. Of the twenty-eight students who were in his year at Balliol, only one other classmate survived the Great War. Hearing that his university friends had been butchered to a man, Macmillan, sorrowfully noting that Oxford would never be the same, chose not to finish his studies. This was a man with a high regard for how unthought-of events can determine the future.

Greatly regretting the damage he had personally done, which had led to the diminution of Britain's standing in the world over Suez, Macmillan used his premiership to make a grand effort to repair British foreign policy. First, realizing the Empire was on its last legs, Macmillan set about the process of decolonization, especially in sub-Saharan Africa, in as painless a way as possible.

Second, when forced to choose between France/Europe and the United States, Macmillan came down strongly on the side of Washington setting about rebuilding the "special relationship." One of the many ways he did this was to jointly work with the American nuclear program. In fact,

[7]Ibid., p. 57.

his staunch unwillingness to disclose US nuclear secrets to France contributed to Paris's veto of Britain's proposed entry into the European Economic Community.[8]

Shorn of its empire and cut off (by France) from Europe, Macmillan had put all of his strategic eggs in the American basket. As he somewhat arrogantly went around saying in this new post-Suez era, Britain would function as the wily Greeks had done for the young thrusting Romans—serving as wise, experienced, world-weary interpreters for their powerful but naive patrons regarding how running the world really worked.[9]

But for a third time in his life, unforeseen events hurtled down on him, threatening Macmillan's celebrated equanimity. Once again, the "special relationship"—the buttress that was now all that was sustaining Britain's post-Suez standing in the world—was in danger of collapsing, and all over the inadvertent cancellation of an obscure missile program.

Skybolt, a ballistic missile jointly developed by the United Kingdom and the United States during the early 1960s, had run well over projected costs. Without giving any thought to the broader strategic symbolism of Skybolt—the fact that it served as a concrete illustration of the enduring US-UK strategic partnership—President Kennedy unilaterally canceled the program because it had become enormously expensive, and also because it was so far behind schedule that it would have been obsolete before it was deployed.

However, utterly unexpectedly, the cancellation of Skybolt provoked a crisis of confidence between the United States and Britain. The optics of the cancellation caused unthought-of tensions in US-UK relations, as it looked as if the United

---

[8] Richard Lamb, *The Macmillan Years 1957–1963: The Emerging Truth* (London: John Murray, 1995), pp. 14–15.

[9] Alistair Horne, *Macmillan: The Official Biography* (London: Macmillan), p. 160.

States was yet again unilaterally cutting Britain down to size, this time high-handedly divesting London of its independent nuclear deterrent. Given that Macmillan had staked everything strategically on the centrality of the "special relationship," the Skybolt crisis came to be seen as a litmus test of the true post-Suez value of the US-British alliance.

Throughout the autumn of 1962 and especially after the cancellation of Skybolt in November 1962, the British minister of defense, Peter Thorneycroft, and the US secretary of defense, Robert McNamara, had constant talks on Skybolt and the implications of its cancellation. Addressing Parliament on December 17, 1962, just ahead of the Nassau Conference, Thorneycroft said, "I have stressed throughout my talks with Mr. McNamara the serious consequences for the United Kingdom of a cancellation of this project, and I can assure the House that the United States Government can be in no doubt on that aspect of the matter."[10]

Macmillan was left to walk a very fine diplomatic line at the Nassau Conference. He was eager not to alienate the Americans, but also absolutely needed to ensure Britain's independent nuclear deterrent. Failure to do so would call the value—from a British point of view—of the whole "special relationship" into question, and along with it, Macmillan's government itself. The prime minister had to either convince Kennedy to countermand his original order and retain Skybolt, or secure a viable replacement. Britain's perceived status as a great power hung in the balance.

At the beginning of the conference, Kennedy, still not understanding the strategic and political implications for Britain, appeared reluctant to provide London with the Polaris missiles which the British government regarded as the only realistic substitute for Skybolt.

---

[10] *Hansard*, House of Commons, December 17, 1962, vol. 669, pp. 893–900.

Fortunately for the prime minister, he was just the sort of man Kennedy instinctively liked: brave, stylish, witty, and unflappable. They were even distantly related by marriage to the aristocratic Cavendish family, which included Macmillan's wife Dorothy and Kennedy's favorite sister, Kathleen.

It was at this pivotal moment, with Kennedy wavering, that Macmillan successfully managed to save his world this third time it was threatened by unforeseen events. Standing to speak, Macmillan invoked his own horrendous experiences in the Great War and eloquently detailed what Britain had sacrificed for the world in its storied past in the greater cause of preserving Western civilization.

After tugging at the president's heartstrings by rightfully reminding him of what Britain had given and meant to the "special relationship," the prime minister dropped the hammer. "Macmillan . . . demanded Polaris and threatened an 'agonizing reappraisal' of British policy if he did not get it."[11]

In a conversation with the British ambassador to Washington, Kennedy at last realized how devastating the Skybolt controversy was for Macmillan in particular, and for the "special relationship" in general.

So, at the Nassau Conference, Macmillan managed to save face. In the end, an agreement was reached, with the United States providing Britain with Polaris missiles on extremely favorable terms. The post-Suez "special relationship" looked like it delivered the goods for Britain after all, and London's status as a great power was salvaged. Harold Macmillan had (just) managed to stop random events from upsetting his world yet another time.

Macmillan had a parting geopolitical risk warning for the dashing young president. Since their first encounter back in

---

[11] Marc Trachtenberg, *A Constructed Peace: The Making of the European Settlement, 1945–1963* (Princeton, NJ: Princeton University Press, 1999), p. 360.

1961, Macmillan had been somewhat taken aback by Kennedy's reliance on his vast, and ever-present, team of advisers. In Nassau in December 1962, on the evening they arrived in the Bahamas, Kennedy and Macmillan—at the prime minister's urging—walked alone together for a long time.

They immediately hit it off, talking not only about the Skybolt crisis and domestic politics but also about their shared interest in history and the things in their lives that both found ridiculous, funny, or deadly serious.

It was during this intimate walk that Macmillan queried Kennedy as to what he feared most. Kennedy, ever the literal rationalist, admitted that nuclear weapons and the American balance-of-payments deficit were the two issues that most frightened him. Kennedy was scared of the known.

However, when the president asked Macmillan what frightened him the most, the prime minister (perhaps mythically) replied, "Events, dear boy, events."[12] Macmillan, unlike the modern, cerebral president, knew from bitter experience that it is the unknown that is to be most feared by analysts of all stripes, as it can—at a stroke—upend the best-laid plans of mice and men.

The Present Tinderbox
in the Waters Surrounding China

And it is just this danger of unforeseen circumstances that today threatens Deng's thoughtful calculations on behalf of his country in the seas ringing China. Given its obvious preoccupation with sustaining economic growth and social

---

[12] There is no conclusive proof that Macmillan said this to Kennedy. He might well have said, "The opposition of events," a phrase that, given his history, he was fond of using. See Elizabeth Knowles, *What They Didn't Say: A Book of Misquotations* (Oxford: Oxford University Press, 2006), p. 33.

stability, Chinese foreign policy has long been guided by Deng Xiaoping's basic precept that it is best to defer major conflicts with outside powers for at least another generation so that China can grow ever relatively stronger compared with its rivals.

However, such a policy has recently been called into question, particularly in Beijing's Asian backyard. China is currently involved in territorial disputes in the South China Sea with nearly all its neighbors and has recently been growing ever more bellicose in staking its claims. In 2010, China reportedly conveyed to the United States that the South China Sea now constituted a "core interest," implying that China's stance there was non-negotiable.

Secretary of State Hillary Clinton replied that the United States had "a national interest in freedom of navigation, open access to Asia's maritime commons and respect for international law in the South China Sea." She called for a multilateral mechanism to resolve disputes there, a stance warmly welcomed by the states of the Association of South East Asian Nations (ASEAN).

Unimpressed by the usual Chinese claims of dominance, as recently as March 2013, Vietnam accused Beijing of firing on one of its fishing vessels in the waters around the Chinese-occupied Paracel Islands, over which the two countries went to war in January 1979.

Beijing is creating muscle to match its more confident diplomacy. China increased its defense spending by 10.7 percent in 2013, to $121 billion, and now has what amounts to the second-largest military budget in the world after the United States, which, however, still spends six times more on defense.

But the problem with Xi Jinping's newly aggressive strategy is that it has almost entirely backfired, driving many of China's neighbors into America's waiting arms. This is the context in which China viewed the Obama administration's "Asia Pivot" so suspiciously.

In the wake of these maritime disputes, ties between Vietnam and America have become almost unimaginably close. Long-time ally Australia has allowed the actual stationing of US Marines in its country for the first time. Habitual South Korean protests about American basing have given way to an eloquent silence. Increasingly riled by escalating disputes over the Senkaku-Diaoyu Islands in the East China Sea, the Abe government in Japan is increasing defense spending for the first time in years, all the while enmeshing itself further in Japan's long-standing alliance with America.

To the other major players in the region (with the conspicuous exception of the Philippines), Washington as a faraway off-shore balancer looks eminently preferable as the dominant power in the region to being pushed around by an all-too-close Chinese neighbor.

The more assertive foreign policy presently being implemented by Xi is conditioned entirely on the great success of Deng's generation. From 1991 to 2013, China's share of global exports of manufactured goods increased from a minuscule 2.3 percent to 18.8 percent. Average real income over that time rose from 4 percent of the American level to fully 25 percent today. Almost overnight, China is a great power once more.

Now that China is domestically secure and economically powerful, Xi has the luxury to cast his eyes to China's near abroad in the South China and East China Seas. But this natural moving away from Deng's methodical, considered foreign policy carries with it the seeds of great danger.

Deng's views on foreign policy can be summed up in the aphorism: "Hide your strength, bide your time."[13] China

[13] Robert A. Manning, "Sun Tzu Would Disapprove of China's Strategy," *National Interest*, August 3, 2013.

has financed deep-water Indian Ocean Rim (IOR) ports in Myanmar, Sri Lanka, and Pakistan and has been displaying an interest in port projects in Kenya, Tanzania, and Bangladesh, emulating the "string of pearls" naval strategy of nineteenth-century Britain.

Quietly, China has been establishing a resource-extraction empire throughout sub-Saharan Africa to link up with these ports. At present, China is constructing a two-ocean commercial strategy in the IOR and the South China Sea, a key step on its road to great power status.

China hysterics are wrong to see this more muscular, adventurous policy as some sort of blueprint for global domination; rather the policy is as old as the Greeks. China is embracing a more bellicose foreign policy because that is what all emerging great powers—such as the United States in the late nineteenth century—end up doing. With endemic internal chaos no longer weakening China, the next logical step is to dominate its near abroad.

While this may be the almost inevitable consequence of China's rise, it does create two major problems for the present leadership. First, an utterly unresolvable structural tension lies at the heart of the increasing controversies in the waters surrounding China: the United States is the dominant power in East Asia, and China wants to be the dominant power in East Asia. Nothing can wish this basic strategic friction away.

In the words of the great American lyricist Johnny Mercer, "somethin's gotta give." China and America are presently frenemies: there is both intense economic cooperation as well as ever-growing strategic competition between them. As such, the present geopolitical position is not sustainable in the long-term; over time the relationship will drift one way or the other.

The Chinese themselves have happened upon a better historical metric for judging how their country's amazing rise should be viewed in the new multipolar era. Speaking on a visit to Washington on September 20, 2013, Wang Yi, China's foreign minister, referred to a Chinese study of fifteen different countries that were geopolitically rising in various eras throughout recorded history.

In eleven cases, confrontation and war broke out between emerging and established powers. The Chinese leadership are right to point to the Thucydides study—so named for an early case study in geopolitical risk analysis, of an emerging Athens fighting an established Sparta in the Peloponnesian War—as confirmation of history's gloomy reality: that quite often established and emerging powers go to war.

This geopolitical problem is what the rest of the world is up against in confronting China. Far more creative diplomacy by America and the rest of the world will be required to beat these daunting odds, instead making Beijing a true stakeholder in the world that lies ahead.

Beijing's second headache is that East Asia itself has grown used to—and has been comforted by—Deng's "softly, softly" approach to foreign policy. Xi Jinping's much more bellicose stance—creating facts on the ground through land reclamation projects on islands in the South China and East China Seas, which China then militarizes—has backfired badly. Suddenly, America has found itself in a stronger strategic position in East Asia simply because of China's increased aggressiveness.

In addition to the cementing of long-standing alliances with Japan, Australia, and South Korea, Washington under President Obama found itself much closer to pivotal India, the ASEAN countries, and even Vietnam and Myanmar. While the whole region is undoubtedly dependent on China as the hub of its astounding economic development, diplomatically and strategically East Asia has hedged its bets (as smaller powers historically so often do) by looking to far-away (and relatively benign) Washington as its primary strategic partner. To put it mildly, this is not something that Beijing desires.

Today's Asia as 1914

Perhaps most hauntingly for geopolitical risk analysts, the structural outline of the present order in Asia resembles nothing so much as the supposedly "unsinkable" pre-1914 world. Both eras are characterized by a particularly peculiar form of multipolarity in which the major players are far from equal in terms of their power, yet the most powerful country in the world (Britain then, the United States now), though in relative decline, remains chairman of the global board by a long way.

For alone amongst great powers, Britain and America have been omnipresent—both economically and in terms of their first-class navies—if not omnipotent; playing a key role in every region of the world, these two countries have been the only true global players on the international scene in the last two centuries. As distant observers of the pivotal Eurasian landmass, in a sense both follow a similar, simple geopolitical imperative: let no competitor dominate either Europe or Asia and all will be well.

Carrying on with the distressingly apt analogy, China fits the bill as the new version of Kaiser Wilhelm's Germany: a rising economic and military power bristling with nationalist indignation at perceived slights—both real and imagined—and increasingly believing that its rise cannot be accommodated by the present international order. Such a point of view leads to states becoming revolutionary powers that are determined to unseat the status quo powers holding them down over the long-term in order to ensure their "place in the sun."

If Beijing makes for a worryingly effective *Kaiserreich*, Prime Minister Shinzō Abe's Japan is Third Republic France to a tee. As obviously declining regional powers—beset by economic torpor and falling relatively ever further strategically behind—they are both directly threatened by scary, aggressive, next-door neighbors. Both countries placed their strategic hopes in alliances with the declining hegemons, Great Britain (in France's case) and the United States (in Japan's).

India is also a convincing stand-in for Czarist Russia—powerful, slightly geographically removed from the situation, yet capable of playing a pivotal role. The aptness of the analogy leaves little room for strategic comfort.

Even the milieu in which the Great War analogy operates is hauntingly similar. Currently, China is exploiting incidents—particularly in the East China and South China Seas—to test the willingness of the United States to stand behind its treaty commitments to Japan, just as in the ten years before 1914 the kaiser provoked a series of international crises to see if Britain would really come to the defense of France under the gun.

Ironically in both cases, the rising power miscalculated, making a general war far more likely as arms races broke out: Japan and East Asia, like France early in the last century, have quickly armed themselves to the teeth in response to their menacing foes. At Davos in January 2014, Abe made precisely this point, comparing the growing strategic rivalry with China to the pre–World War I situation, particularly in regards to the current arms race brewing in Asia.

Then as now, there are almost no significant multilateral security organizations in the region to cushion normal geostrategic blows. So Asia today, like Europe then, is about nationalistic states, with armies and navies, determined to throw their weight around. The leaders of the three major regional powers—Prime Minister Abe of Japan, Prime Minister Modi of India, and Chinese President Xi Jinping—are all strong nationalists.

As was true in 1914, it is easy to see that, with nationalism in all three countries rising to a fever pitch, fundamental issues of strategic credibility would rather quickly be on the line for everyone; turning back (as was true in 1914) would be almost impossible, despite the fact that no one really wants the calamitous war that would ensue.

This lack of multilateral shock absorbers is mainly down to the fact that the Japanese elite have never managed to face up to their country's World War II atrocities. (Their proclivity to pray at the Yasukuni shrine, which commemorates a number of war criminals, could be laughed off as bizarre if it didn't terrify both the South Koreans and the Chinese; imagine how the French would feel if the Germans prayed at the Goebbels shrine.)

South Korea in particular should be, on geopolitical merits alone, Japan's best regional ally (both working together balancing against a resurgent China), but has unnecessarily fraught relations with Tokyo, stemming from Japan's historical amnesia. So instead the still-dominant Americans are forced to shuttle bilaterally between their various Asian allies, scuttling about like a headless chicken trying to keep the geostrategic show on the road.

Like pre-1914 Wilhelmine Germany, China is on the strategic march, especially throwing its weight around the South China Sea, where more than $5 trillion in trade passes through its waters each year. The problem is that Vietnam, Brunei, Malaysia, and Taiwan also have competing claims and increasingly chafe at China's high-handed treatment there, where Beijing is constructing military bases.

At last bearing it no longer, in the summer of 2016 the Philippines took Beijing to court; The Hague ruled that China's preposterous claims to seven-eighths of the South China

Sea (based on the so-called nine-dash line) has no basis in international law. However, China, to the horror of its neighbors, simply ignored the court's decision. The mask has well and truly slipped, revealing China's naked power grab in this most dangerous region in the world.

As was also true in 1914, major powers find themselves locked into treaty commitments, severely hampering their strategic flexibility. Over the disputed Senkaku-Diaoyu Islands in the East China Sea, present US Secretary of Defense James Mattis has made it clear that, while the United States takes no ultimate position over ownership, it regards Japan's present control of the islands as covered by the mutual defense treaty between the allies. Its obligations to Tokyo would compel America to go to war with China if Beijing forced a change in the islands' status.

As such, this central hot spot in Asia—perhaps the most dangerous real estate in today's world—could easily lead to a general war. In essence, Deng's thoughtful foreign policy is at the daily mercy of a drunken Chinese sea captain.

Consider the plausible scenario. A drunken, nationalist Chinese commercial sea captain plants a flag on one of the disputed islands in the East China or South China Sea and is shot by over-zealous government forces from one of the neighboring countries with conflicting claims. China, in turn, demands that the aggressors be handed over to Beijing for justice, based on its ownership of the island. Tokyo refuses, calling on the United States for support. And we are very close to World War III.

As happened with the assassination of Archduke Franz Ferdinand in Sarajevo, such an incident alone might be enough to strike the match. A major crisis could occur at any moment for the United States, crucially one in which it has already subcontracted its sovereign decisions about war and peace to either a newly bellicose Japan or simply to fate itself.

In any case, Washington would find itself under almost unendurable pressure to respond, and in so doing would condemn the world to another cataclysm. At a bare minimum, given the stakes and the doleful pre–World War I example of fixed alliances leading to an abdication of judgment, Washington must conduct endless vigilance of both Beijing and Tokyo so as not to effectively hand over control of America's foreign policy.

Deng's laudable, rational foreign policy system—and perhaps world peace itself—is precariously balanced at the edge of the precipice, dependent on the gods and fate—in other words favorable "events"—to avert catastrophe in Asia every single day.

History Is Never Finished

None of this means that geopolitical risk analysts should give up their day jobs. Sound, creative, systemic analysis of the world they see before them remains the name of the game. However, the telling example of Deng Xiaoping—that even the most rational, reasonable, effective foreign policy analysis is at the mercy of events beyond human control—should give them pause in two basic ways.

First, however good any of us are, humility—a central realist virtue—is in order. The unforeseen can always radically alter even the best analysis. Second, suppleness, the ability to revisit and revise geopolitical risk calculations again and again in light of new (and perhaps jarring) events, is the final hallmark of any first-rate analyst or policy-maker. History, the recording of human events as they occur, is never finished. Neither is the job of the geopolitical risk analyst.

CHAPTER TWELVE

Conclusion: Back to the Pythia's Lair

MASTERING GEOPOLITICAL RISK

Can the Future Be Foretold?

The great goal, the Everest of this book, has been to identify the historical elements that comprise the rules of the road for mastering geopolitical risk analysis and to holistically put our ten commandments to use in explaining the baffling world we presently live in. Having discovered these elements—and illuminated them through the use of historical story-telling, placing them in real-world policy situations throughout the ages—their order of analytical use completes the typology of geopolitical risk analysis, getting us to the Holy Grail of actual understanding. We can now conclude by answering our original Delphic question: Can the future indeed be foretold? And if so, in what circumstances and with what limitations? Our bold Drakean reply follows on naturally from this bold Drakean narrative.

Kenneth Waltz and the Systemic Realism Underlying Geopolitical Risk Analysis

As we have seen, a striking feature of modern geopolitical risk analysis is that most of its prominent practitioners tend to be realists of one sort or the other, analysts who are comfortable talking about power and its role—for good or ill—in the world. Most realists also place a high value on the importance of political systems, believing that the sort of world we find ourselves in (and countries' specific place in it) largely determines what will historically happen.

So unipolar worlds (such as Imperial Rome or China at the height of its regional pomp) work in one fashion, bipolar worlds such as the 1945–1991 US-Soviet era in another, and the multipolar world of today in still another. Such analytical insights flow from a structural realist philosophy—an intellectual sub-set of realism that is widely adhered to by most leading geopolitical risk practitioners out there today in both the political and commercial worlds.

Building on the earlier realist thinking of E. H. Carr, Hans Morgenthau, and Reinhold Niebuhr, Kenneth Waltz, in his ground-breaking work, *Theory of International Relations*, laid the cornerstone for modern geopolitical risk analysis with his illuminating focus on the central role of global political systems in determining action.[1] If Morgenthau is the hero of the history-first wing of geopolitical risk analysts, Waltz is the standard-bearer for the political scientists. But this should not be seen as a binary choice. As this book has shown, the best kind of geopolitical risk analysis fuses the insights of the two disciplines.

Waltz agreed with earlier realist leading lights that, owing to the anarchic nature of the international system—the lack of a global referee to keep the peace—the perennial competition between states would continue on forever, with warfare being a permanent part of international life.

Conflict has been endemic since the days of the ancient Greeks, and realists wearily point out that there is no sign whatsoever—based on the anarchic nature of the world order—that the endless empirical historical record is likely to ever alter. This explains why, rather than wringing their

---

[1] Kenneth Waltz, *Theory of International Relations* (Reading, MA: Addison-Wesley, 1979).

hands and wasting their intellectual efforts in a fruitless search for perpetual peace, geopolitical risk analysts instead get on with analyzing the world as they actually find it, warts and all.

However, unlike Hans Morgenthau's almost Freudian psychological focus on human nature and the specific characters of major world leaders, Waltz took a far more Olympian view.[2] He posited that both the nature of the global system that any country finds itself in as well as the country's specific position within that system poses significant real-world constraints on its foreign policy actions. In other words, if you are Ringo in the Beatles, you don't get to decide who sings lead.

Waltz argued that these systemic constraints largely determined countries' general foreign policy behavior at any given moment in history. Strikingly, of the various possible global systems, Waltz believed that a bipolar world was the most stable: with fewer significant actors, there is far less chance than in a multipolar system of miscalculation leading to great power war.[3]

For modern geopolitical risk analysts, this line of thought— that a multipolar system is less stable than a bipolar world— perfectly explains why political risk analysis is presently coming into its own commercially, as the world is now historically transitioning from the bipolar US-Soviet competition to the more complicated multipolar world our children will inherit.

A less stable system means more political risk, and more political risk points to a greater need for political risk analysis. The stunning commercial rise of modern political risk analysis is ironically confirmed by the very geopolitical theoretical backdrop such analysts hew to in the first place.

[2] Morgenthau, *Politics Among Nations*, pp. 4–15.
[3] Waltz, *Theory of International Relations*, p. 133.

The Ten Commandments of Political Risk

Know Thyself

1. Know the nature of the world you live in.
2. Know your country's place in that world.
3. Know when you are the geopolitical risk.
4. Know when game-changers occur.

Nothing in Excess

5. Balance is the key to foreign policy.
6. Game out lunatics.
7. Game out chess players.

Make a Pledge and Mischief Is Nigh

8. Avoid the losing gambler in Vegas syndrome.
9. Avoid the promised land fallacy.
10. Prepare for the butterfly effect.

"Know Thyself" as the Base of the Geopolitical Risk Analysis Typology

Waltz's systemic insight mirrors the thinking of the ancient Greeks, taking us back to the dank cave of the Pythia, where our adventure began. For a systemic power assessment of the world—knowing the nature of the world one actually lives in and one's place in it—is undoubtedly where all geopolitical risk analysis begins, the trunk of our analytical tree being the ancient admonition to "know thyself." As such, the systemic commandments we have derived from history amount to the building blocks for mastering geopolitical risk as a whole.

Knowing whether the global power system is stable or in flux, and crucially assessing changes over time in that structure that can alter its very nature, must be the first basic commandment of geopolitical risk analysis. In our terms, we must start with the trials and tribulations of George Harrison and the Beatles, as well as the surprising longevity of their friendly rivals, the Rolling Stones. In the mid-1960s, the Beatles were rightly seen as the best of friends, the epitome of hippy togetherness. By contrast, the Stones were snarky about the world and surly about each other.

Yet the bipolar Beatles system, dominated by John Lennon and Paul McCartney, collapsed in a blink of an eye, as its power structure, with the rise of the creative talents of George Harrison (and the increasing disinterest of John), no longer reflected the band's creative realities. In other words, the overall power realities of the system changed over time, even as the decision-making structure within the group did not. This is the classic definition of a failed, unstable global system, a lesson today's leading power, the United States, would do well to learn from.

Meanwhile, in ruthlessly jettisoning their founder, the tragic and flailing Brian Jones, the Stones—under the leadership of Mick Jagger and Keith Richards—moved from an unstable multipolar mess to a remarkably durable bipolar system that perfectly reflected the Jagger-Richards songwriting dominance.

This stable order survived numerous drug busts, massive addictions, and girlfriend swapping precisely because it was so rooted in the creative realities of the group. Getting the nature of the global system precisely right—be it unipolar, bipolar, or multipolar—and then constantly assessing any changes over time that can alter that system is where it all begins for geopolitical risk analysis.

The second commandment of geopolitical risk analysis under the "know thyself" imperative, is that, once the overall nature of a global system has been determined, is to precisely assess a country's place within that global system and, crucially, to act on this knowledge. Here the story of Lord Salisbury—the unlikely but true hero of this book—shows us the way forward.

In late Victorian England, Salisbury had both the bravery and the intellectual integrity to see that Britain's place in the world was changing. This meant that while Britain remained the dominant global power by a long way—being the only great power that was omnipresent in every region of the globe—it was in the throes of a long relative decline, with Germany, Japan, and the United States slowly gaining on it, year on year.

Ignoring the usual complacent analysis that flows from most leading powers that their country's dominant position will be unchallenged forever (look at American commentators today), Salisbury instead brilliantly adapted British foreign policy to fit the world he actually found himself living in. Rather than taking on rising powers America and Japan, instead Salisbury skillfully co-opted them, most particularly by defusing the war drums beating in the 1890s between Washington and London over the issue of Venezuela.

A generation later, Salisbury's unsung but far-sighted foreign policy reached its apogee as Japan and the United States rode to Britain's rescue in 1918, decisively tipping the Great War Britain's way and ensuring that it remained a great power.

This was only accomplished because Salisbury then—as geopolitical risk analysts must do now—had the courage to clearly look at his country's evolving position in the world order and adapt British foreign policy to specifically match this change. Seeing what a country can and ought to do based on its overall strategic position in the existing global order is an indispensable step to take in any successful geopolitical risk analysis.

Likewise, at about the same time, the *Genrō* in late-nineteenth-century Japan learned the bitter lesson from their humiliations at the hands of Western powers in opening up their country that they were relatively weak in comparison. The revitalization of Japan on the global stage became the basis for the remarkable, breakneck reforms its elite set in motion, a conservative revolution that within a generation transformed the country's global prospects. By correctly and honestly identifying its structural international weakness, Japan transformed itself through the Meiji Restoration, which set the country on course for a dramatic about-face, becoming the greatest regional power in Asia.

The third necessary commandment of geopolitical risk analysis also flows on from the ancient Greek's admonition to "know thyself": to look in the mirror and know when we ourselves are the political risk in the global system. As the great historian Edward Gibbon made clear in *Decline and Fall of the Roman Empire,* in the end the Romans were not victims of external events but rather were primarily undone by endemic domestic problems that occurred within their empire.

More specifically, the Romans' decadent inability to wean themselves off their dependence on foreign mercenaries to defend their empire left them at the mercy of the very people they had hired to man the gates. As far back as the ascendancy of Sejanus during the pivotal reign of Tiberius, the power of the Praetorian Guard—the emperor's personal bodyguard— had grown to unhealthy proportions, leading to perpetual political instability over time and domestic chaos that prevented Rome from dealing with its many and growing problems.

Geopolitical risk analysts are called upon to apply their analytical craft to domestic matters as they so routinely do to foreign affairs, as a great power's inability to solve its own problems—the current dismal state of the EU leaps to mind—over time can weaken its foreign policy initiatives and even its position as a great power itself.

It takes a real talent for introspection for analysts to realize that geopolitical risk is not just something that happens to other people and to instead turn the powerful analytical lens on their own country, to which most people have more emotional ties than they realize. Recognizing that we ourselves might be the problem is a hard but imperative element of modern geopolitical risk analysis—as is presently the case with the West, where much of the world's geopolitical risk, in the age of both Donald Trump and European sclerosis, is coming from.

The fourth major commandment of geopolitical risk analysis under the "know thyself" banner is to discern when everything has changed—to separate the historically essential from all the noise the twenty-four-hour news cycle throws at all of us every single day.

Despite the many undoubted towering intellectual geniuses that graced America's founding, it was only John Adams who really saw the game-changing historical significance of what was going on in Philadelphia in the summer of 1776. While Jefferson was writing at the time about his desire to buy a barometer, and his rival Alexander Hamilton (at an improbably young age) was helping George Washington direct the war effort, Adams alone had the clarity of mind to see, in that blisteringly hot early July, that the American Revolution had profound historical ramifications that would change the world order.

Likewise, during the stirring month of December 1941, with the Nazis at the very gates of Moscow and the Japanese devastating the American Pacific Fleet at Pearl Harbor, it was Winston Churchill alone amongst the Big Three leaders (Churchill, Stalin, and Roosevelt) who saw through all the tumult that Japan's ill-judged attack had been the key event that fundamentally altered the global strategic balance of power—by ensuring American entry into the war on the side of the Allies, thus decisively shifting the correlation of forces in their direction. Many important things were going on that fateful December, but only one crucially changed the trajectory of the war and all that was to follow. Churchill, like Adams, possessed the out-of-body analytical ability to see the world at a higher, structural level and to see what made it change.

The creative ability to sift the intellectual wheat from the chaff, discerning which events are game-changers, which are important, and which are interesting but basically irrelevant, is an absolutely vital skill for any first-rate geopolitical risk analyst to possess.

"Nothing in Excess" as a Branch of the Geopolitical Risk Analysis Typology

Branching off from the "know thyself" base of the geopolitical risk elemental tree is the second admonition in the Pythia's gloomy lair to do "nothing in excess." A lack of what the ancient Greeks would describe as intellectual balance lies behind many of the myths of Greek culture, where monomania in all its forms predictably leads to tragic disaster. In our more modern world, as we have seen, the same has held true for untold policy-makers, as well as for geopolitical risk analysts.

A fifth major geopolitical risk commandment (and the first under the "nothing in excess" banner) is that, having discovered one motive force of history, all too often geopolitical risk analysts as well as policy-makers stop wondering whether there might be others. Intellectual balance is absolutely necessary if geopolitical risk analysis is to be truly useful to either governmental or corporate clients. Here modern Marxists are the obvious, and worst, offenders.

Yes, it is certainly true that economic motivations and the notion of class had been shamefully under-studied before Marxism came along. But having discovered and championed a major new driver of analysis, Marxists' subsequent lack of further intellectual curiosity has proven disastrous, both intellectually and practically, for a victimized humanity that suffered through the doleful real-world consequences of their failure.

But rather than reconsider, Marxists made a fetish of their discovery—championing economic determinism to the exclusion of all else, closing off the possibility of seeing clearly the more complicated real world in front of them. Global political decisions and outcomes are self-evidently the result of the interaction of economic, political, military, sociological, historical, religious, and cultural forces, the weighting of which varies case to case. It is this bouillabaisse of factors—and not exclusively one of them—that determines real-world policy decisions and outcomes, and that should govern the geopolitical risk analysis that flows from them.

Just as Napoleon managed to easily defeat the long-lived glittering Republic of Venice in the 1790s because it had gormlessly ceased to believe it had need of an army and navy, so his overcorrection of France's recent past—and the subsequent over-militarization of French society—led to the great man's doom. It should be obvious that robust economic and military attributes are both important factors in any great power's success, and that both are essential. But as history so often illustrates, what should be obvious is so often not.

The riveting story of Napoleon should serve as a warning for all specialized studies experts who specifically focus on military, economic, or political power (or a specific region of the world), to the exclusion of everything else. At best, their myopic analysis can only accurately provide the dots of our overall holistic painting as to how the world really works—dots that should then be interpreted by more generalist geopolitical risk analysts who can answer the more important riddle as to what the painting actually looks like. At worst, in their short-sightedness, these specialists—without realizing they have only part of the answer—will attempt to universalize their parochial, limited analysis. In so doing, they can but meet their own intellectual Waterloo.

The sixth geopolitical risk commandment rests on realizing that the groups and the leaders under study always vary. The analytical weighting of the geopolitical risk tool-box by necessity alters case by case precisely because the groups being assessed are endlessly different in our maddening, fascinating, beguiling world. It is centrally important for geopolitical risk analysts to remember the truism that not all human beings are the same.

As our striking example of the highly effective Assassins during the time of the Third Crusade makes clear, geopolitical risk analysts have a particularly hard time gaming out people they believe to be lunatics. Yet whether the group in question be the Assassins, Charles Manson's hideous "Family," or the present-day ISIS death cult, deeming them simply bonkers is a dangerous intellectual trap.

For, to quote Shakespeare, there is almost always method to these groups' madness, intellectually foreign and irrational as they may appear at first glance. To decide that a group is crazy all too often lets geopolitical risk analysts off the hook: such a characterization implicitly means that analysis is simply impossible, as the group in question is not sane enough to be explained and assessed rationally. This is almost always lazy nonsense. Analysts do not have to accept that a "crazy" group's goals will ever be met—as is the case for ISIS and was the case for Manson—to be able to study them. For while a group's ultimate goals may be unattainable, once these goals are understood, the manner in which it goes about trying to realize them is almost always rational enough to be looked at. I don't have to believe that ISIS's efforts to establish a universal caliphate are achievable to be able to assess its administration of large swaths of Syria and Iraq and its strategic planning in the Middle East.

In the case of the Assassins, the intellectual failure was even more egregious. For as strange and intellectually bizarre as the Assassins' tactics seemed to the Crusaders, they actually accomplished their primary strategic goal and decisively blunted Western efforts to retake the Holy Land. Beneath the scary (and to Western eyes unfathomable) tactic of in essence medieval suicide bombings, the Assassins were utterly rational in their understanding of the politics of their Crusader enemies.

By killing Conrad, king of Jerusalem, the Old Man of the Mountain proved to be a highly rational and utterly successful political risk analyst. Seeing that the fragile Western Crusader coalition was likely to fall apart without the glue of Conrad's kingship to keep it together, the Assassins removed the Crusaders' keystone, and the political edifice that was the Westerners' alliance came tumbling down.

Far from being "mad," the Old Man of the Mountain's highly rational strategy was crowned with success. Geopolitical risk analysts would do well to remember this salutary historical example before ever writing off the need to analyze a group as impossible owing to the fact that it is simply too crazy to do so.

If some groups seem too random to assess at all, geopolitical risk analysts also often fail at the other extreme: in the chaos of far too much daily information being thrown their way, they overlook the hidden patterns of behavior of the highly rational chess players in their midst. This amounts to the seventh commandment of geopolitical risk analysis, also grouped under the "nothing in excess" admonition of the far-away Pythia.

While many groups and political actors on the foreign policy scene never get beyond the level of using tactics to further their immediate well-being (German Chancellor Angela Merkel leaps to mind as such an example), there are chess players in our midst, foreign policy actors who engage in strategic thinking, having long-term plans in place that they methodically try to reach through the use of varied tactics along the way.

Such rare birds (Russian President Vladimir Putin is a modern-day example) are continually worth looking for, as if an analyst can discover them, what they are going to do next becomes easily identifiable. The strength of chess players is that their strategic thinking allows them to have a foreign policy compass readily to hand, guiding them sure-footedly along the international relations path.

Whatever random events occur, this strategic advantage allows chess players to respond quickly and decisively, as they have no need (as most mortals do) to re-orient themselves to whatever specific crisis has arisen. The downside for them, however, is that if their hidden strategic patterns are discovered by a good analyst, an assessment of what they will do in the future becomes readily apparent and their future actions can be gamed out.

But identifying chess players is certainly very difficult, as the vast majority of the groups and leaders looked at by geopolitical risk analysts are no more than garden-variety tacticians. The story of the hapless Niccolò Machiavelli's man-crush on the dashing, dark, unscrupulous Cesare Borgia is a case in point. Beguiled by Cesare's dark luster, Machiavelli forgot to notice that Borgia was ultimately spectacularly unsuccessful and was actually no more than a good-looking, somewhat mediocre, tactician.

Instead, lurking right in front of the supposed supreme master of the dark arts of politics was a genuine and highly successful chess player, Pope Julius II, who easily bested both Borgia and Machiavelli in their real-world contest for power.

Julius may have lacked Borgia's star power, but he more than made up for this with his systematic strategic *nous* and the decisive tactical moves that flowed naturally from it. While the shallow, tactical Borgia may have blinded Machiavelli, it was the methodical, hyper-rational Julius who carried the day. Modern-day geopolitical risk analysts will find it well worth their while to hunt for these elusive, and often successful, creatures.

"Make a Pledge and Mischief Is Nigh" as a Branch of the Geopolitical Risk Analysis Typology

Along with "nothing in excess," "make a pledge and mischief is nigh" is the other major sub-heading to branch off from "know thyself" in the geopolitical risk analysis elemental typology. To put it in modern terms, it was the Pythia's way of warning those who encountered her terrible presence to check, and forever re-check, the assumptions upon which they based the decisions they made in their lives. As we have seen, throughout history this admonition has an eternal, timeless quality that geopolitical risk analysts and policy-makers alike must always keep in mind.

This means avoiding common logical fallacies beyond all else. Both Robert E. Lee's storied Army of Northern Virginia and the Vietnam War decision-makers in the Johnson administration fell prey to the "losing gambler in Vegas" syndrome. This amounts to the eighth modern geopolitical risk commandment.

Having invested so much in victory at Gettysburg and in Indochina, respectively, both groups of decision-makers adopted the utterly illogical rationale that because there were so many poker chips already on the table, they had to keep playing come what may. In both cases, the result was utter, predictable disaster.

The problem for both Lee and LBJ was that they never stopped to wonder why they had yet to be successful; rather than see that their failure had enduring structural causes, they in essence merely decided that they had been unlucky, in policy terms. Vegas-style, they assumed that their luck would somehow even out if they just kept committing more troops and wherewithal to the battle at hand.

Tragically, neither Lee nor Johnson was able to focus on the analytical reasons for his failure: the North had an advantage in terms of both men and a strong defensive position at Gettysburg, and Ho Chi Minh had the magic elixir of domestic political legitimacy that the South Vietnamese government painfully lacked. It was not "luck" that explained the failures of the South at Gettysburg and the US intervention in Vietnam; rather, there were all too real analytical reasons for them, obstacles that were never sufficiently scrutinized, let alone overcome.

The danger is that both analysts and policy-makers end up doing the same wrong thing over and over again. Successful policy initiatives are not merely a matter of will. Rather, warnings should start flashing when geopolitical risk analysts say (as I heard with frightening regularity over the Iraq War) that so much has already been committed to a specific policy that has failed up until now that we simply must keep on with it. This is the moment when geopolitical risk analysts take off their thinking caps and instead indulge in wish fulfillment, a form of policy voodoo that almost always has disastrous consequences.

Our ninth commandment in the study of the rules of the road governing geopolitical risk analysis—also hovering under the "make a pledge and mischief is nigh" typological sub-heading—is to avoid another logical trap, the "promised land" fallacy. The able (but almost always wrong) father of the modern German navy, Alfred von Tirpitz, managed to convince his excitable kaiser that at a single stroke—by directly challenging the vaunted British Royal Navy for dominance—Berlin could force London into a cowed acceptance of Germany's parity with the British Empire, Wilhelm's most fervent strategic dream.

The simplicity of this one-shot strategy proved as beguiling as it was wrong-headed. Alarmed by the crash German naval build-up, the British responded in kind, making it impossible for von Tirpitz to catch up. At the same time, by appearing overtly warlike and directly threatening British dominance, the Germans unwittingly made an enemy of Britain, an enmity that spelled their ruin in the Great War.

Likewise, Soviet premier Nikita Khrushchev's somewhat half-hearted efforts—combining a generally cautious foreign policy with blood-curdling statements—did not lead to the success of his "wars of national liberation" strategy. Instead, the over-blown rhetoric regarding this strategy merely steeled American and Western resolve against the Soviets without beginning to prove to be the decisive strategic game-changer the Soviet leader had so confidently predicted.

Geopolitical risk analysts and policy-makers who adopt the promised land fallacy should be viewed with deep analytical suspicion, as rarely is one strategic move capable of decisively altering a country's global position. Simply too many political, economic, military, and cultural elements go into determining a country's strategic place in the world for one factor to overturn the need to account for complexity in geopolitical risk analysis.

Instead, as was surely the case with Khrushchev, followers of the promised land strategy are more likely betraying signs of their psychological desperation as they search for an easy (often non-existent) way out of their usually unfavorable strategic position. This fallacy is another example of the illogical snake oil that invariably leads to poor analysis and should be avoided like the plague by any first-rate geopolitical risk analyst.

The tenth and final commandment necessary for mastering geopolitical risk (also grouped under the "make a pledge and mischief is nigh" sub-heading) is to remember the historical adage that however good the analysis, random, unforeseen, and devastating events can humble it (and its authors) at a moment's notice, changing everything.

Prime Minister Harold Macmillan—a man whose aristocratic friends and indeed way of life had been blotted out in an instant in the carnage of the Great War—was acutely aware of this butterfly effect in international relations. Trying to protect Britain's sliding structural position as a great power, and convinced that the well-meaning but unaware Kennedy administration was unintentionally creating damning new facts on the ground over nuclear policy—whose unforeseen consequences would thoughtlessly (but definitively) harm Britain's global credibility—Macmillan had the analytical foresight to mitigate the Skybolt nuclear crisis.

At the Nassau Conference of December 1962, the aging representative of a bygone era managed to gently tutor the embodiment of a new one on the likely doleful consequences of unforeseen events and to head off a crisis that could have ended the "special relationship" between the two great powers. As is so often the case, Macmillan's strategic insight was born of his own biography: unforeseen events in his life, both large and small, had shown him in a personal way that they could analytically change everything.

Likewise, the epic story of Deng Xiaoping, paramount leader of China and the architect of its astonishing economic and strategic rise, is in many ways the history of modern China itself. After (just) surviving the murderous purges of his political rival Mao Zedong, Deng turned China completely around in the course of a generation, taking it from the madness of the Cultural Revolution to great power status in seemingly an instant.

Complementing his economic reforms, Deng crafted a restrained, subtle foreign policy designed to keep China out of geopolitical trouble as it put all its energies into the economic growth strategy that became the envy of the modern world. Deng was a first-rate strategic and analytical thinker, and his carefully calibrated foreign policy has surely been crowned with success. Yet with today's increasing tensions between a more aggressive China and its fearful neighbors in the East China and South China Seas, Deng's successful foreign policy strategy is in many ways at the mercy of events that neither Beijing nor anyone else can control.

Regionally, the current strategic configuration in East Asia resembles nothing so much as Europe in 1914, hardly a confidence-inspiring reality, as locked-in alliances operate on what amounts to a military hair-trigger. As we have seen, a single drunken sea captain in this most dangerous region in the world could unwittingly bring the temple down on all Deng's masterful strategic handiwork.

Thus, the old ethical realist imperative of humility in the face of uncontrollable events must be the response of any first-rate geopolitical risk analyst.[4] However good you are at mimicking the Pythia, and however far-sighted

[4] See Lieven and Hulsman, *Ethical Realism*.

your strategic analysis has proven (as with Deng), there is never a moment to rest on your laurels. The relentless forward surge of history, of new events that can confound old analytical truisms, requires that analysts always remain intellectually supple and endlessly restless with the best of their handiwork.

So the answer to the Pythia's challenge is this. If it proves possible for a heroic figure to hew to these ten daunting commandments—a modern-day intellectual Labor of Hercules—then over the medium-term, and only for a time, the future can indeed be foretold in certain specific cases. There are so many caveats and pitfalls to even this limited statement that for any aspiring geopolitical risk analyst, it is best to begin thinking about mastering geopolitics where this book ends—dwelling on the importance of humility.

Saying this, we should also not under-sell what can be intellectually accomplished either. My own political risk firm called the "shocking" Brexit referendum correctly, just as I analytically knew that the Iraq War was doomed to failure, and that the recent December 2016 Italian referendum on political reform was heading towards a decisive defeat. It is not merely luck that some firms have a far better record of prediction for their clients than others. As is true in baseball, over a period of time the best teams win the most games in geopolitical risk analysis.

Geopolitical risk analysis is not an exact science, and even the best analysts in the world can be wrong. But it should not be disparaged for this lack of perfection. For in all its wondrous artistry, from the days of the Pythia until now, the world's best geopolitical risk analysts add a tremendous amount of value for any business or government looking to understand the world. In other words, there is a reason all those Greeks for all those centuries sacrificed herds of sheep at the foot of Mount Parnassus.

The End of the Pythia and the Beginning
of Political Risk Analysis

As every able geopolitical risk analyst knows, eventually history changes all things. Ironically, the world's first geopolitical risk firm was undone by structural changes in global
politics, as Rome supplanted Greece as the ordering power
in the Mediterranean and the Empire itself transitioned from
paganism to sponsoring Christianity.

Eventually, these global changes spelled the end for even
the first and most long-lived political risk firm. Late in the
reign of the Roman Emperor Theodosius I, in 390 AD, militant
Christian monks—emboldened by the emperor's decision
a decade earlier to end official state support for polytheist
religions and customs—stormed and destroyed the complex
at Delphi, after over 1,100 years of worship.

The last Pythia, a position that without doubt had been
the most powerful held by a woman in the classical world,
fled in terror in the face of these anti-pagan zealots. The
first successful political risk consulting firm tumbled into
the beautiful, poignant state of disrepair that we see today.

Yet her record remains, as does the suddenly trendy
modern iteration of what she attempted to do so long ago—
using special advantages (then spiritual, now intellectual) to
divine the future for her anxious clients.

Just as in ancient Greece no event of consequence was
undertaken without consulting the Pythia, today the world's
leading businesses and governments tread carefully to the
major political risk firms to get the best independent, outside
advice they can find on managing the vagaries of the world,
avoiding the pitfalls, and creatively taking advantage of global
circumstances. In other words, little has really changed.

However, unlike the Pythia's dependence on hallucinogenic gases, we have uncovered in this book the rich, unique

historical seam for mastering geopolitical risk analysis across the ages, allowing us through our ten commandments to creatively update the Pythia's ground-breaking work.

In traveling far from home, as Sir Francis Drake bid us to do in the swashbuckling, mesmerizing prayer that opened this book, our journey through history has been bountifully rewarded. For yes, within limits, the future can be foretold through the use of geopolitical risk analysis. Truly venturing far from our intellectual shore, in daring more boldly, we have come to see the stars.

❖ ACKNOWLEDGMENTS ❖

Nothing is as hard as writing a book; *To Dare More Boldly* is the fourteenth I have written all or part of. Oddly enough, what I remember most from each of these daunting, mammoth undertakings is not what I was writing or thinking, but the real world that swirled around me as I was doing so. *To Dare More Boldly*, in my mind my own *Pet Sounds*, is easily the most important and the best of them all, despite my great fondness for several of the others. Arrestingly, it has been a genuinely happy book to write, which is all the stranger given that it was created as my personal life fell apart.

For this almost miraculous experience, I have to thank the many people listed here, who did not just talk about love and friendship but actively exhibited these qualities through the long, rewarding years that made *To Dare More Boldly* a reality. I can never thank you enough, and I will never forget that we rode out the storm together.

First, to my "Gang of Ten" (the list expanded as the book progressed, but the Chinese nickname stuck), who gave up their busy lives to read every word of the text and comment, I owe you a great debt. Lucio Caracciolo, James Frayne, Will Schirano, Lara Palay, Dan Lyons, Martin Baber, Raleigh Addington, Dario Fabbri, Robert Kahn, and Periklis Thivaios, in their friendship and commitment, made work on this project nothing but a pleasure.

Three other members of the Gang of Ten deserve special praise. My long-time friend and colleague Teun van Dongen questioned every intellectual link made in this book with unremitting zeal and great skill, undoubtedly making *To Dare More Boldly* far better. Further, another great friend,

Jim Zanotti, pushed me to ever greater heights over the revolutionary new elemental links I have made here—our ten commandments. Tom Welsh, my comrade and long-time intellectual collaborator at *City AM*, out of nothing but love and friendship painstakingly helped me line-edit every word of the text. Serving in his good-humored, perpetually helpful creative role as my George Martin, Tom has excelled even himself here.

My daily companions Ella Britton and Martin Baber shared a cottage with me in the Cotswolds as I wrote *To Dare More Boldly*, living and dying with me through this vast undertaking, commiserating over every hurdle and rejoicing over every breakthrough. Serving as my emotional ballast and my family, their love and endless loyalty (along with the warm help of Koby, their West Highland Terrier) have made this project the great joy it has been.

My great friend and collaborator Peter Dougherty, my fearless, creative editor (as well as director of Princeton University Press), has functioned as village priests used to do, serving as friend, mentor, champion, and creative foil (in a Lennon-McCartney sort of way) ever pushing me to make this book the creative and intellectual breakthrough that it is. Peter has been with me both emotionally and intellectually since the first sentence; it is not too much to say that *To Dare More Boldly* would not exist without him, and for this and his endless warm and creative support, I am eternally in his debt.

Finally, this book is dedicated to my three glorious children, Benjamin, Matilda, and Samuel, who remind me constantly of the stakes we are always playing for, and to the great love of my life, Sara. Your love keeps me grounded in the world of today, even as I spend much of my time thinking about the lessons of the past. You remind me that John Lennon was so entirely right: "Love is the answer."

❖ BIBLIOGRAPHY ❖

Akamatsu, Paul. *Meiji 1868: Revolution and Counter-Revolution in Japan* (New York: Harper and Row, 1972).

Armitage, David. *The Declaration of Independence: A Global History* (Cambridge, MA: Harvard University Press, 2007).

Baum, Richard. *Burying Mao: Chinese Politics in the Age of Deng Xiaoping* (Princeton, NJ: Princeton University Press, 1996).

Beasley, William G., *The Meiji Restoration* (Stanford, CA: Stanford University Press, 1972).

The Beatles. *The Beatles Anthology* (San Francisco: Chronicle Books, 2000).

Blake, Robert. *The Conservative Party from Peel to Churchill* (New York: St. Martin's Press, 1970).

———. *Disraeli* (London: Eyre and Spottiswoode, 1966).

Branagh, Kenneth, *Beginning* (New York: W. W. Norton & Co., 1989).

Bremmer, Ian. *Every Nation for Itself: Winners and Losers in a G-Zero World* (New York: Portfolio, 2012).

———. *The J Curve: A New Way to Understand Why Nations Rise and Fall* (New York: Simon & Schuster, 2006).

Bugliosi, Vincent, with Curt Gentry. *Helter Skelter: The True Story of the Manson Murders* (New York: W. W. Norton and Co., 1974).

Calenza, Christopher S. *Machiavelli: A Portrait* (Cambridge, MA: Harvard University Press, 2015).

Capponi, Niccolò. *An Unlikely Prince: The Life and Times of Machiavelli* (Boston: Da Capo Press, 2010).

Chernow, Ron. *Washington: A Life* (New York: Penguin Books, 2010).

Clark, Christopher. *The Sleepwalkers: How Europe Went to War in 1914* (London: Allen Lane, 2012).

Clayson, Alan. *George Harrison* (London: Sanctuary, 2003).

Coote, Stephen. *Drake: The Life and Legend of an Elizabethan Hero* (New York: St. Martin's Press, 2003).

Cummins, John. *Francis Drake: Lives of a Hero* (London: Palgrave Macmillan, 1997).

Daftary, Farhad. *The Ismailis: Their History and Doctrines* (Cambridge: Cambridge University Press, 1990).

Daily Telegraph. "Jean-Claude Juncker's Most Outrageous Political Quotations," July 15, 2014.

Dardis, Tom. *The Thirsty Muse* (London: Abacus, 1990).

Dikoetter, Frank. *Mao's Great Famine: The History of China's Most Devastating Catastrophe* (London: Walker & Co., 2010).

Dio, Cassius. *Delphi Complete Works of Cassius Dio* (East Sussex: Delphi Classics, 2014).

Doggett, Peter. *You Never Give Me Your Money: The Beatles After the Breakup* (New York: HarperCollins, 2009).

Donaldson, Robert H., and Joseph L. Nogee. *The Foreign Policy of Russia: Changing Systems, Enduring Interests* (London: M. E. Sharpe, 2009).

Elkins, Stanley, and Eric McKitrick. *The Age of Federalism* (Oxford: Oxford University Press, 1995).

Ellis, Joseph. *American Sphinx: The Character of Thomas Jefferson* (New York: Alfred A. Knopf, 1996).

———. *Founding Brothers: The Revolutionary Generation* (London: Vintage Books, 2000).

———. *Passionate Sage: The Character and Legacy of John Adams* (New York: W. W. Norton and Co., 2001).

Esdaile, Charles, and Andrew Roberts. "Debate: Was Napoleon Great?" *British Journal of Military History*, vol. 1, issue 3, June 2015.

Ferguson, Niall. *The Pity of War* (London: Penguin, 1999).

Ferling, John E. *Setting the World Ablaze: Washington, Adams, Jefferson, and the American Revolution* (Oxford: Oxford University Press, 2000).

Fitzgerald, F. Scott. *The Great Gatsby* (Ware, Hertfordshire, UK: Wordsworth Editions, 1992).

Fontenrose, Joseph. *The Delphic Oracle: Its Responses and Operations, with a Catalogue of Responses* (Berkeley: University of California Press, 1981).

Foote, Shelby. *The Civil War: A Narrative*, vol. 2, *Fredericksburg to Meridian* (New York: Random House, 1958).

Frater, Stephen. "December 11, 1941: Hitler and Arguably the Most Insane and Pivotal Decision in History," *The History Reader*, December 11, 2011.

Friedman, George. "How Important Is the US President—or Any Leader?" *Geopolitical Futures*, November 10, 2016.

———. *The Next 100 Years: A Forecast for the 21st Century* (New York: Doubleday, 2009).

Friedman, George, with Meredith LeBard. *The Coming War with Japan* (New York: St. Martin's Press, 1991).

Fursenko, Aleksandr, and Timothy Naftali. *Khrushchev's Cold War* (New York: W. W. Norton and Co., 2006).

Gibbon, Edward. *The History of the Decline and Fall of the Roman Empire* (Ware, Hertfordshire, UK: Wordsworth Editions, 1998).

Gillingham, John. *Richard the Lionheart* (London: Weidenfeld and Nicolson, 1978).

Goodwin, William. *Lives of the Necromancers* (London: F. J. Mason, 1876).

Gould, Jonathan. *Can't Buy Me Love: The Beatles, Britain, and America* (New York: Three Rivers Press, 2007).

Grier, Peter. "Pearl Harbor Attack: How Did Winston Churchill React?" *Christian Science Monitor*, December 7, 2015.

Hamshere, C. E. "Drake's Voyage Round the World," *History Today*, vol. 17, issue 9, September 1967.

Hitchens, Peter. "Britain Can No Longer Afford to Pay the Extortionate Cost of the Welfare State." *DailyMail.com*, January 13, 2013.

Holland, Tom. *Persian Fire: The First World Empire and the Battle for the West* (London: Little, Brown, 2005).

Halberstam, David. *The Best and the Brightest* (New York: Ballantine Books, 1993).

Horne, Allistair. *Macmillan: The Official Biography* (London: Macmillan, 2000).

Huffman, Herbert B. "The Oracular Process: Delphi and the Near East," *Vetus Testamentum*, vol. 57, issue 4, 2007, pp. 449–60.

Hulsman, John. "Forget the Neocons: How Lawrence of Arabia Can Help Save Iraq from Chaos," *City AM*, June 19, 2014.

———. "How to Defeat ISIS: We Already Have a Playbook for Beating These Extremists," *City AM*, July 7, 2014.

———. "Paris Terror Attacks: We Must Not Give ISIS the Narrative It Craves," *City AM*, November 16, 2015.

———. "Realism and the Apocalypse of 1914," *Limes* (Italian monthly), May 2014.

———. *To Begin the World Over Again: Lawrence of Arabia from Damascus to Baghdad* (New York: Palgrave Macmillan, 2009).

Jagger, Mick, Keith Richards, Charlie Watts, and Ronnie Wood. *According to the Rolling Stones* (San Francisco: Chronicle Books, 2003).

Jansen, Marius B. *Sakamoto Ryōma and the Meiji Restoration* (New York: Columbia University Press, 1994).

Jensen, Merrill. *The Founding of a Nation: A History of the American Revolution* (Oxford: Oxford University Press, 1968).

Jones, Dan. *The Plantagenets: The Kings Who Made England* (London: William Collins, 2013).

Kelly, Patrick J. *Tirpitz and the Imperial German Navy* (Bloomington: Indiana University Press, 2011).

Kelsey, Harry. *Sir Francis Drake: The Queen's Pirate* (New Haven, CT: Yale University Press, 1998).

Kennedy, Paul M. *The Rise of Anglo-German Antagonism: 1860–1914* (New York: Prometheus Books, 1980).

Kermode, Frank. *Concerning E. M. Forster* (London: Weidenfeld & Nicolson, 2010).

Kissinger, Henry A. *A World Restored: Metternich, Castlereagh, and the Problems of Peace, 1812–22* (Boston: Houghton Mifflin Company, 1996).

———. *Diplomacy* (New York: Pocket Books, 1994).

Lamb, Richard. *The Macmillan Years 1957–1963: The Emerging Truth* (London: John Murray, 1995).

Lampedusa, Giuseppe Tomasi di. *The Leopard* (London: Vintage Books, 2007).

Lenin, Vladimir. *Imperialism: The Highest Stage of Capitalism* (London: Penguin Classics, 2010).

Lewis, Bernard. *The Assassins: A Radical Sect of Islam* (Oxford: Oxford University Press, 1967).

Lewisohn, Mark. *The Beatles: All Those Years*, vol. 1, *Tune In* (New York: Crown Archetype, 2013).

Liang, Zhang, Andrew Nathan, and Perry Link. *The Tiananmen Papers* (New York: Public Affairs, 2001).

Lieven, Anatol, and John Hulsman. *Ethical Realism: A Vision for America's Role in the World* (New York: Pantheon Books, 2006).

MacFarquhar, Roderick, and Michael Schoenhals. *Mao's Last Revolution* (Cambridge, MA: Harvard University Press, 2006).

Machiavelli, Niccolò. *The Prince* (Norwalk, CT: Easton Press, 1980).

Madden, Thomas. *Venice: A New History* (New York, Viking, 2012).

Maier, Pauline. *American Scripture: Making the Declaration of Independence* (New York: Alfred A. Knopf, 1997).

Markham, Felix. *Napoleon* (New York: Mentor Books, 1963).

Massie, Robert K. *Dreadnought: Britain, Germany, and the Coming of the Great War* (New York: Random House, 1991).

Mattingly, Garrett. *The Armada* (Boston: Houghton Mifflin, 1959).

McCullough, David. *John Adams* (New York: Simon & Schuster, 2001).

McLynn, Frank. *Napoleon* (New York: Pimlico, 1998).

McPherson, James M. *Battle Cry of Freedom: The Civil War Era* (New York: Oxford University Press, 1988).

Meisner, Maurice J. *The Deng Xiaoping Era: An Enquiry into the Fate of Chinese Socialism* (New York: Hill and Wang, 1996).

Morgenthau, Hans J. *In Defense of the National Interest* (Lanham, MD: University Press of America, 1982).

———. *Politics Among Nations: The Struggle for Power and Peace* (New York: Alfred A. Knopf, 1978).

———. *Truth and Power: Collected Essays 1960–1970* (New York: Praeger, 1970).

Norman, Philip. *Shout!: The Beatles in Their Generation* (New York: Fireside, 1996).

Norwich, John Julius. *A History of Venice* (New York: Alfred A. Knopf, 1982).

Odom, William E. *The Collapse of the Soviet Military* (New Haven, CT: Yale University Press, 1998).

Peplow, Mark. "Battle of Marathon Date Revised," *Nature*, July 19, 2004.

Polo, Marco. *The Travels of Marco Polo* (London: J. M. Dent and Sons, 1918).

Richards, Keith, with James Fox. *Life* (New York: Little, Brown, 2010).

Roach, John. "Delphi Oracle's Lips May Have Been Loosened by Gas Vapors," *National Geographic News*, August 14, 2001.

Roberts, Andrew. *Napoleon: A Life* (London: Penguin Group, 2014).

———. *Salisbury: Victorian Titan* (London: Faber and Faber, 2012).

Sabatini, Rafael. *The Life of Cesare Borgia* (London: Stanley Paul, 2013).

Schama, Simon. "Napoleon Bonaparte; French Emperor," *Financial Times*, June 19, 2015.

Sears, Stephen W. *Gettysburg* (Boston: Houghton Mifflin, 2003).

Seutonius. *The Twelve Caesars* (London: Penguin Classics, 2007).

Sharaa, Michael. *The Killer Angels* (Edinburgh: Polygon, 2013).

Shaw, Christine. *Julius II: The Warrior Pope* (London: Wiley-Blackwell, 1997).

Snow, C. P. *The Two Cultures* (Cambridge: Canto, 1993).

Southey, Robert. *English Seamen: Howard, Clifford, Hawkins, Drake, Cavendish* (London: Methuen & Co., 1897).

Spiegel Online. "The Guttenberg Plagiarism Scandal: German Society Is Applying a Double Standard," February 28, 2011.

Tacitus. *The Annals of Imperial Rome* (London: Penguin Classics, 2003).

Taubman, William. *Khrushchev: The Man and His Era* (New York, W. W. Norton and Co., 2003).

Thompson, J. M. *Napoleon Bonaparte: His Rise and Fall* (Oxford: Oxford University Press, 1954).

Thompson, William J. *Khrushchev: A Political Life* (New York: St. Martin's Press, 1995).

Thorpe, D. R. *Supermac* (London: Chatto & Windus, 2010).

Time. "Elder Careless," September 24, 2003.

Vogel, Ezra. *Deng Xiaoping and the Transformation of China* (Cambridge, MA: Belknap Press of Harvard University Press, 2011).

Waltz, Kenneth. *Theory of International Politics* (Reading, MA: Addison-Wesley, 1979).

White, Mark. *Kenneth Branagh* (London: Faber and Faber, 2005).

Woolsey, Matt. "Top-Earning Pirates," *Forbes*, September 9, 2008.

Wyman, Bill, with Ray Coleman. *Stone Alone: The Story of a Rock 'n' Roll Band* (New York: Da Capo Press, 1997).

Yang, Benjamin. *Deng: A Political Biography* (London: Routledge, 1997).

al-Abadi, Haider, 83
Abbey Road (record; Beatles),
    249–50
Abe, Shinzō, 280–81
Adams, Abigail, 123
Adams, John, 37; at Continental
    Congress (1776), 122–23,
    125–32, 291; Jefferson and,
    143, 145–46
Adams, John Quincy, 204
Addington, Henry, 163
African Americans, 144; Helter
    Skelter philosophy on, 74–76;
    as slaves, 142
Agnadello, Battle of (1509), 118
Alexander I (czar, Russia), 162
Alexander VI (pope; Rodrigo
    Borgia), 100, 113, 116, 117
All Things Must Pass (record;
    Harrison), 250, 252
al-Qaeda, 79, 80
al-Qaeda in Iraq (AQI), 80–81
American Revolution, 124–32,
    141–43, 291
Antietam, Battle of (1862), 171
Armistead, Lewis, 185–86
Asia: current political climate in,
    279–83, 301. *See also* China;
    Japan
Asquith government (UK), 230,
    231
assassinations: of Conrad, 89–90;
    by *Hashashin*, 71; policies not
    changed by, 89n13
Assassins (*Hashashin* movement),
    295; Conrad as target of, 88,

89; dismissed as lunatics, 294;
    Saladin as target of, 85–86;
    under Sinan, 70–72, 91
Athena (deity), 5
Athens (ancient), 1–6
Augustus (emperor; Roman
    Empire), 44, 46
Australia, 276
Austria, 153–55

Balfour, Arthur, 208
Ball, George, 178
Band (rock band), 238
Bank of France, 158–59
baseball, 10–11
Beatles (rock band), 233–34, 288;
    as analogy for West, 250–51;
    collapse of, 234–36; decline
    of, 246–50; in Manson's
    philosophy, 75–76; rise
    of, 237–38; Rolling Stones
    compared with, 242
The Beatles ("The White Album";
    record), 247–48
Beria, Lavrentiy, 224
Bethmann-Hollweg, Theobald
    von, 229–30
Boer War (1897), 212
Borgia, Cesare, 95, 99–103,
    296–97; Julius versus, 116, 117
Borgia, Gioffre, 100
Borgia, Giovanni, 100
Borgia, Rodrigo. *See* Alexander VI
Borodino, Battle of (1812), 162
Bremmer, Ian, 15–18, 22; on Brexit
    and Trump election, 25, 26

Brexit (British exit from European Union), 25–26, 302
Brezhnev, Leonid, 228
Britain. *See* Great Britain
Britain, Battle of (1940), 136
Bugliosi, Vincent, 73–77
Bundy, McGeorge, 175–79
Burke, Edmund, 49
Burnside, Ambrose, 171
Bush, George W., 14, 148
butterfly effect (random events), 39, 254–55, 300
Byrds (rock band), 237

Caligula (emperor; Roman Empire), 47, 65
Campoformio, Treaty of (1797), 154
Caracalla (emperor; Roman Empire), 65
Castelli, Bernardino, 151
Castro, Fidel, 226
Chamberlain, Joshua Lawrence, 168–70, 172–74, 182, 184
Charles VIII (king, France), 116
Charlotte d'Albret, 101
Chernow, Ron, 108
chess players, 36–37, 92–93, 98, 119–20, 296
Chiang Kai-Shek, 260
China, 251; current foreign policies of, 274–79, 281–83; under Deng Xiaoping, 255–56, 263–65, 301; Deng Xiaoping's foreign policy for, 256–59; economic boom of, 53–54; Economist Intelligence Unit in, 13; under Mao Zedong, 260–63; Tiananmen Square crisis in, 265–66; as world power, 279–80

Chinese Communist Party (CCP), 256–57, 260–62; under Deng Xiaoping, 263–67
Chirac, Jacques, 51
Christianity and Christians: destruction of Delphi by, 303; in Roman Empire, 44–45. *See also* Third Crusade
Churchill, Winston, 122, 134–38, 140–41, 291–92
Civil War (US; 1861–65), 168–74, 181–87, 298
Claudius (emperor; Roman Empire), 65
Cleveland, Grover, 204, 205
Clinton, Hillary, 275
Colonna family, 118
Common Sense (Paine), 125
communism, 218, 220
Communist Party (China). *See* Chinese Communist Party
Concert for Bangladesh (1971), 252
Congo, 222
Congress of Vienna (1815), 155
Conrad of Montferrat (king, Jerusalem), 86–91, 295
conscription: in France, under Napoleon, 157; in Japan, 202
Constantine (emperor; Roman Empire), 66
Continental System, 160–62
Council on Foreign Relations, 196
Cuba, 222; Missile Crisis in, 226–28
Cultural Revolution (China), 261–63

Darius (king, Persia), 1
Declaration of Independence (1776), 121–24, 129–32, 141–45

Della Rovere, Giuliano. *See* Julius II

Delphi (Greece), 2–6; destroyed, 303

Deng Pufang, 262

Deng Xiaoping, 39, 53, 301; Chinese foreign policy of, 256–59; current Chinese foreign policies and, 274–77; economic policies of, 266–67; as leader of Chinese Communist Party, 263–66; Mao Zedong and, 259–63; unforeseen events faced by, 255–56, 283

Depardieu, Gérard, 59

Dickinson, John, 127–28, 131, 132

Didius Julianus (emperor; Roman Empire), 65

DiMaggio, Joe, 11

Disraeli, Benjamin, 190, 193

Donaldson, Robert, 221

Drake, (Sir) Francis, 304

HMS *Dreadnought* (British ship), 215

dreadnoughts (class of ships), 215, 216, 230

Drusus the Younger, 47

Dylan, Bob, 237, 238, 252

Eagleburger, Lawrence, 13

economic determinism, 293

Economist Intelligence Unit (EIU; firm), 12–14

Eden, Anthony, 268, 269

Egypt, Suez Crisis in, 268–69

Eight Elders (China), 264, 266

Eisenhower, Dwight D., 225, 268–69

elderly people: in Europe's demographic crisis, 54–56; in French heat wave of 2003, 49–52

elections (US): of 1972, 26; of 2016, 25–26

Ellis, Joseph, 108

embargoes, 160

England. *See* Great Britain

Epstein, Brian, 246–47

Esdaile, Charles, 164

ethylene (chemical), 3–4

Eurasia Group (firm), 15–18

Eurasia Group Global Political Risk Index (GPRI), 15

Europe: current economic decline of, 52–54; debt crisis in, 59–60; future of, 61–64; heat wave of 2003 in, 49–52; social spending in, 54–56

European Economic and Monetary Union (EMU), 61

European Union (EU): British exit from (Brexit), 25–26, 302; euro crisis in, 55

euro zone, 62

Ewell, Richard, 170

Faithfull, Marianne, 245

Family (Manson cult), 73–77

Fatherland Party (Germany), 232

feudalism: abolished in Japan, 202; ended in France, 158

First Coalition, 154

Florence, Republic of, 93, 95–96, 114

France: allied with Britain, 216–17, 231; during American Revolution, 128–29; economic crisis in, 61, 64; expelled from Italy, 118–19; fall of Napoleon in, 161–65; heat wave of 2003 in, 49–52; Muslim refugees in, 82; under Napoleon, 155–60; Revolution in (1789), 104; Suez invaded by, 269; Venice conquered by, 151–55, 293

France, Battle of (1940), 136
Frankfurt Proposals (1813), 164
Franklin, Benjamin, 129
Franz Ferdinand (archduke,
    Austria), 254, 282
French Front National (FN), 82
French Revolution (1789), 104,
    158
Friedman, George, 10, 18–21; on
    Brexit and Trump election, 25
Fursenko, Aleksandr, 219, 227

Galba (emperor; Roman Empire),
    65
game-changers, 37
Gang of Four (China), 263
Geithner, Timothy, 13
Genrō (Japan), 201–3, 207,
    289–90
Geopolitical Futures (firm), 21
geopolitical risk analysis, 6–8;
    chance in, 10; definition of,
    6n; elements of, 31–32, 36–39;
    gaming out chess players in,
    92–93; Gibbon's contributions
    to, 66–67; "know thyself" in,
    287–92; of lunatics, 72–73,
    84; "make a pledge and
    mischief if nigh" in, 297–302;
    Morgenthau's contributions
    to, 30–31; in multipolar
    systems, 286; "nothing in
    excess" in, 292–97; promised
    land fallacy in, 209; random
    events in, 254–55
geopolitics, 10
George III (king, England), 105,
    128, 141
Germany: demographic crisis in,
    54; economic crisis in, 62–63;
    Guttenberg plagiarism scandal
    in, 57–59; militarization
    of, under Hitler, 160; naval
    competition between Britain
    and, 207, 209–17, 219–20,
    229–31, 299; in World War
    I, 232; in World War II, 133,
    138–41
Gettysburg, Battle of (1863),
    168–74, 181–87, 298
Gibbon, Edward, 42–45, 48, 56,
    66–67, 290
Grant, Ulysses S., 187
Great Britain: American
    Revolution against, 124–32,
    141–43; decline of empire
    of, 38; at end of nineteenth
    century, 188–89; France,
    under Napoleon, versus,
    160–63, 166; Japan and,
    206–7; Jay Treaty between US
    and, 104–8; leaves European
    Union (Brexit), 25–26, 302;
    under Macmillan, 269–74,
    300–301; naval competition
    between Germany and, 209–
    17, 229–31, 299; Salisbury's
    foreign policy for, 193–97,
    289; Suez Crisis and, 268–69;
    Venezuela and, 203–6; as
    world power, 279; in World
    War I, 232; in World War II,
    135–38, 140–41, 291–92
Great Leap Forward (China),
    260–61
Greece (ancient): destruction of
    Delphi in, 303; geopolitical
    risk analysis in, 31–32, 39–40;
    internal decay of, 65–67;
    Pythia of Delphi (Oracle of
    Delphi) in, 2–6
Greece (modern), 61, 63
Guttenberg, Karl-Theodor zu,
    57–59
Guy of Lusignan (king,
    Jerusalem), 85–88

Halberstam, David, 175, 177–80
Haldane, Viscount, 230–31
Hamilton, Alexander, 98, 104–5, 107, 109, 257, 291
Hancock, John, 121
Hancock, Winfield Scott, 184, 185
Harriman, Averell, 135
Harrison, George, 38, 234–36, 288; death of, 252–53; during decline of Beatles, 247–50; post-Beatles, 251–52; rise of, 236–38
Harrison, Olivia, 252
Hashashin movement (Assassins). See Assassins
Hattin, Battle of (1187), 85
Helter Skelter (Manson's philosophy), 74–77
Henry II of Champagne (king, Jerusalem; Count of Champagne), 68–69, 90
Herodotus, 2
Hindenburg, Paul von, 232
history: in geopolitical risk analysis, 31; Gibbon's methods in, 42; lessons from, 8–10
Hitchens, Peter, 53
Hitler, Adolf, 133, 136, 138–40; Napoleon compared with, 159–60
Ho Chi Minh, 177, 222, 298
Hollande, François, 59, 64
Hood, John Bell, 171, 173–74
Hooker, Joseph, 171
Hua Guofeng, 263, 264
hubris, 167
Hu Yaobang, 264–66

imperialism, 222; Suez Crisis and, 268–69; wars of national liberation against, 218
impressment, 105

India, 195, 280; economic boom of, 53–54; Harrison's popularizing music and philosophy of, 237; Khrushchev's visit to, 221–22; Orissa famine in, 192
Iran, Chinese policy toward, 259
Iraq, ISIS in, 78, 80–81, 83
Iraq War, 81, 148, 167–68, 302; losing gambler syndrome in, 298
Ireland, 61
Isabella (queen, Jerusalem), 88, 90
ISIS (Islamic State), 78–84, 251, 294, 295
Islam: Hashashin movement (Assassins) in, 70–72; of ISIS (Islamic State), 78–84; Third Crusade defeated by, 86–91
Israel, Suez invaded by, 269
Italy, under Napoleon, 154

Jackson, Thomas Jonathan "Stonewall," 170, 184
Jagger, Mick, 238–45, 253, 288
Japan: current policies of, 276, 280, 281; Genrō in, 201–3, 289–90; Great Britain and, 206–7; Meiji Restoration in, 197–201; Pearl Harbor attacked by, 133–35, 137–38, 291–92; on Senkaku-Diaoyu Islands dispute, 282; in World War II, 138–39
Jascius (Archbishop of Tyre), 87
Jay, John, 105–6
Jay Treaty (1794), 104–12
J Curve, 16–17
Jefferson, Thomas, 104; Adams and, 145–46; at Continental Congress (1776), 123–30, 291; Declaration of Independence

Jefferson, Thomas (*continued*)
    written by, 141, 143–45;
    Hamilton and, 108
Jerusalem, Kingdom of, 86–90
Jiang Qing, 263
Jiang Zemin, 267
John C. Hulsman Enterprises (firm),
    21–23; on Trump election, 26
Johnson, Lyndon B., during
    Vietnam War, 168, 175–78
Johnson (LBJ) administration,
    losing gambler syndrome of,
    37, 175, 177–79, 297–98
Johnston, Joseph E., 170
Jones, Brian, 38, 238–46, 288
Joseph Bonaparte (king, Spain), 161
Julius II (pope; Giuliano
    Della Rovere), 93, 95, 99,
    115–19; elected pope, 101–2;
    Machiavelli on, 112–15, 297
Juncker, Jean-Claude, 60
Junot, Jean-Andoche, 152

Kael, Pauline, 26
Kaganovich, Lazar, 223, 224
Kennan, George, 28, 29
Kennedy, John F., 89n13, 254;
    Macmillan and, 273–74, 300–
    301; Skybolt missile program
    canceled by, 271–73
Kennedy administration: in Cuban
    Missile Crisis, 226–28; losing
    gambler syndrome of, 37
Khrushchev, Nikita, 38, 223–25;
    brinkmanship of, 217–22;
    in Cuban Missile Crisis,
    226–28; promised land fallacy
    of, 299–300; removed from
    power, 228–29
King, Martin Luther, Jr., 143, 144
Kissinger, Henry A., 7, 13–15
Kissinger Associates, 13–15
Krenwinkel, Patricia, 77

Kuomintang (China), 260
Kurds, in Iraq, 83

Lampedusa, Giuseppe Tomasi
    Di, 62
Laos, 222
Law, Evander, 173
Lee, Richard Henry, 128, 129,
    131
Lee, Robert E.: at Battle of
    Gettysburg, 37, 168–72, 174,
    186; Longstreet and, 181–84;
    losing gambler syndrome of,
    187, 297–98
Leipzig, Battle of (1813), 163
Lenin, Vladimir Ilyich, 58, 218
Lennon, John, 234–38, 246–49,
    288; murder of, 252
Leoben, Peace of (1797), 154
Leopold (king, Austria), 88
Le Pen, Marine, 64
Let It Be (record; Beatles), 248
Lexington and Concord, Battles
    of (1775), 125
Lieven, Anatol, 196
Lincoln, Abraham, 143, 144, 169
Li Peng, 266
Liu Shaoqi, 261, 262
Livilla, 47
Livingstone, Robert, 129
Long Island, Battle of (1776),
    124
Long March (China; 1934–35),
    260
Longstreet, James, 171, 172,
    181–86
losing gambler syndrome, 37,
    167–68, 187, 297–98; at Battle
    of Gettysburg, 171, 182–84,
    186; in Vietnam War, 174–75,
    177–81
Louis XVIII (king, France), 155
Ludendorff, Erich, 232

Lumumba, Patrice, 222
lunatics, 36, 69, 84, 294–95; ISIS
    (Islamic State) as, 78–79;
    Manson as, 74; Sinan as,
    70–72

Machiavelli, Niccolò, 93–99,
    296–97; on Cesare Borgia,
    101; on Julius, 112–15
Machiavellianism, 97
Macmillan, Harold, 225, 254,
    268–74, 300–301
Macrinus, Marcus Opellius
    (emperor; Roman Empire), 65
Madison, James, 104
Maier, Pauline, 144
Malenkov, Georgy, 224
Manin, Ludovico Giovanni,
    151–53
Manson, Charles, 72–77, 294
Mantion, Stephane, 49
Mao Zedong, 256, 260–63, 301
Marathon, Battle of, 1
Marco Polo, 72
Marxists, 292–93
Mason, George, 141
Mattei, Jean-François, 50, 51
Mattis, James, 282
McCartney, Paul, 76, 234–38,
    288; during decline of Beatles,
    246–50; post-Beatles, 252–53
McClellan, George B., 170, 171
McGovern, George, 26
McNamara, Robert, 175–79, 272
Meade, George Gordon, 172
Medici family, 93, 96
Meiji Restoration (Japan; 1868–
    1912), 197–202, 289–90
mercantilism, China's policy of,
    257–59
Mercer, Johnny, 277
Merkel, Angela, 62, 63, 83, 296
Michelangelo, 112

Middle East: Chinese policies in,
    258–59; ISIS in, 78–84, 295
militarism, in France, under
    Napoleon, 156–57, 159, 164
Milne, A. A., 244
Mitchell, Wess, 28
Modi, Narendra, 281
Monroe Doctrine, 204–6
Morgenthau, Hans J., 28–31, 285,
    286
Morris, Robert, 132
Moscow, Battle of (1941), 133

Naftali, Timothy, 219, 227
Napoleon Bonaparte (emperor,
    France), 166; fall of, 161–65;
    France under, 155–60; Venice
    conquered by, 151–55,
    293–94
Napoleonic Code (France),
    157–58
Nassau Conference (Bahamas;
    1962), 268, 272–74, 300
Nasser, Gamal Abdel, 268, 269
National Commission on
    Terrorism, 14
national interest, 29–30
National People's Party
    (Germany), 232
Naval Defense Act (UK, 1889),
    193
Nero (emperor; Roman Empire),
    65
Ney, Michel, 155–56
Niebuhr, Reinhold, 28, 205
Nixon, Richard, 26, 180
Nizari Ismaili (Islamic sect), 70,
    85, 91
Nogee, Joseph, 221
nuclear weapons: Khrushchev's
    policies on, 220–21, 225;
    Macmillan on, 270–71
Nymphidius Sabinus, Gaius, 65

Obama, Barack, 148
Obama administration, 276
Odom, William, 218
off-shore balancing policy, 194–97
Oldham, Andrew Loog, 241–43
Old Man of the Mountain. *See*
Rashid ad-Din Sinan
Olney, Richard, 204–5
Ono, Yoko, 246, 252
Oracle of Delphi. *See* Pythia of
Delphi
Orbison, Roy, 252
Orsini family, 118
Ottoman Empire, 149

Paine, Thomas, 125
Pallenberg, Anita, 243, 245
Paris (France), heat wave of 2003
in, 49–52
Paris, Treaty of (1783), 105
Pauline Kael fallacy, 26
Peace of Leoben (1797), 154
Pearl Harbor (Hawaii), 133–35,
137–38, 291–92
Peninsular War, 161–62
Perry, Matthew C., 198, 201
Pertinax (emperor; Roman
Empire), 65
Petraeus, David, 80
Petty, Tom, 252
Philip II (king, France; Philip
Augustus), 86, 88
Philip of Beauvais, 88–89
Philippines, 281–82
Pickett, George E., 168, 184–86
Pius III (pope), 102, 116
Plato, 98
Plutarch, 3–4
Polaris missiles, 272, 273
political risk analysis: history of
firms in, 11–27; by Pythia of
Delphi, 5. *See also* geopolitical
risk analysis

political risk firms, 11–12;
Economist Intelligence Unit,
12–13; Eurasia Group, 15–18;
Geopolitical Futures, 21;
Kissinger Associates, 13–15;
smaller firms, 21–23; Stratfor,
18–21
political science, 7, 19; applied by
Eurasia Group, 15
Pope, John, 170–71
Portugal, 61, 161
Praetorian Guard (Roman
Empire), 44, 46–47, 65–66,
290
Prato, Battle of (1512), 93, 96,
114
praxis, 52, 74, 77
The Prince (Machiavelli), 94,
96–99; on Cesare Borgia, 101,
113; on Julius, 114–15
promised land fallacy, 38, 209,
299–300
Proudhon, Pierre-Joseph, 56–57
psychology, 31
Putin, Vladimir, 82, 92, 251, 296
Pythia of Delphi (Oracle of
Delphi), 2–6, 39–40, 297,
302; end of, 303; Ten
Commandments of Political
Risk of, 41, 287

Quarrymen (rock band), 236–37

Rabin, Yitzhak, 89n13
Raffarin, Jean-Pierre, 50, 51
random events (butterfly effect),
39, 254–55, 300
Rashid ad-Din Sinan (Old Man
of the Mountain). *See* Sinan,
Rashid ad-Din
realist school of thought, 27–30,
284–86; Machiavelli in, 96–98
refugees, Syrian, 82–83

Renaissance, 93
Revolutionary War. *See* American Revolution
Revolver (record; Beatles), 235
Ribbentrop, Joachim von, 139
Richard I (king, England; the Lion-Heart), 86, 88, 90
Richards, Keith, 238–45, 253, 288
Roberts, Andrew, 156, 158
Rodney, Caesar, 132
Rolling Stones (rock band), 238–39, 288; Jones in, 239–46
Roman Empire: Gibbons on decline of, 42–45, 290; Sejanus and decline of, 46–49
Rome (Italy), 117–18
Roosevelt, Franklin, 134, 135, 137, 140
Rubber Soul (record; Beatles), 235, 237
Rush, Benjamin, 145
Russia: allied with Britain, 231; Napoleon's war on, 161–63; under Putin, 92, 251; Syria policy of, 82. *See also* Soviet Union
Russo-Japanese War (1904–1905), 202, 207
Rutledge, Edward, 131–32

Sahwa movement (Iraq), 80–81
Sakamoto Ryōma, 199–201
Saladin (sultan, Egypt and Syria), 85–87, 90, 91
Salam, Hassan Ala Dhikrihi, 70
Salamis, Battle of, 6
Salisbury, Lord (Robert Gascoyne-Cecil), 38, 188–93, 198, 289; end of policy of, 216; foreign policy of, 193–97, 207–8; during Venezuela crisis, 205–6
samurai (Japan), 199, 202

Sancha of Aragon, 100
Satsuma rebellion (Japan), 202n
Schama, Simon, 159
Scowcroft, Brent, 13
Sejanus, 46–49, 65, 66, 290
Semichastny, Vladimir, 228–29
Senkaku-Diaoyu Islands dispute, 282–83
Sgt. Pepper's Lonely Hearts Club Band (record; Beatles), 235, 237
Shakespeare, William, 294
Shankar, Ravi, 252
Sherman, Roger, 129
Shia Muslims, 83
Sickles, Dan, 172
simony, 116
Sinan, Rashid ad-Din (Old Man of the Mountain), 68–73, 295; Crusaders versus, 88–91; Saladin versus, 84–86
Singh, V. P., 53
Sino-Japanese War (1894–1895), 202
Sixtus IV (pope), 115
Skybolt (US-UK missile program), 271–74, 300
slavery and slaves: Declaration of Independence references to, 129, 142; taken by Great Britain after Revolutionary War, 105–6
Snow, C. P., 150
Sonnō Jōi (Japan), 201
South China Sea, 275–76, 281–82, 301
South Korea, 281
Souvanna Phouma, 222
Soviet Union: in Cuban Missile Crisis, 226–28; under Khrushchev, 217–26, 299; wars of national liberation supported by, 228–29; in World War II, 133, 136. *See also* Russia

Spain, 61; under Napoleon,
161–62
Sparhawk, John, 123
Stalin, Joseph, 98, 219; Khrushchev
and, 223–24; during World
War II, 134, 140
Stalingrad, Battle of, 220, 223
Starr, Ringo, 235, 247, 248
Stratfor (firm), 18–21
Stuart, J.E.B., 182
Suez Canal (Egypt), 195; Crisis in
(1956), 221, 268–69
Sunni Muslims, 83
Syria: Chinese policy in, 259;
ISIS in, 78, 82; refugees from,
82–83

Tacitus, 47, 48
Taylor, Maxwell, 178–79
Their Satanic Majesties Request
(record; Rolling Stones), 243
Themistocles, 5–6
Theodosius I (emperor; Roman
Empire), 303
Third Crusade (1189–92), 68, 70,
72; assassination of Conrad
and, 86–91; Battle of Hattin
in, 85; defeated by Assassins,
294, 295
Thompson, J. M., 159
Thorneycroft, Peter, 272
Tiananmen Square crisis (China;
1989), 264–65
Tiberius (emperor; Roman
Empire), 46–48, 290
Tokugawa Yashinobu, 200
Traveling Wilburys (rock band),
252
Trenton, Battle of (1777), 169
Trump, Donald; election of,
25–26; Putin and, 82
Turkey, 227
Tyre (Lebanon), 87

Ukraine, 223
United Kingdom. *See* Great
Britain
United States: in American
Revolution against Great
Britain, 124–32, 291; Civil War
in, 168–74, 181–87; in Cuban
Missile Crisis, 226–28; current
foreign policy of, 196–97;
current relationship between
China and, 275–79; Declaration
of Independence of, 121–24,
141–45; early economic growth
of, 257; in Iraq, 83; Jay Treaty
between Great Britain and,
104–8; Monroe Doctrine of,
204–5; on Senkaku-Diaoyu
Islands dispute, 282–83;
Soviet Union versus, 220, 222;
special relationship between
Britain and, 270–73, 300–301;
Suez Crisis and, 269; treaties
between Japan and, 198; during
Venezuela crisis, 205–6; in
Vietnam War, 174–81; wars of
national liberation against, 218;
as world power, 279; in World
War I, 232; in World War II,
133–40, 291–92

Vandenberg, Arthur, 138
Venezuela, 203–7, 289
Venice, Republic of, 118,
147–49, 165–66; conquered
by Napoleon, 151–56, 293;
decline of, 149–51
Vietnam, 222; current relations
between United States and,
276; dispute between China
and, 275
Vietnam War, 168, 174–81; losing
gambler syndrome in, 37, 187,
297–98; Morgenthau on, 29

von Tirpitz, Alfred, 38, 209–17, 299; Haldane mission and, 229–32

Waltz, Kenneth, 28, 285–87
Wang Yi, 278
war games, 22–23
Warren, Gouverneur K., 172
wars of national liberation, 217–19, 221, 222, 226–29, 299
Washington, George, 98; during American Revolution, 124, 126, 143, 169, 291; farewell address of, 108–12; Jay Treaty of, 103–8
Waterloo, Battle of (1815), 165
Waters, Muddy, 239
Watkins, Paul, 74–77
Watson, Charles "Tex," 77
Watts, Charlie, 240, 244
Wellington, Duke of (Arthur Wellesley), 155, 161, 165
Westmoreland, William, 174
whites, Helter Skelter philosophy on, 74–76
Wilhelm (kaiser, Germany), 211, 214, 232, 299
Williams, Ted, 11
William V of Montferrat, 87

Wilson, Brian, 33
Wilson, Dennis, 76
Winant, Gil, 135
Winnacker, Ernst-Ludwig, 57
World War I, 208, 216, 217, 289; current Asian situation and, 279–81, 301; events leading to, 254; Germany in, 232; Japan in, 207; Macmillan during, 269–70, 273
World War II: Great Britain in, 135–38, 291–92; Khrushchev during, 223; Pearl Harbor attacked in, 133–35; United States in, 139–41
Wyman, Bill, 240, 241, 244

Xerxes (king, Persia), 1–2, 5
Xi Jinping, 255, 257, 281; foreign policies of, 275–76

Yorktown, Battle of (1781), 143
young people, unemployment among, 64

Zeus (deity), 5
Zhao Ziyang, 264, 266
Zhou Enlai, 260, 261